Building Teacher Capacity in English Language Teaching in Vietnam

This timely volume opens a window on issues related to English language education in Vietnam. The authors consider that teacher quality is the key factor to be considered if the national English language curriculum outcomes are to be achievable. Aiming to shed light on key issues recently observed in the Vietnamese landscape of English language education, the volume examines the complexity of the institutionalisation of the standardised English proficiency policy, which has been in force since 2008. That policy uses the Common European Framework of References for Languages (CEFR) as the model to set the standards and levels of proficiency for teachers, learners, and state employees.

The book presents both the theoretical and practical aspects of the standardisation movement in English language education. The contents comprise a series of extended research-based chapters written by experts of language-in-education policy and planning in and about Vietnam from a range of perspectives including teachers, English language curriculum developers, and teacher educators and researchers. The rich coverage of the book includes the current discussion on English language education in Vietnam ranging from policy to practice, making it highly relevant to English teachers, teacher educators, and scholars, in Vietnam and worldwide, who aspire to broaden their horizons and professionalism.

Le Van Canh is an associate professor in applied linguistics at Vietnam National University, Hanoi. He has been involved in English language teacher education in Vietnam for the past 40 years. His publications centre on second language teacher education in response to the enactment of innovation in Vietnamese ELT. For the last few years, he, as a teacher educator, promotes teacher research among Vietnamese ELT teachers in an attempt to bridge global disciplinary discourses with local practices. His research interests are teacher education, language planning and policy, and context-based TESOL pedagogy.

Hoa Thi Mai Nguyen is a senior lecturer in the School of Education at The University of New South Wales, Australia, and specialises in teacher education and development, mentoring, TESOL, and sociocultural theory. She has experience teaching and training pre-service and in-service teachers in Asia and Australia. She has had two authored books, two edited books and over 15 book chapters and 20 articles in well-regarded peer-reviewed journals and international prestigious publishers. She is also an honorary research fellow at the University of Sydney and a visiting scholar at King's College London.

Nguyen Thi Thuy Minh is an associate professor in the English Language and Literature Academic Group at the National Institute of Education, Nanyang Technological University, Singapore. Her research interests include pragmatics in language teaching and learning, interactional competence development, language pedagogy and language teacher education. She has published widely in mainstream TESOL and applied linguistics journals and reputable edited books, and co-authored several teachers' handbooks and school resource materials. She is currently serving on the editorial board of the *Asian Journal of English Language Teaching* published by the Chinese University of Hong Kong.

Roger Barnard is an associate professor in applied linguistics at the University of Waikato, New Zealand. Over the past 15 years, he has worked with academics in Vietnam and many other Asian universities on collaborative research projects, resulting in several publications, most recently, R. Barnard & Z. Hasim (Eds.), *English Medium Instruction Programmes: Perspectives from South East Asian Universities* (2018).

Routledge Critical Studies in Asian Education
Series Editors: S. Gopinathan, Wing On Lee
and Jason Eng Thye Tan

Literature Education in the Asia-Pacific
Policies, practices and perspectives in global times
Edited by Chin Ee Loh, Suzanne Choo and Chatherine Beavis

English Tertiary Education in Vietnam
Edited by James Albright

English Language Teacher Preparation in Asia
Policy, research and practice
Edited by Subhan Zein and Richmond Stroupe

Lesson Study and Schools as Learning Communities
Asian school reform in theory and practice
Edited by Atsushi Tsukui and Masatsugu Murase

The Asian EFL Classroom
Issues, challenges and future expectations
Edited by Soo-Ok Kwen and Bernard Spolsky

Teacher Education for English as a Lingua Franca
Perspectives from Indonesia
Edited by Subhan Zein

The Governance and Management of Universities in Asia
Global influences and local responses
Chang Da Wan, Molly N.N. Lee, and Hoe Yeong Loke

Building Teacher Capacity in English Language Teaching in Vietnam
Research, Policy and Practice
*Edited by Le Van Canh, Hoa Thi Mai Nguyen, Nguyen Thi Thuy Minh,
Roger Barnard*

For more information about this series, please visit: www.routledge.com/
Routledge-Critical-Studies-in-Asian-Education/book-series/RCSAE

Building Teacher Capacity in English Language Teaching in Vietnam

Research, Policy and Practice

Edited by Le Van Canh, Hoa Thi Mai Nguyen, Nguyen Thi Thuy Minh, Roger Barnard

Routledge
Taylor & Francis Group
LONDON AND NEW YORK

The
HEAD
Foundation

First published 2020
by Routledge
2 Park Square, Milton Park, Abingdon, Oxon OX14 4RN

and by Routledge
52 Vanderbilt Avenue, New York, NY 10017

Routledge is an imprint of the Taylor & Francis Group, an informa business

First issued in paperback 2021

British Library Cataloguing-in-Publication Data
A catalogue record for this book is available from the British Library

Library of Congress Cataloging-in-Publication Data
A catalog record for this book has been requested

ISBN: 978-1-138-31386-6 (hbk)
ISBN: 978-1-03-209067-2 (pbk)
ISBN: 978-0-429-45737-1 (ebk)

Typeset in Galliard
by Apex CoVantage, LLC

Contents

Figures and tables

Figures

Tables

Foreword

Andy Kirkpatrick

In 2009, the Association of Southeast Asian Nations (ASEAN), which is made up of ten member states (Brunei, Cambodia, Indonesia, Malaysia, Myanmar, Laos, the Philippines, Thailand, Singapore, and Vietnam), formally made English the sole working language of the group. Article 34 of the ASEAN Charter reads: "[T]he working language of ASEAN shall be English." In declaring this, it merely ratified what was already common practice. Indeed, at the founding meeting of ASEAN in 1967, delegates explained that there was no official discussion on what should be the working language of the group as "the idea of English as the common language came out automatically" and "we took it for granted" (Okudaira, 1999, pp. 95–96). The role that English plays as the sole working language of ASEAN has further heightened the perceived importance of English among member states. In addition to the usual arguments that English allows participation in modernisation and globalisation, there is a strong regional imperative for member states to promote English. As a minister in the Cambodian government pointed out more than a decade ago:

> We need to know English so that we can defend our interests. . . . ASEAN is not some kissy-kissy brotherhood. The countries are fiercely competitive, and a strong knowledge of English will help us protect Cambodian interests.
> (Clayton, 2006, p. 230)

It is also worth noting that the minister went on to say, "When we use English we don't think about the United States or England. We think only about the need to communicate" (Clayton, 2006, p. 233).

I suggest that this second comment is worth noting for the following reason. One of the developments in the use of English worldwide when it comes to the learning and teaching of English, one that has been appreciated by the Cambodian minister, is that English is now used more by people for whom English is an additional language and whose cultures are not native-speaking Anglo-centric ones than it is by native speakers of the language. For such learners, knowing about English-speaking cultures may not be as important as knowing about the cultures of the people with whom they will most frequently be using English. Thus, while it is understandable why Vietnam's recently developed English Teacher

Proficiency Framework (ETFC) lists "knowledge of English speaking cultures" in the domain knowledge of subject matter (Vu & Dudzik, Chapter 2, this volume), the focus on English-speaking cultures is misplaced, as it is with people from a wide variety of different cultural backgrounds with whom Vietnamese users of English need to communicate, not least, of course, as already noted by the Cambodian minister, with fellow members of ASEAN. As Le (Chapter 4, this volume) argues, there is a need, therefore, to move away from the native speaker model as the target for English learners in Vietnam. Indonesian scholars have also persuasively presented this argument in a forthcoming book entitled *Teacher Education for English as a Lingua Franca: Perspectives from Indonesia* (Zein, in press). There, Hamied, Mustafa, and Zein make four recommendations. The first is that the objectives of English language education be reoriented so that the focus of the classroom switches from its current concentration on native speaker varieties of English to varieties used in the region and English as a lingua franca. English as a lingua franca (ELF) can be defined as "any use of English among speakers of different first languages for whom English is the communicative medium of choice" (Seidlhofer, 2011, p. 7). Their second recommendation is that teachers and students should be empowered as users of English as a lingua franca. To achieve this, "Pre-service teacher education must prepare teachers with exposure to the varieties of English used in the ASEAN context and [illustrate that] communication can be accomplished without adherence to the native-speaking norms." Mustafa, Hamied and Zein's third and fourth recommendations are that policies for developing teachers' English language proficiency are needed and that a ministerial-level task force should be created to oversee the implementation of these polices. It seems that the challenges facing Indonesia in promoting English language education are similar to the challenges faced in Vietnam, as are the suggestions put forward by experts for overcoming these challenges. Indeed, many of these challenges are faced by the majority of ASEAN's member states, and it is therefore surprising that ASEAN has not set up a task force comprised of regional experts to address them. As I shall argue later in this chapter, a regionally established and accepted set of English language teacher and learner competency benchmarks would go some way in providing legitimacy to these recommendations, while also facilitating staff and student mobility across ASEAN.

Both the Indonesian-based volume and the current volume on the challenges facing the teaching and learning of English in the region stress the need to move away from a focus on native speaker norms as the learning targets or goals and to consider adopting an approach that sees the learner as a multilingual user of English as a lingua franca. It is therefore worth briefly reviewing the regional English language learning and teaching contexts that have given rise to this call to re-evaluate the goals of English language learning and teaching. The first point to reiterate is that English is currently acting as the sole working language of ASEAN. As such, English is being used as a lingua franca by multilinguals from within ASEAN.

The adoption of English as the sole working language of ASEAN means that English is clearly expected to play a major role in ASEAN, and this includes creating a sense of ASEAN identity. English is seen as an essential tool for reinforcing the three ASEAN pillars of (1) the ASEAN political security community (APSC), (2) the ASEAN economic community (AEC), and (3) the ASEAN sociocultural community (ASCC) (Widiati & Hayati, 2015, Stroupe & Kimura, 2015). The crucial role of English in this enterprise was recently emphasised by the then Secretary General of ASEAN himself, Le Luong Minh:

> With the diversity in ASEAN reflected in our diverse histories, races, cultures and belief systems, English is an important and indispensable tool to bring our Community closer together. . . . Used as the working language of ASEAN, English enables us to interact with other ASEAN colleagues in our formal meetings as well as day-today communications. . . . In order to prepare our students and professionals in response to all these ASEAN integration efforts, among other measures, it is imperative that we provide them with opportunities to improve their mastery of the English language, the language of our competitive global job market, the lingua franca of ASEAN.
>
> (ASEAN, 2013)

It is important to reiterate that this role of English does not involve interacting with native speakers. Rather, it involves interacting in English with fellow multilinguals from ASEAN. This means that it is more important for those who are using ELF in ASEAN to be familiar with the cultures of ASEAN. As Widiati and Hayati (2015) point out, instead of teaching the cultures traditionally associated with British or American English, professional development programmes need a shift in emphasis to a lingua franca curriculum in which the cultures of ASEAN or ASEAN plus three (i.e., plus China, Japan, and Korea) are covered. Earlier, Widiati and Hayati (2015) reviewed teacher education in Indonesia and suggested that "there needs to be more explicit integration of the ASEAN curriculum so that in-service and pre-service teachers have adequate knowledge and skills on how to educate their future students about ASEAN identity and ASEAN integration through their English classes" (2015, p. 138). They also recommend the *ASEAN Curriculum Sourcebook* as providing examples of relevant materials. It is indeed surprising that more use is not made of this sourcebook as the materials are specifically designed to help students become engaged with and identify with the ASEAN sociocultural community. A focus on establishing the ability to communicate successfully using English as a lingua franca with fellow multilinguals across ASEAN is likely to be more motivating for learners of English than the setting of targets of native speaker proficiency. The current policy in Vietnam is "English for everyone," but which English has not been discussed. It has been assumed that the aim is for learners to aim for native speaker proficiency, but, as previously noted, this is unlikely to be the most appropriate model for Vietnamese learners in these contexts. As also suggested, Vietnamese learners of English are more likely to be stimulated by the prospect of being able to use English successfully with people of different linguistic and cultural backgrounds (Le & Barnard, Chapter 11, this volume; Nguyen & Cao, Chapter 9, this volume).

Yet the idea of the native speaker as model remains firmly entrenched in the minds of policymakers and educators, including English language teachers and teacher educators, and this presents a significant challenge. It is hard to convince policymakers and stakeholders that adopting an English-as-a-lingua-franca approach to English language teaching will lead to more successful learning outcomes. In this context, it is helpful to remember that learning English needs to be based on its contextual use. In broad terms, "the global learning of English needs to be based on its global use," and this means that the goal of being able to use English as a lingua franca "corresponds more closely to what is real for learners, and is a more realistic objective for them to achieve" than is an attempt to approximate native speaker norms (Seidlhofer and Widdowson, in press). In the context of ASEAN, ASEAN meetings are routinely attended by Asian multilinguals who are able to communicate successfully with one another, even though their English does not adhere to native speaker norms. That the English of these multilinguals may indicate that their first language is Vietnamese, Malay, or Thai, does not mean that they are any less able to communicate successfully than native speakers. Indeed, research over several decades has shown that non-native speakers of English can be more intelligible than native speakers in multilingual contexts (e.g., Smith & Rafiqzad, 1979; Deterding & Kirkpatrick, 2006). The Asian corpus of English (ACE) – which is a corpus of Asian multilinguals using English as a lingua franca in naturally occurring settings collected by the author and several data collection teams across East and Southeast Asian, including one team based at SEAMEO RETRAC in Ho Chí Minh city – is evidence that Asian multilinguals communicate successfully using ELF in a variety of different settings. There are few instances where communication breaks down, and on the rare occasions when it does, the communication is quickly repaired by the adoption of communicative strategies. These communicative strategies can be divided into "listener" and "speaker" strategies, as illustrated in below.

Communicative strategies of ASEAN ELF speakers (Kirkpatrick, 2010, p. 141)

Strategy type (listener)

Lexical anticipation
Lexical correction
Lexical suggestion
Don't give up
Request repetition
Request clarification
Let it pass
Listen to the message
Participant paraphrase
Participant prompt

Strategy type (speaker)

Spell out the word
Repeat the phrase
Be explicit
Paraphrase
Avoid local/idiomatic referents

Using material from ACE, which is freely available at http://corpus.ied.edu. hk/ace, and showing learners of English how these Asian multilinguals use ELF and the communicative strategies they adopt to ensure successful communication would, I feel, be more useful and appropriate for Vietnamese learners than materials designed to enable learners to achieve native speaker proficiency. Instead of seeing learners of English as people trying to attain native speaker proficiency, it is more validating for both learners and teachers to see the aim of English lessons as being to develop multilinguals by adding English to their multilingual repertoire. This point is underlined in a recent volume edited by Sifakis and Tsantila (2019), which describes how the ELF approach is being adopted in a variety of different contexts around the world.

One possible reason why Vietnam's current NFLP2020 (National Foreign Language Project 2020) policy has knowledge about English-speaking cultures as a key component of the subject knowledge domain and why it is proving hard to successfully implement – indeed the timeframe by which the various benchmarks are to be met has recently been extended from 2020 to 2025 – is that it has been a strictly top-down policy. As Nagai and O'Dwyer (2011, p. 46) have noted:

> While top-down implementation brings the benefits of integrated, effective decision-making and curriculum control; there is a risk of the loss of teacher autonomy and their resulting indifference to the reform. For successful use of the imported framework of language proficiency such as the CEFR on the national scale, teacher capacity must be built through diverse culturally appropriate approaches. These approaches need to be developed with the amalgam of top-down and bottom-up strategies supported by a strong leadership.

Although Nagai and O'Dwyer's recommendations are for the implementation of the CEFR in Japan, this view is, interestingly reiterated by Le (Chapter 4, this volume), who, in suggesting how INSET (in-service [teacher] training) in Vietnam should change, asserts that "what is needed for enhancing teacher capacity for successful implementation of the ELT initiative in Vietnam, and in other similar contexts, is a strong leadership that can orchestrate the interaction between top-down control and bottom-up autonomy."

The importance of engaging the teachers in the decision-making process is also noted by the authors of the Vietnam chapter in the forthcoming *Routledge*

International Handbook of Language Education Policy and Practice in Asia (Nguyen & Nguyen, forthcoming). They note that, although:

> the government's decision to invest in enhancing the language competence of English teachers is a judicious step toward improving the quality of its English education in general. . . . [T]eachers under training and educational observers have expressed apprehension toward the CEFR-based levels prescribed for English teachers, claiming that these benchmarks are likely beyond teachers' ability, especially for those in rural areas.

They conclude that these centralised policies, which fail to take into consideration feedback from the community, such as teachers, students, parents, or administrators (Nguyen, 2011), have resulted in mismatches between decisions made by policymakers and what teachers and students actually need for improved teaching and learning performance.

As the chapters in this volume, along with other sources noted, show, there is currently a serious shortfall between the stated aims in terms of teacher proficiency in the NFLP2020 project and reality. As Le (Chapter 1 this volume) argues it is imperative for Vietnam to invest more in teacher education and materials and to redefine the goals of English language education. As already noted, a discernible trend that can be observed both worldwide and within ASEAN itself is towards the adoption of an ELF approach to English language teaching in contexts suited for such an approach. I contend that Vietnam offers a suitable context for such an approach, a context that thus requires the goals of English language education to be redefined. At the same time, many other member states of ASEAN also provide suitable contexts for the adoption of a new ELF-related approach to English language teaching. The recent volume on the topic by Indonesian scholars previously cited is evidence of this. It might be mutually beneficial, therefore, as intimated earlier, for ASEAN to establish a task force comprised of regional experts to consider ways in which common English teacher and learner competencies might be established within the framework of an ELF approach to language teaching. This would lead to some form of consistency across ASEAN, together with a shared sense of ownership, and allow for staff and student mobility within ASEAN's member states.

References

ASEAN. (2013). Keynote address by H. E. Le Luong Minh, Secretary-General of ASEAN at the British Council Conference on '*Educating the next generation of workforce: ASEAN perspectives on innovation, integration and English*'. Bangkok, June 24, 2013.

Clayton, T. (2006). *Language choice in a nation under transition: English language spread in Cambodia*. Boston: Springer.

Deterding, D., & Kirkpatrick, A. (2006). Emerging Southeast Asian Englishes and intelligibility. *World Englishes, 25*(3–4), 391–409.

Kirkpatrick, A. (2010). *English as a lingua franca in ASEAN: A multilingual model.* Hong Kong: Hong Kong University Press.

Musthafa, B., Hamied, F. A., & Zein, S. (in press). Enhancing the quality of Indonesian teachers in the ELF era. In S. Zein & Z. Sakhiyya (Eds.), *Teacher education for English as a lingua franca: Perspectives from Indonesia.* London: Routledge.

Nagai, N., & O'Dwyer, F. (2011). The actual and potential impacts of the CEFR on language education in Japan. *Synergies Europe, 6*, 141–152.

Nguyen, T. M. H. (2011). Primary English language education policy in Vietnam: Insights from implementation. *Current Issues in Language Planning, 12*(2), 225–249.

Nguyen, X. N. C. M., & Nguyen, V. H. (forthcoming). Vietnam. In A. Kirkpatrick & A. Liddicoat (Eds.), *The Routledge international handbook of language policy and practice in Asia.* London and New York: Routledge.

Okudaira, A. (1999). A study on international communication in regional organizations: The use of English as the "official" language of the Association of South East Asian Nations (ASEAN). *Asian Englishes, 2*(1), 91–107.

Seidlhofer, B.(2011). *Understanding English as a Lingua Franca.* Oxford: Oxford University Press.

Seidloher, B., & Widdowson, H. (in press). ELF for EFL: A change of subject? In N. Sifakis & N. Tsantila (Eds.), *ELF for EFL contexts.* Clevedon: Multilingual Matters.

Sifakis, N. C., & Tsantila, N. (Eds.). (2019). *ELF for EFL contexts.* Bristol: Multilingual Matters.

Smith, L. E., & Rafiqzad, K. (1979). English for cross-cultural communication: The question of intelligibility. *TESOL Quarterly, 13*(3), 371–380.

Stroupe, R., & Kimura, K. (Eds.). (2015). *ASEAN integration and the role of English language teaching.* Phomh Penh: IDP.

Widiati, U., & Hayati, N. (2015). Teacher professional education in Indonesian and ASEAN 2015: Lessons learned from English language teacher education programs. In R. Stroupe & K. Kimura (Eds.), *ASEAN integration and the role of English language teaching* (pp. 121–148). Phnom Penh: IDP.

Zein, S. (Ed.). (in press). *Teacher education for English as a lingua franca: Perspectives from Indonesia.* London: Routledge. (2,996 words).

Contributors

Roger Barnard is an associate professor in applied linguistics at The University of Waikato, New Zealand. Over the past 15 years, he has worked with academics in Vietnam and many other Asian universities on collaborative research projects, resulting in several publications, most recently, R. Barnard & Z. Hasim (Eds.), *English Medium Instruction Programmes: Perspectives from South East Asian Universities* (2018).

Le Van Canh is an associate professor in applied linguistics at Vietnam National University, Hanoi. He has been involved in English language teacher education in Vietnam for the past 40 years. His publications centres on second language teacher education in response to the enactment of innovation in Vietnamese ELT. For the last few years, he, as a teacher educator, promotes teacher research among Vietnamese ELT teachers in an attempt to bridge global disciplinary discourses with local practices. His research interests are teacher education, language planning and policy, and context-based TESOL pedagogy.

Diana Dudzik is an English teacher educator and curriculum consultant from the United States who received her PhD from the University of Minnesota. Diana has conducted research on education policies, curriculum reform and teacher development in Djibouti, and teacher education in Vietnam. She has taught ESL at the adult, university, secondary and primary levels. Diana has written curriculum, evaluated programs, and facilitated teacher development in Vietnam, Laos, Djibouti and the US. In Djibouti, she worked with educators to develop a contextual student textbook. In Laos, she led a team to develop a medical English curriculum and materials. In Vietnam, she worked as an NGO volunteer, Senior English Language Fellow, and Fulbright Scholar to build teacher capacity, evaluate national curriculum, and design blended teacher development. Diana is the key author of Vietnam's *English Teacher Competency Framework*, the nation's first subject-specific teacher standards. She received a *Bằng khen* in 2013 and a *Ky niem chuong vi su nghiep giáo duc*, Medal for the Course of Education, from Vietnam's Ministry of Education and Training in 2017. Her research interests focus on effective, accessible teacher education and development in international settings.

Donald Freeman is Professor of Education, University of Michigan, where his work has focused on understanding and designing equitable professional development opportunities in ELT that are accessible to teachers across diverse teaching circumstances and contexts. He directs the *Learning4Teaching Project*, a series of national research studies of ELT public-sector teachers' experiences in professional development conducted in Chile, Turkey, and Qatar. He is Senior Advisor on the *ELTeach Project* (National Geographic Learning), which provides on-line professional development to ELT public-sector teachers, and author, most recently, of *Educating Second Language Teachers*, (Oxford, 2016). He is a past president of TESOL, and member the International Advisory Council for Cambridge ESOL, and immediate past chair of the International Research Foundation for English Language Teaching (TIRF).

Laura Grassick is Teaching Fellow in TESOL in the School of Education, University of Leeds, UK. She holds a PhD in Education from the University of Leeds. She has extensive experience in teacher education in many contexts around the world, with a particular interest in Vietnam. Her research area focuses on English language curriculum change and the interconnected relationships involved in successful implementation of educational reform. She is co-editor (with Martin Wedell) of the book: *International Perspectives on Teachers Living with Curriculum Change*. Her interest in curriculum change and teacher education also extends to the area of young learners and the policy and practice of teaching languages in the primary school curriculum.

My Hau Thi Ho, EdD, received her doctoral degree and her master's degree from La Trobe University, Australia. She is currently Lecturer and Head of the Department of International Studies, Hue University of Foreign Languages, Vietnam. Her research interests are intercultural communication, Vietnamese applied linguistics, and English as a Lingua Franca.

Anne Katz has worked for over thirty years in second language education with a focus on assessment, curriculum design, and standards development. Her publications have centered on classroom uses for assessment, the development of academic English, effective classroom practices for English language learners, and functional frameworks of language proficiency. Her most recent research has explored the relationship between English language proficiency and student performances on achievement tests in English. She is co-designer and Senior Consultant to ELTeach, an on-line professional development program for public-sector teachers (National Geographic Learning and Educational Testing Service). As a teacher educator, she promotes linkages between research and school contexts to support active and collaborative professional development.

Manh Duc Le (PhD, UNSW) works as a language teacher trainer and English lecturer at Vietnam Maritime University. Manh obtained his Ph.D degree from the University of New South Wales, Australia in 2018. He has some publications on language policy implementation and language teacher empowerment. His recent work is published in an edited book *Global Perspectives on Language Education Policies* (Routledge, 2018). Manh's current research interests include positive psychology in language classrooms, language teacher education and professional development.

Nguyen Thi Thuy Minh is an associate professor in the English Language and Literature Academic Group at the National Institute of Education, Nanyang Technological University, Singapore. Her research interests include pragmatics in language teaching and learning, interactional competence development, language pedagogy and language teacher education. She has published widely in mainstream TESOL and applied linguistics journals and reputable edited books, and co-authored several teachers' handbooks and school resource materials. She is currently serving on the editorial board of the Asian Journal of English Language Teaching published by the Chinese University of Hong Kong.

Nguyen Thi Hong Nhat is a lecturer of English and a teacher educator at Hanoi Pedagogical University 2, Vietnam. She holds a Doctor degree from the University of Queensland. She has been conducting a number of workshops for language teachers on teaching English with technologies. Her research interest is in the teaching of listening as a foreign language skill, technology-mediated task-based language teaching, EFL materials development, teacher education in Computer-Assisted Language Learning, and educational change.

Lê Thị Thùy Nhung works as a lecturer of English in the Department of Foreign languages at Banking University, Ho Chi Minh City. She holds a Master of Arts in TESOL studies from the University of Queensland, Australia and a PhD in English language education from the University of Newcastle, Australia. She has involved in postgraduate training and research as a supervisor, thesis examiner, course convener and as an editor and peer reviewer for some EFL journals. Dr. Le is a frequent speaker/presenter at conferences and workshops for English language teachers in Ho Chi Minh city. She has published chapters in books and journals on TESOL and language teacher education.

Hanh Thi Nguyen, PhD, is Professor of Applied Linguistics in the TESOL Program at Hawaii Pacific University, USA. Her research interests are the development of interactional competence in professional settings, second language learning, and child language development; classroom discourse; the social aspects of second language learning; and Vietnamese applied linguistics. She is the author of *Developing Interactional Competence: A Conversation Analytic Study of the Patient Consultation in Pharmacy* (Palgrave-Macmillan, 2012) and the co-editor of *Conversation Analytic Perspectives on English Language Learning, Teaching and Testing in Global Contexts* (Multilingual Matters, 2019), *Pragmatics of Vietnamese as a Native and Target Language* (University of Hawaii Press, 2013), *Pragmatics and Language Learning Vol. 12* (University of Hawaii Press, 2010), and *Talk-in-Interaction: Multilingual Perspective*

(University of Hawaii Press, 2009). Her work has also appeared in several book chapters and journals such as *Applied Linguistics, The Modern Language Journal, Journal of Pragmatics, Text & Talk, Learning, Culture and Social Interaction,* and *Language and Education.*

Hoa Thi Mai Nguyen is a senior lecturer in the School of Education at The University of New South Wales, Australia, and specialises in teacher education and development, mentoring, TESOL, and sociocultural theory. She has experience teaching and training pre-service and in-service teachers in Asia and Australia. She has had two authored books, two edited books and over 15 book chapters and 20 articles in well-regarded peer reviewed journals and international prestigious publishers. She is also an honorary research fellow at the University of Sydney and a visiting scholar at King's College London.

Tram Do Quynh Phan is a lecturer of English and TESOL at University of Foreign Languages, Hue University, Vietnam. Tram is completing her PhD student in Language Education at University of New South Wales, Sydney, Australia. Her doctoral study investigates EFL teachers' responses to the language curriculum in Vietnam under the perspective of cultural historical activity theory. Her research interests include language teacher education, professional learning, educational innovation and sociocultural theory.

Cao Thi Hong Phuong (Phuong Cao) currently works as a teacher trainer at the faculty of English, Hanoi National University of Education, Vietnam. She earned her MA in TESOL from Victoria University of Wellington, New Zealand. Her teaching and research interests include testing and assessment, teaching and learning vocabulary, and ELT methodology. She has regularly presented her research papers at both national and international conferences in TESOL.

Hai Ha Vu has been a lecturer of English and English language teaching methodology, as well as a TESOL trainer at the University of Languages and International Studies (Vietnam National University, Hanoi) since 2007. He has also been the leader of four national (sub-)projects and active participants in many others under the Vietnam's National Foreign Language 2020 Project since 2010. His research interests and publications revolve around English language teacher education, English language teaching, critical pedagogy, and code-switching studies.

Abbreviations

ASEAN	Association of Southeast Asian Nations
CALL	computer-assisted language learning
CBT	competency-based training
CBTE	competency-based teacher education
CC	communicative competence
CEFR	Common European Framework of Reference for Languages
CLIL	Content and Language Integrated Learning
DOET	Departments of Education and Training
EAP	English for Academic Purposes
EFL	English as a foreign language
ELF	English as lingua franca
EIL	English as an international language
ELT	English language teaching
ELTs	English language teachers
EMI	English medium instruction/English-as-medium-of-instruction
ETCF	English Teacher Competencies Framework
FL	foreign language
IELTS	International English Language Testing System
ICC	intercultural (communicative) competence
INSET	in-service (teacher) training
LT	language teaching/language teacher
LSP	Language for Specific Purposes
MOET	Ministry of Education and Training
NFLP2020	National Foreign Language Project 2020
NS	native speaker
NNSs	non-native speakers
PD	professional development
PL	professional learning
PELTE	pre-service English language teacher education
TE	teacher education
TEYL	teaching English to young learners
TOEFL	Test of English as a Foreign Language

TOEIC	Test of English for International Communication
VLPF	Vietnamese Language Proficiency Framework
VNIES	Vietnam National Institute for Educational Sciences
VSTEP	Vietnamese Standardised Test of English Proficiency
WTO	World Trade Organisation

Introduction

Under the influence of globalisation and neoliberalism, English becomes "a way of securing economic advancement, elevated status and prestige and trans-national mobility" (Singh, Kell, & Pandian, 2002, pp. 53–54). As part of this global commodification of English, developing countries have associated English proficiency with national economic development, modernisation, and participation in the global economy. Vietnam is a case in point.

In 2008, the landscape of English language education in Vietnam was marked by the government's initiative to reform the English language education within the national education system, which is known as the National Foreign Languages 2020 Project (NFLP 2020). This is to achieve an ambitious goal that "by the year 2020 most Vietnamese youth whoever graduate from vocational schools, colleges and universities gain the capacity to use a foreign language independently" (Ministry of Education & Training, 2008, p. 1). Towards that goal, "English for Everyone" and "the earlier-the-better" approaches (Enever & Moon, 2010; Hamid, 2010; Sayer, 2015; Wedell, 2008) have been adopted. Overnight, English became the most preferred foreign language across the country. For policymakers, parents and students, English proficiency is less a "choice" than a necessity for success in education, employment, and economic mobility and prosperity. Most of parents in economically developed urban areas consider investment in their children's learning English as "early investment" and, as a result, English language academies for young children run by foreigners have mushroomed in most urban areas. Street advertisements and signboards in English have become part of the urban linguistic landscape.

Within the state educational system, while young children may have their first English lesson at the kindergarten as an optional activity, English is a compulsory subject from grade 3 of the primary school level to tertiary level. Innovations such as learner-centred, task-based pedagogy, blended learning, English-as-medium-of-instruction (EMI), technology-assisted language learning all have been promoted.

Among the strategies that have been enacted is the establishment of National English proficiency benchmarks, which have been upgraded to a more international standard based on the Common European Framework of Reference for Languages (CEFR) scale. Accordingly, school and university graduates are expected to achieve Level B1. For teachers, upper secondary (senior high school) teachers are required to reach Level C1 while both lower secondary (junior high school) and primary teachers are expected to reach the B2 Level, with a provisional B1 Level for primary teachers. The required level of English proficiency is set at Level C1 for both university lecturers who teach English as the major and content university lecturers who use English as a medium of instruction. In addition, masters and doctoral candidates are respectively required to be certified as users of English at the B1 and B2 Levels in order to be eligible for admission. A huge investment of resources has been prioritised for the development of the new curriculum, textbooks, and teachers' professional competence. After a decade of implementation, much of the targeted outcome of Project 2020 remains to be desired, and it is time to examine empirically and critically why the project fails to meet its expectations.

The impetus for this edited volume arose from the recent significant changes and debates in English language education policy in Vietnam. As language teachers, teacher educators, and teacher education researchers who are either working in Vietnam or familiar with what is happening in English language education and English language teacher education in this country, we come to realise that a volume on this issue remains desired despite a number of relevant publications by both Vietnamese and non-Vietnamese scholars. Thus, it becomes apparent that an edited volume of the present kind would provide state-of-the-art insights into current strategies, issues, and challenges for those who are both scholars and policymakers interested in Vietnamese experience in innovating English language education.

It must be made clear that our intention is not to criticise or challenge the recent initiative in English language education in Vietnam. On the contrary, we strongly believe that it is a worthwhile endeavour. Therefore, the proposition underlying this volume is that failure in educational innovation, including innovation in English language education, constitutes a learning process to achieve long-term success. To turn failure into a learning process, reflection is required. This is critical given the complexity of educational innovation as well as that of English language teaching and learning. With this view in mind, the editors and contributors hope that this volume will be celebratory in the sense that it informs a thoughtful and effective process that lays a stepping stone towards the expected long-term success. It is in this realm that we hope that the chapters in this volume provide reflective space that allows not only inspiration and imagination to thrive and results in creative ways to improve English language education in the age of globalisation and neoliberalism.

The structure of the volume

As its central theme is teacher capacity building as essential for developing learners" target language competence, the volume touches upon a variety of related issues such as the competence-based model of teacher training, teacher in-service training, the implementation of EMI and technology-assisted pedagogy, and so on. The concept of this volume is founded on the view that the anchoring factor in the success of the second/foreign language education policy is teacher competence, but teacher competence should be viewed as contextually situated and relational to contemporary social, political, cultural, economic, and classroom realities. Effective approaches to building teacher competence cannot be decontextualised.

In Chapter 1, Le Van Canh explores the recent innovation in English language education in Vietnam, which is aimed at strengthening the country's economic competitiveness. He discusses major challenges that emerge from the analysis of the nexus of the ideology behind the innovation, the sociocultural and educational context within which the innovation is embedded and the adequacy of language teacher competence to the requirements of the innovation. He then presents recommendations for addressing those challenges. Le Van Canh concludes his chapter asserting that, in order for English language education in the country to take off, Vietnamese educational policymakers need to contest the colonial mentality that motivates them to copy, apply and appropriate Western models uncritically. Instead, they need to look out for global professional discourses on the one hand and be grounded in the country's culture and mind, histories and geopolitics, on the other.

In Chapter 2, Hai Ha Vu and Diana L. Dudzik, using Vietnam's English Teacher Competencies Framework (ETCF), the country's first set of subject-specific teacher standards, present a case study that examines the current pre-service English language teacher education (PELTE) curriculum implemented in one of the leading language teacher education institutions in Vietnam. Through an analysis of syllabus documents, a survey of pre-service teachers, and follow-up interviews and focus groups with pre-service teachers, teacher educators and programme managers, the authors discuss the strengths of a competency-based teacher education curriculum and a balance among theory, practice and context and then recommend how to address the identified curricular gaps by embedding competencies throughout the curriculum as well as creating more opportunities for situated and authentic practice in the PELTE programme.

In Chapter 3, Laura Grassick explores the feelings of a group of seven primary English language teachers in Vietnam as they grapple with making sense of the new requirements and changes to their professional knowledge and practice brought about by the National Foreign Language 2020 Project (NFLP 2020) curriculum and language policy. The data show how feelings of uncertainty and vulnerability emerge from teachers' perceptions of risk in relation to challenges to their professional selves and changes in the contextual demands of their work, brought about by the new language policy. Laura Grassick suggests that a better understanding of teachers' feelings might improve the kind of support provided for teachers during the implementation process, helping to ensure its success.

In Chapter 4, Le Van Canh reports on a study that explores the complexity of teacher learning in the context of top-down mandatory INSET. Data were collected through focus group interviews and classroom observation and analyzed qualitatively. Findings show that teachers' uptake was varied, unpredictable, and conditioned by the relational interdependency of teachers' classroom experiences, cognition, emotion, and action. It is also revealed in the study that only a surface manifestation of resulting change was observed in teachers' instructional practices. Le argues that mandatory top-down INSET should continue to serve as one of the leading models of professional development for Vietnamese EFL teachers for many compelling reasons but needs to be reoriented to capture the complexity of teacher learning. This reorientation ties together the construction of teacher education as learning and teacher education as policy in sophisticated and intriguing ways so as to create more conducive conditions for teacher learning and teacher change to emerge from the bottom up.

In Chapter 5, Hoa Thi Mai Nguyen, Tram Do Quynh Phan, and Manh Duc Le examine the professional learning experiences of EFL teachers in the context of changes in English education policy in Vietnam. Using qualitative research design in the light of activity theory, the study aims to explore how in-service teachers experience their professional learning in their school contexts. By discussing the data from multiple sources, the authors argue for the need to provide teachers and their schools opportunities to exercise their agency in carrying out their professional learning activities that are relevant to their needs and teaching contexts. The study has made a contribution in using activity theory to suggest changes in designing and implementing PL activities for EFL teachers in the current context.

Donald Freeman and Anne Katz, in Chapter 6, point out the challenge of providing effective professional development to large numbers of teachers who will be implementing the intended curricular innovation. According to them, programmes designed to help teachers develop English skills for teaching English have been implemented but with little evidence of success. As a result, they offer a different framework for content and participation, which reframes the problem of scale in training. Snapshots of three implementations in Saudi Arabia, Vietnam, and India illustrate how this framework is used to build their teachers' capacity to provide English instruction in English. This strategy "leverages" teachers' classroom knowledge to successfully create scalable professional development opportunities.

The teaching of academic content courses and programs through the medium of English is becoming common in Vietnam's higher education sector, driven in large part by the government's National Foreign Language 2020 project. Lê Thị Thùy Nhung, in Chapter 7, presents a qualitative study that was set to explore the implementation of English Medium Instruction (EMI) in Vietnamese universities through lecturers' perspectives. An analysis of interviews with 22 lecturers delivering business courses at four universities in a major city in Vietnam suggests that the lecturers were in favour of EMI as they pointed to benefits of this approach to their profession. However, the participants acknowledged several factors hindering the delivery of subjects through English. Based on these findings, Lê Thị Thùy Nhung argues that the current EMI implementation in Vietnamese universities produces more challenges than opportunities and recommends that successful EMI practice requires adequate institutional support pertaining to the

English proficiency of both lecturers and students, teacher training, and sufficient resources for teaching and research.

In Chapter 8, Nguyen Thi Hong Nhat reports on a qualitative case study on the impact of a computer-assisted language learning (CALL) training course on the teacher participants' teaching practice. As revealed in the study, contextual factors that affected teachers' actual CALL practice include educational, administrative, and logistical issues. The author argues that changes on the part of both individual teachers and the system are needed for teacher autonomy in the effective introduction of CALL.

In Chapter 9, Nguyen Thi Thuy Minh and Cao Thi Hong Phuong examine a series of new English textbooks that have been developed for use in Vietnamese schools in the context of the NFLP 2020 aiming at renovating teaching practices and cultivating students' abilities to communicate effectively in intercultural situations. The aim of the study is to identify the extent to which the new textbook series enable teachers to achieve the aim of developing competent intercultural speakers. As indicated in the chapter, the books do not fully enable teachers to develop intercultural awareness among their students despite an attempt to globalise their cultural contents. Minh recommends that teachers need to be supported in how to work with textbooks for intercultural teaching. And in order to assist teachers in this aspect, greater autonomy should be given to them in terms of textbook modification and adaptation.

In Chapter 10, My Hau Thi Ho and Hanh Thi Nguyen report on issues related to the teaching and use of English as a lingua franca (ELF) in Vietnam as perceived by university teachers, full-time students, working part-time students, and working graduates in two Vietnamese cities. In-depth interviews with focus groups revealed that the participants held ambivalent views towards ELF, with positive views more often expressed by working students and working graduates, who have more exposure to English varieties. By discussing the participants' views, the authors recommend that future policies need to be connected with the reality of language teaching and learning in Vietnam, where NNS varieties are more relevant than NS standards. In keeping with local reality, language policies should not normalise and perpetuate linguistic imperialism.

The volume is concluded with a discussion by Le Van Canh and Roger Barnard, who discuss the need to take a holistic view of assisting teachers to build up the capacity to act on their knowledge base in their teaching arenas.

In sum, by presenting insights from empirical studies on the practices of building teacher competence for the improved quality of English language education in Vietnam, contributors of this volume emphasise that the success of any initiative in ELT depends on people, not things. No matter how well intentioned an ELT initiative might be, no matter how great the investment in resources might be, the gap between policy and implementation remains, leading to the waste of resources, unless sufficient affordances are provided for teachers to engage cognitively and emotionally with the initiative and the resources. To be more specific, the implementation of top-down initiatives in ELT must be accompanied or even preceded by compatible innovation in teacher education, especially in the professional development of teachers of which the key goal is to promote effective teaching that results in learning gains for all students.

References

Enever, J., & Moon, J. (2010). *A global revolution? Teaching English at primary school.* London: British Council.

Hamid, M. O. (2010). Globalisation, English for everyone and English teacher capacity: Language policy discourses and realities in Bangladesh. *Current Issues in Language Planning, 11*(4), 289–310.

Ministry of Education & Training. (2008). *Decision no. 1400/QĐ-TTg: 'Teaching and learning foreign languages in the national education system, period 2008 to 2020'.* Retrieved from www.chinhphu.vn/portal/page/portal/chinhphu/hethongvanban? class_id=1&_pa ge=18&mode=detail&document_id=78437

Sayer, P. (2015). "More & earlier": Neoliberalism and primary English education in Mexican public schools. *L2 Journal, 7*(3), 40–56.

Singh, M., Kell, P., & Pandian, A. (2002). *Appropriating English: Innovation in the global business of English language teaching.* Oxford: Peter Lang.

Wedell, M. (2008). Developing a capacity to make "English for everyone" worthwhile: Reconsidering outcomes and how to start achieving them. *International Journal of Educational Development, 28*(6), 628–639.

1 English language teaching in Vietnam

Aspirations, realities, and challenges

Le Van Canh

Introduction

The global expansion of English, accompanied by the neoliberal discourses, has given rise to the universal association of English to economic and educational opportunities. According to Wedell (2011, p. 275):

> The rapid expansion of English language teaching into state education systems worldwide over the past 20 to 30 years has been an obvious trend. For the first time in foreign language teaching history, national governments and individuals worldwide seem to see teaching a language (English) to all learners in state schools as an important means of increasing human capital on which future national economic development and political power depends.

Within the Asia-Pacific region, Nunan's (2003) survey conducted in China, Hong Kong, Japan, Korea, Malaysia, Taiwan, and Vietnam indicated that English became compulsory at a lower age despite limited resources and the lack of qualified English language teachers. Particularly, as English has been adopted as the working language of ASEAN countries, it is imperative that "citizens of the Member States [are pushed to] become proficient in the English language so that the citizens of the ASEAN region are able to communicate directly with one another and participate in the broader international communities" (ASEAN Secretariat, 2009, p. 3).

Vietnam, like many other countries from within and outside ASEAN, encounters many challenges in its endeavour to expand English language education to the national educational system, the greatest challenge being the lack of well qualified teachers (Wedell, 2008). This chapter examines a recent innovation in English language education called the National Foreign Languages 2020 Project (NFLP, 2020). Although the innovation has its supporters, it has been subject to considerable criticism in Vietnam for setting overambitious and unrealistic goals. The chapter falls into five sections. The first provides brief background information about the country in order to contextualise the subsequent analysis of the country's current English language education landscape. The second section describes the most recent innovation in English language education policy.

The third section examines language teacher education and teacher competence. Next, the chapter describes the gap between the intended goals and the reality of the implementation of the innovation. The fifth and final section discusses the challenges and recommendations for addressing those challenges.

Background

Vietnam is located in South East Asia. It has a population of more than 90 million composed of more than 50 different ethnic groups with their own languages. While Vietnamese is the official language, the country is, in reality, multilingual and multicultural. Throughout the country's many-thousand-year-long history, education has constantly featured prominently as a critical strategy for advancing human capital development in the government's strategies for socio-economic development. Meanwhile in the minds of the Vietnamese, education has always been greatly valued as the significant symbolic capital for social and economic upward mobility.

In Vietnam, compulsory schooling begins at the age of six and involves nine years from primary to lower secondary school. Students have 12 years of full-time schooling. The educational system in Vietnam is highly centralised. The Ministry of Education and Training (MOET) takes the initiative for curriculum design, development, revision and review, and textbook writing and assessment, usually in response to policies motivated by social, economic, and political forces and changing trends in educational theory and practice. A one-size-fits-all approach is always adopted to centrally mandated curricular changes, and teachers are expected to faithfully implement those changes in their classroom teaching. This approach to educational planning leads to proactive government intervention even at the classroom level. Understandably, most of the teachers teach the coursebook, not the students (Le, 2012). As a result, a great number of Vietnamese students view the covering of the content of the coursebook as their aim of learning rather than using English for real-life communication (Ton & Pham, 2010).

Since the turn of the century when Vietnam has moved more rapidly towards a full market-driven economy for more comprehensive integration into global processes, there have been several changes in the country's educational policies and practices. Neoliberalism, which frames education as primarily a site for human capital building and economic productivity (Block, Gray, & Holborow, 2012), has implicitly proliferated as an organising principle of social life in the country. Traditional teacher values are increasingly in conflict with the quasi-marketisation of the educational system. Teacher integrity and students and parents' attitudes towards teachers are negatively influenced.

In addition to the influence of the market economy, the prolonged mismanagement in education has reduced public credibility in domestic education, and this in its turn has led to the unanticipated rise in the number of outbound students. More and more middle-class families and nouveau riche choose to send their children overseas for tertiary education. The most preferred destinations for these outbound students are the United States of America (22,400), Australia (19,700), Canada (14,200), and Britain (5,000), according to 2017 statistics by the New York–based Institute of International Education (*Thanh Nien*, May 30, 2018). As English is the gatekeeper for these students, parents invest a great amount of their financial resources in their children learning English in private English language centres or foreigner-run schools. By contrast, in the mountainous areas, school students and their parents prefer staying away from schools to work in the fields despite teachers' advice (D. C. Nguyen, Le, Tran, & T. H. Nguyen, 2014).

Recent innovation in English language education

English did not foreground the foreign language education landscape in Vietnam until the early 2000s when the country moved away from a centrally planned socialist economy to a market-driven economy in the wake of the collapse of the Soviet Union bloc. The new economic policy, which was officially adopted in the late 1980s, attracted an ever stronger flow of direct foreign investment. This led to the pressing need of a labour force with a good command of English. The need became far greater following the country's membership of the Association of Southeast Asian Nations (ASEAN) in mid-1995 and of the World Trade Organisation (WTO) in early 2007. Naturally, English became synonymous with economic growth and prosperity (Holborow, 2012) in the political, educational, and public discourses, creating "English language fever" throughout the country.

Influenced by neoliberal ideology, which is "understood as an ideology within language education that views language as a commodity and promotes the idea that FL [foreign language] learning is connected to the acquisition of wealth, social status, and professionalism" (Ennser-Kananen, Escobar, & Bigelow, 2016, p. 16). Vietnamese politicians and parents reify English as inherently useful and essential for full participation in global society. In politicians' minds, English proficiency is a critical resource for Vietnam's competitiveness in the global economy. Put another way, a good command of English is perceived as "essential" and an "economic imperative" for the country's "*employment opportunities, economic development, modernization, internationalization, participation in the global economy* and to become an *economic global player*" (Sayer, 2015, p. 50, original emphasis). In the mass media, English proficiency has become an expression of "pride" associated with the power of a successful citizen, with economic, material gain, and opportunities for a better future. In effect, the English language has been viewed as one of the key strands of today's Vietnamese education, alongside mathematics and information technology.

A significant landmark that has recently been staked out in English language education in Vietnam is the NFLP 2020. The Project was approved by the government in 2008 with a budget of nearly US$500 million, targeting English proficiency as a comparative advantage in successfully facing the economic challenges of a globalised, multilingual, and multicultural world for all Vietnamese school-graduates and university graduates by 2020. To achieve this target, an

"English for Everyone" approach (Wedell, 2008) was adopted. English has thereby become a compulsory subject in the school curriculum and an optional activity in kindergartens or nursery schools.

A phased approach is adopted to ensure a smooth introduction of English to the primary school curriculum starting at grade 3. Accordingly, English is to be taught to 70% of grade 3 classes by 2015 and available nationwide by 2019. English teaching hours are set to double, and maths are to be taught in a foreign language in 30% of high schools in major cities by 2015. Although it was not until 2011 that English was officially introduced as a compulsory primary school subject throughout the country in grade 3, many state primary schools and private schools based in urban areas had been at the forefront of the movement without knowledge of how young children learn a second language in the context of classroom instruction. A good number of private schools introduce English as a compulsory subject as early as first grade in response to parents' demands. These private schools employed either untrained or inadequately trained native-English-teachers to attract fee-paying students from well-to-do parents, who tend to associate English proficiency to their children's better future. As Nguyen (2011, p. 225) has observed:

> The emergence of English as a global language has had a considerable impact on language planning policy in many non-English-speaking countries, including Vietnam, leading to more English teaching in primary schools. As English has become increasingly prominent, there has been an urgent need to keep proficiency in this foreign language high to enhance Vietnam's competitive position in the international economic and political arena.

Within the public educational sector, alongside the increase of weekly instructional hours from 2 class hours (45 minutes each) to 4 hours, the starting age for English language learning is lowered to the age of 9 (grade 3) ranging from 2 to 4 class hours a week depending on the existing human resources. A new series of textbooks have been written by Vietnamese authors in partnership with Pearson using the leading learner-centred task-based approach. The textbooks are published both in print and electronically. Innovative pedagogies such as learner-centred, task-based learning, blended learning, English-as-medium-of-instruction (EMI), technology-assisted language learning all have been promoted. Technologies such as interactive whiteboards and video-based instructional materials are provided for schools in the belief that these will maximise learners' exposure to English for communication within and outside the classroom.

Driven by the desire to set standards for what teachers and students at different levels of education should be able to do with their English, a six-level proficiency framework, a modification of the Common European Framework of Reference (CEFR), has been adopted as an assessment blueprint, and the locally developed language proficiency test called Vietnamese Standardised Test of English Proficiency (VSTEP) is used as an assessment tool. It is stipulated that upper secondary school and university graduates, irrespective of their major area of study, are supposed to reach the third level (CEFR B1) in order to be eligible for graduation. Ironically, the same proficiency benchmark (CEFR B1) is applied to both secondary school graduates and university graduates. Although a great amount of money was budgeted to the development of VSTEP, many universities have opted for TOEFL (Test of English as a Foreign Language), IELTS (International English Language Testing System), or TOEIC (Test of English for International Communication) because of the credibility gap in the quality of the locally produced test and test administration (Le, 2017a).

Language teacher education and teacher competence

In Vietnam, the teacher education system, like the educational system itself, is also highly centralised. The training of teachers for all subjects and all types of schools is regulated by national legislation. Teacher training is provided at universities of education. The prototypical training route for teaching any school subject including foreign languages is a four-year undergraduate programme. The basic entrance requirements into universities of education is the certified completion of 12 years of schooling and passing the national entrance examination after the upper secondary school. Due to the negative influence of the market economy, high achievers in the secondary school graduation examination are no longer attracted to teaching careers, and consequently the entry score at teacher training universities is ever lower (*VN Express*, August 8, 2017). The teacher education curriculum (both pre-service and in-service) is largely preoccupied with what content and pedagogy teachers need to master. Nguyen (2013) compared the second language teacher education programme in one Australian university with that in a Vietnamese university and found that the Vietnamese university's curriculum devoted most of its input load to English proficiency and subject matter knowledge but little to contextual knowledge including knowledge of the learners. In addition, the practicum is not organised enough to make it a useful learning experience for prospective teachers because of limited resources (Le, 2014; Nguyen, 2015). The result is that most graduates from teacher training universities are not sufficiently equipped with classroom practical skills when they are placed in schools (*Vietnam News*, March 24, 2010).

The hasty and ideologically driven replacement of the previously dominant Russian with English in the educational system and the introduction of English into the primary school curriculum in the early 1990s led to the serious problem of teacher shortage. To solve the problem, the government decided to retrain a great majority of Russian-language teachers to teach English and simultaneously gave a green light for universities to offer *tai chuc* (off-campus or extension) fee-paying courses of English language teacher training for secondary school graduates who were not academically qualified for university admission. As training courses of this type brought in huge profits to both training universities and hosting institutions, they mushroomed in every corner of the country, leading to problems of quality management. The graduates from these courses became "half-skilled" teachers (i.e., those with limited English and pedagogical competence) yet were placed in various schools. This constitutes an unresolved problem in terms of teacher quality facing educational administrators even today.

While pre-service teacher training is inadequate, the ongoing professional development of teachers is largely top-down with mandatory in-service training (INSET) being the dominant approach. INSET courses for teachers are intensively delivered during the summertime when students are on holiday. These courses focus on two key goals: upgrading teachers' English proficiency to the required level and updating their pedagogical practices with the teaching approaches that are in vogue and promoted in the current literature. Trainers in these courses are sent by contracted universities and senior colleges, and the great majority of them are young lecturers who have never been trained to be teacher educators and who as a result have little understanding of the teachers' teaching contexts and their practical needs. Little emphasis is placed on factors that have been documented as being effective to teachers' acquisition of professional knowledge such as time, reflection, and follow-up in the form of "long-term support, coaching in teachers' classrooms, or ongoing interactions with colleagues" (Ball, 1996, pp. 501–502).

Aware of teacher competence as key to the success of Project 2020, 80% of the total budget of US$446.43 million for the Project was allocated to teacher training. The top priority is to raise teachers' English proficiency. The required threshold level for primary and lower secondary school teachers is Level 4 (CEFR B2) and for upper secondary school and university teachers Level 5 (CEFR C1). VSTEP has been used for the assessment of teachers' proficiency, and English-majored university lecturers are commissioned to be examiners. The mandated threshold level has been described as ambitious and unrealistic, and it has sparked heated controversy among Vietnamese scholars (Bui & Nguyen, 2016; Le, 2015; Le & Do, 2012), classroom teachers, and international consultants. For example, Dennis Berg, who has worked as an educational consultant in Vietnam for over 20 years, said in an interview in the Vietnamese *Thanh Nien* (July 10, 2013) newspaper:

> If we look at the quality of English teaching in Vietnam and the lack of support in terms of salaries, resources and service training, I would have to say that the targets do not look very achievable to me. . . . Without faculty development and changes in teacher training programs, the project will never meet its goals.

The results of the baseline screening test showed that more than 87% of the 80,000 English teachers in state schools have low proficiency as measured through the nationwide assessment in 2011–2012. Eighty-three per cent were primary school teachers, 87% were junior high school teachers, and 92% were high school teachers (Nguyen, 2013). In an attempt to raise teachers' levels of English proficiency, concentrated in-service language improvement courses involving 400 training hours were offered to English teachers of all educational levels. These training programs were often run by different agencies, such as universities, colleges, departments of education and training, and international agencies such as the British Council, National Geographic (Cengage), and the American Regional Language Office.

Despite intensive training, by the end of 2015 the percentage of teachers who met the proficiency requirement, which was measured by VSTEP, was far from the expected target (Nguyen, 2013). A full report on the results of teacher proficiency assessment (Dudzik & Nguyen, 2015, p. 48) shows:

> As a part of the NFLP 2000 [National Foreign Language Project 2020], an unprecedented, widespread assessment of teacher proficiency has been conducted since 2011 among public school English teachers. Findings from these assessments are alarming when compared to the new proficiency benchmarks. Assessment statistics for 2011 indicate that 97% of the 3,591 primary school teachers tested fell below the B2 benchmark set by the government, 93% of the 3,969 lower secondary school teachers who were assessed fell below the B2 level, and 98% of the 2,061 high school teachers fell below the C1 benchmark. . . . 44,995 English teachers [approximately half the total population of English language teachers nationwide] had been assessed to date since 2011. The results of those assessments show that 83% of primary English teachers' English proficiency levels fell below the B2 benchmarks, 91.8% of the upper-secondary English teachers assessed did not meet the C1 benchmark, nor did 4.6% of college and university English teachers.

A great number of teachers felt frustrated as they had to repeatedly take the test without showing significant progress in test scores. These teachers experience the feelings of humility when they are classified as substandard or unqualified teachers (*giao vien khong dat chuan*) in both public and professional discourses. These discourses have resulted in a form of self-deprecation that negatively affect teacher emotions and professional identities, leading to their demotivation in trying to reach the proficiency level that is believed to be too challenging for them (Le, 2017b; also Chapter 4 in this volume).

Despite this fact, the government has aimed at the target of 100% of teachers at all levels meeting the proficiency threshold level (CEFR B2 for primary and lower secondary school teachers and CEFR C1 for upper secondary school and university teachers) by 2019. However, Nguyen and Mai (2015, p. 1840) state that these outcomes, if achieved, are likely to "soothe the surface cut without touching the deep root of the problem" because it is not clear whether the teachers' improved English proficiency leads to their improved classroom practices.

The tension between aspiration and reality

The recent English language education policy in Vietnam, which is part of the country's larger educational reform, is more driven by supranational discourses of the value of English in the nation's economic competitiveness (Ricento, 2012) than by a careful analysis of the country's socio-economic, educational, and sociolinguistic ecology (Bui & Nguyen, 2016; Hamid & Erling, 2016; Kirkpatrick & Bui, 2016). Particularly, it fails to consider the complexity of the interdependence between centralised and localised forms of management of educational innovation (Wedell, 2009) comprising policymakers, English language teaching (ELT) administrators, teachers, teachers educators, and the sociocultural and economic structure of the country. What has happened in Vietnam lends further support to Qi's (2009, p. 119) observation of the English teaching outcomes in Japan, Korea, China, and Taiwan:

> Countries in East Asia are investing considerable resources in providing English, often at the expense of other aspects of the curriculum, but the evidence suggests that these resources are not achieving the instructional goals desired. It would seem advisable, then, for governments and educational bureaucracies to review their policies in ELT.

Vietnam's highly centralised education system is characterised by the flow of reform initiatives from the Ministry of Education and Training (MOET) down through the schools and then into the classroom, while contextual complexity tends to be ignored. The curriculum is prescribed, and examinations are high-stake. English examinations are usually designed to assess students' reading comprehension, knowledge of grammar rules, and vocabulary. As a result, teaching and learning overemphasise the acquisition of knowledge about English at the expense of the development of communicative ability. In spite of this, students' performance in high-stake examinations remains frustrating. Because the exam was composed of only multiple-choice questions and did not include listening, speaking, and writing skills, the inherent complex calibration of the test score to the CEFR or even to the local six-level proficiency framework becomes unresolvably demanding.

In the classroom, while teachers have to follow the nationally mandated syllabus, a good number of learners, especially those from economically disadvantaged areas, can hardly process the teaching content because it does not match their "built-in" syllabus. Seeing no progress in their English proficiency and little evidence for English use in their local community, these students seem to perceive English as "an outlandish irrelevance" (Bruthiaux, 2002, p. 292). Therefore, their instrumental motivation is questioned (Le, 2015).

At the tertiary level, Le's (2017a) study revealed a number of contextual constraints on the attainment of the espoused objectives. These include learners' low entry level of proficiency, their perceived needs of English, inadequate instructional time, the lack of strategies to bridge in-class learning with out-of-class independent learning, a lack of institutional support for teacher professional development, and teachers' unsupportive attitudes towards the mandated outcome, which is CEFR B1 or Level 3 on the local proficiency scale. Ton and Pham (2010) reported that most Vietnamese university students tended to have a vague idea about the goal of learning English. They seemed to believe that they were learning English in order to achieve the objectives set in the coursebook rather than for real-life use. In other words, many students were learning English simply because it is a subject in the curriculum. This finding is supported by Humphreys and Wyatt (2014), who investigated the perception of autonomy by a group of Vietnamese EAP (English for Academic Purposes). The authors recommended that teachers needed to support these students developing goal setting and self-reflection. Nguyen, Fehring, and Warren (2015) reported the result of their case study on a group of university teachers' perception of factors affecting English language learning and teaching in their own institution. Among the inhibiting factors is the limited opportunity for the professional development of teachers.

After nine years of implementation, the expected achievements had not been reached, and on November 16, 2016, MOET reported to the National Assembly that the project failed to meet its goals within the planned 2008–2020 period. The failures were anticipated right at the birth of the project 2020, but the scholarly warnings were not seriously considered. In the recent national review seminar, constraints that were voiced by scholars and researchers included unrealistic benchmarks, inadequate instructional time, students' and teachers' low and varied starting points, lack of appropriate approaches to implementation, and a rigid syllabus and teaching methodology (*Vietnam News*, January 8, 2018). In December 2017, the government, without reviewing the policy, approved an extension of the project to 2025 instead of the originally planned termination in 2020 and urged the continuation of the new English curriculum and proficiency standards and the English-for-everyone target.

Challenges and recommendations

Raising up English proficiency levels to the expected national benchmarks is unquestionably a hard struggle in contemporary Vietnam because of the inequality of access to English and to high-quality teachers (Bui & Nguyen, 2016; Nguyen et al., 2014). Despite recent remarkable economic growth, there remain great sociocultural and economic variations across geographical areas, especially between the rural and urban areas and between the mountainous countries where different ethnic minority groups reside and the rest of the country. Students in disadvantaged areas do not have exposure to English except for few weekly hours of formal instruction, and they may not have the immediate need of English because they do not see how English is connected to their present and future lives. These students are likely to be "vulnerable to, and affected by, discourses that [they] never choose" (Butler, 2016, p. 24). Bui and Nguyen (2016) have argued that the promotion of English threatens not only social, educational, and economic development among the ethnic minority groups but also their linguistic and cultural ecology, rather than bettering their socio-economic conditions. Given this contextual complexity, the challenge is how teachers can create optimal conditions for language learning by teaching their students to adapt their language resources to changing situations (Larsen-Freeman, 2014). As teaching and learning are interdependent, it is argued that Vietnamese teachers need to acknowledge that teachers are also learners of teaching while working with diverse groups of students. This perspective helps them to develop their situated knowledge that helps them to responsively mediate their students' learning (Le, forthcoming). Learning, therefore, should happen on both sides of the desk.

Teacher quality is essential to any educational innovation (Hamid & Erling, 2016; Hu, 2002; Malderez & Wedell, 2007; Wedell, 2008). While technological resources are necessary, any success is a result of the development of classroom teachers' competencies. As Hu (2002, p. 651) rightly points out:

> Without qualified teachers, no matter how good the curriculum, the syllabus the textbooks and the tests are, the development of English language teaching will be handicapped and quality compromised.

Of all the competencies of an effective EFL (English as a foreign language) teacher, English proficiency is at the forefront though English proficiency itself does not guarantee effective teaching (Le & Renandya, 2017; Pasternak & Bailey, 2004; Richards, 2017). The puzzle is how to help in-service teachers reach the advanced level of proficiency on the one hand and how to support them to maintain their acquired proficiency on the other. In Vietnam, teachers, besides having little exposure to English and minimal experiences of day-to-day English use outside their classrooms, are assigned to teach at one level (primary, lower secondary, upper secondary, and tertiary) throughout their career life (Mai, 2014), while access to expert assistance is limited. Such a circumstance is likely to lead to a plateauing of proficiency or language attrition (Lowie, Caspi, van Geert, & Steenbeek, 2011). Mandating proficiency benchmarks for teachers without taking into consideration these contextual constraints only discourages teachers from making emotional investments, which determine their sense of success and satisfaction, in maintaining and improving their English language proficiency. Given these obstacles and the recognition of teacher classroom English proficiency (Freeman & Katz, Chapter 6 in this volume; Young, Freeman, Hauck, Garcia Gomez, & Papageorgiou, 2014), it would be more practical to invest in improving teachers' ability to use functional English for classroom teaching while providing ongoing support for them to exercise their agency in improving and maintaining their general proficiency according to their own agenda. Defined as "the essential English language skills a teacher needs to be able to prepare and enact the lesson in a standardized (usually national) curriculum in English in a way that is recognizable and understandable to other speakers of the language" (Young et al., 2014, p. 5), the cornerstone of teachers' classroom proficiency is oral proficiency, which needs to be prioritised. Instrumental to the process of developing English proficiency are teacher identities as language users and language educators. It is these identities that mediate their learning behaviours, resulting in the enactment of their agency to self-assess where they are at present, what their next destination is, and how they can arrive there (Nguyen, 2017; Nguyen & Bui, 2016; Obaidul & Nguyen, 2016). From the sociocultural perspective, teacher agency is emergent, dynamic, socially mediated, and contextually situated (van Lier, 2008), rather than something one possesses. Biesta and Tedder (2007, p. 137) note that "the achievement of agency will always result from the interplay of individual efforts, available resources and contextual and structural 'factors' as they come together in particular and, in a sense, always unique situations."

Situating teacher agency in the ecological complexity calls for a concerted effort in both supporting and challenging teachers to adapt to the new professional discourses and to reshape their identity and professional practice. This calls for the need to pay more attention to "the more unpredictable passionate aspects of learning, teaching and leading" (Hargreaves, 1998, p. 558). Therefore, improving teachers' working conditions must be the first priority because the working conditions affect teachers' emotional well-being, which, in turn, affects teachers' professional well-being and identity. As Schulz (2000, pp. 517–518) has pointed out:

> As long as teachers need to find part-time or summer employment to provide the basic material comforts for themselves and their families, as long as they have to face up to five different preparations a day in classes of 25 students and more, as long as they are faced with instructional settings where, at best, they can function as custodians, we will neither attract nor retain a sufficient number of highly qualified and highly motivated teachers.

In contemporary Vietnam, the money-driven lifestyles, the ever widening gap between the rich and the poor, between cities and the country sites, the administrative ineffectiveness, the lack of integrity in quality management, and the increasing social vices have altogether made teachers' lives more physically and emotionally stressful and their working conditions worse. Apart from that, teachers suffer from heavy teaching schedules and do not have access to appropriate social situations that are supportive of the reconceptualisation of their teaching. Institutional policies such as a mandated curriculum, high-stakes assessment, the myth of nativespeakerism, and the discourse of English as economic capital also discourage teachers from enacting their agency (Johnson, 2019). It is not surprising that while a few Vietnamese EFL teachers struggle to maintain growth and motivation, the large majority who do not have the will and/or the energy to struggle give up and settle down in their "comfort zone" by routinising their practices. Thus, conditions and catalysts for teachers to fundamentally change their conceptualisation and their enactment of language teaching need to be created. Alongside the improvement of teachers' working conditions, it is critical that teachers are provided with multiple, mediated, and sustained opportunities to engage in continuous knowledge-building processes throughout their careers in order to reframe their praxis in a dialectical unity of theoretical knowledge and practical knowledge gained from both their access to expert knowledge and their situated experience. In addition, there should be well defined criteria to evaluate how engagement in those knowledge-building processes enhances the development of the language teacher (the person) and language teaching (the activity) expertise (Johnson & Golombek, 2016). It is expected that teachers will be able to adapt to ever changing demands and circumstances in order to acquire new knowledge, skills, and understanding and to refine what they already possess (Pachler & Field, 2001, p. 15) once such opportunities are available.

In summary, the challenges to the success of Vietnam's new initiative in English language education can be addressed through the thoughtful and empirically informed consideration of the interaction and negotiation on three planes: the individual, the interpersonal, and the institutional (Rogoff, 2003). If competent teachers are integral to student achievement, teachers need to be provided with continued effective structural supports and resources not only to maintain but to improve their classroom English proficiency and to develop their expertise simultaneously. Key to the development of teacher expertise is "constant engagement in exploration and experimentation" (Tsui, 2003, p. 277) on the part of teachers through the institutionally framed professional ecology. Barriers to the effective functioning of that professional ecology in contemporary Vietnam are organisational hierarchies deeply rooted in Vietnamese culture, the learning culture, constrained resources, the devaluing of teachers' lived experience in favour of external, decontextualised knowledge, and lack of incentives for teachers' enactment of their agency. Therefore, it is imperative that ecological conditions that not only support and encourage but also challenge teachers to shift to the identity of agentive learner-teachers be created and sustained. Equally important is the legitimation of teacher identities in relation to multilingual, English-as-a-lingua-franca, and intercultural communication paradigms. Towards this goal, Vietnamese educational policymakers need to contest their colonial mentality, which is deeply rooted in Vietnamese culture for historical reasons, that motivates them to copy, apply, and appropriate Western models uncritically. Because each context has its own constraints, affordances, and dynamics that are related to its history and cultural values, educational models are not easily generalisable. Therefore, it is fundamental that Vietnamese policymakers look out for global professional discourses on the one hand and be grounded in their country's culture and mind, histories, and geopolitics on the other. Such endeavours are worthwhile to the development of locally and culturally relevant pedagogy that guarantees sustained successes in local ELT.

Conclusion

For the future success of innovation in ELT, it is necessary to have a holistic picture of what was happening and is happening so as to identify not only the lessons of success but also the barriers to the defined goals. This chapter has attempted to sketch out a range of basic issues relating to ELT and English language teacher education in contemporary Vietnam with regard to the country's recent initiative, which is aimed to raise the level of English proficiency among Vietnam's young generations. As Vietnam is a country member of the ASEAN community in which English has been accepted as a working language and as an active player in the global processes, the role of English in Vietnam will not be just a subject to be learned in the classroom but also a medium for social and practical use. Fully aware of this reality, the Vietnamese government has demonstrated its strong commitment to human capital development at the service of the country's participation in the global economy for national development. The intention behind this policy initiative is unquestionably welcomed because it opens up many opportunities for Vietnamese teachers and learners to develop their English proficiency for their personal benefits and the country's economic prosperity. Unfortunately, the hasty adaptation of the CEFR to the Vietnamese educational context failed to take into consideration the geopolitical, sociocultural, and economic disparity between Vietnam and European countries. Unsurprisingly, the new policy creates unnecessary emotional burdens, tensions, and challenges for teachers and learners, especially those from economically difficult areas. As a result, creating the emotional ecology (Zembylas, 2007) in which teachers' professional well-being is embedded must be a priority if the desire to improve the quality of English language education is realised. Emotional ecology can be created with teacher policies that afford the complex interaction between teachers' professional demands and emotional experiences (e.g. freedom to exercise agency, job satisfaction, and personal feelings of accomplishment), thereby encouraging teachers to continually adapt (and change) their conceptual knowledge to the new contexts. After all, it is professional well-being, constituted through the interaction between teacher emotion and identity, that can move teachers towards greater levels of expertise that inform contextually, theoretically, and pedagogically sound instructional practices on which successful language learning depends.

References

ASEAN Secretariat. (2009). *ASEAN socio-cultural community blueprint.* Jakarta: Author.

Ball, D. L. (1996). Teacher learning and the mathematics reforms: What do we think we know and what do we need to learn? *Phi Delta Kappan, 77,* 500–508.

Biesta, G., & Tedder, M. (2007). Agency and learning in the lifecourse: Towards an ecological perspective. *Studies in the Education of Adults, 39*(2), 132–149.

Block, D., Gray, J., & Holborow, M. (Eds.). (2012). *Neoliberalism and applied linguistics.* New York: Routledge.

Bruthiaux, P. (2002). Hold your courses: Language education, language choice, and economic development. *TESOL Quarterly, 36*(3), 275–296.

Bui, T. T. N., & Nguyen, H. T. M. (2016). Standardizing English for educational and socio-economic betterment: A critical analysis of English language policy reforms in Vietnam. In R. Kirkpatrick (Ed.), *English language education policy in Asia* (pp. 363–388). Cham, Switzerland: Springer.

Butler, J. (2016). Rethinking vulnerability and resistance. In J. Butler, Z. Gambetti, & L. Sabsay (Eds.), *Vulnerability in resistance* (pp. 12–27). Durham, NC: Duke University Press.

Dudzik, D. L., & Nguyen, Q. T. (2015). Vietnam: Building English competency in preparation for ASEAN (2015). In R. Stroupe & K. Kimura (Eds.), *ASEAN integration and the role of English language teaching* (pp. 41–71). Phnom Penh: IDP Education (Cambodia).

Ennser-Kananen, J., Escobar, C. F., & Bigelow, M. (2016). "It's practically a must": Neoliberal reasons for foreign language learning. *International Journal of Society, Culture & Language, 5*(1), 15–28.

Hamid, M., & Erling, E. J. (2016). English-in-education policy and planning in Bangladesh: A critical examination. In R. Kirkpatrick (Ed.), *English Language education policy in Asia* (pp. 25–48). Cham, Switzerland: Springer International.

Hargreaves, A. (1998). The emotions of teaching and educational change. In A. Hargreaves, A. Lieberman, M. Fullan, & D. Hopkins (Eds.), *International handbook of educational change* (pp. 558–575). Dordrecht: Kluwer.

Holborow, M. (2012). What is neoliberalism? Discourse, ideology and the real world. In D. Block, J. Gray, & M. Holborow (Eds.), *Neoliberalism and applied linguistics* (pp. 33–35). London, England: Routledge.

Hu, G. W. (2002). Recent important developments in secondary English language teaching in the P. R. China. *Language Culture and Curriculum, 15*(1), 30–49.

Humphreys, G., & Wyatt, M. (2014). Helping Vietnamese university learners to become more autonomous. *ELT Journal, 68*(1), 52–63.

Johnson, K. E. (2019). The relevance of a transdisciplinary framework for SLA in language teacher education. *The Modern Language Journal, 103*(Suppl. 2019), 167–174.

Johnson, K. E., & Golombek, P. R. (2016). *Mindful L2 teacher education.* New York: Routledge/Taylor & Francis.

Kirkpatrick, R., & Bui, T. T. N. (2016). Introduction: The challenges of English education policies in Asia. In R. Kirkpatrick (Ed.), *English language education policy in Asia* (pp. 1–23). Cham, Switzerland: Springer International.

Larsen-Freeman, D. (2014). Another step to be taken – Rethinking the end point of the interlanguage continuum. In Z.-H. Han & E. Tarone (Eds.), *Interlanguage: Forty years later* (pp. 203–220). Amsterdam: John Benjamins.

Le. V. C. (2014). Great expectations: The TESOL practicum as a professional learning experience. *TESOL Journal, 5*(2), 199–224.

Le, V. C. (2015). English language education innovation for the Vietnamese secondary school: The project 2020. In B. Spolsky & K. Sung (Eds.), *Secondary school English education in Asia: From policy to practice* (pp. 182–200). Florence: Taylor & Francis.

Le, V. C. (2017a). English language education in Vietnamese universities: National benchmarking in practice. In E. S. Park & B. Spolsky (Eds.), *English education at the tertiary level in Asia* (pp. 183–202). Abington and New York: Routledge.

Le, V. C. (2017b). *Báo cáo đánh giá tác động của các chương trình bồi dưỡng giáo viên tiếng Anh về năng lực ngôn ngữ và năng lực sư phạm* [Report on the empirical investigation into the impact of in-service language and pedagogical competence improvement training courses for English language teachers]. Hanoi, Vietnam: National Foreign Languages Project.

Le, V. C. (forthcoming). Remapping the teacher knowledge-base of language teacher education: A Vietnamese perspective. *Language Teaching Research* (Early online version).

Le, V. C., & Do, T. M. C. (2012). Teacher preparation for primary school English education: A case of Vietnam. In B. Spolsky & Y. Moon (Eds.), *Primary school English education in Asia: From policy to practice* (pp. 106–128). New York: Routledge.

Le, V. C., & Renandya, W. A. (2017). Teachers' English proficiency and classroom language use: A conversation analysis study. *RELC Journal, 48*(1), 67–81.

Lowie, W., Caspi, T., van Geert, P., & Steenbeek, H. (2011). Modelling development and change. In M. H. Verspoor, K. De Bot, & W. Lowie (Eds.), *A dynamic approach to second language development: Methods and techniques* (pp. 22–122). Amsterdam: John Benjamins.

Mai, N. K. (2014). Towards a holistic approach to developing the language proficiency of Vietnamese primary teachers of English. *Electronic Journal of Foreign Language Teaching, 11*(2), 341–357.

Malderez, A., & Wedell, M. (2007). *Teaching teachers: Principles, processes and practices.* London: Continuum.

Nguyen, D. C. (2017). Creating spaces for constructing practice and identity: Innovations of teachers of English language to young learners in Vietnam. *Research Papers in Education, 32*(1), 56–70.

Nguyen, D. C., Le, T. L., Tran, H. Q., & Nguyen, T. H. (2014). Inequality of access to English language learning in primary education in Vietnam. In H. Zhang, P. W. K. Chan, & C. Bouyle (Eds.), *Equality in education: Fairness and inclusion* (pp. 139–153). Rotterdam: Sense Publisher.

Nguyen, H. (2015). *The effectiveness of the practicum in EFL teacher education: Case studies of three universities in Vietnam.* Unpublished doctoral dissertation, Australia: RMIT University.

Nguyen, H. T. M. (2011). Primary English language education policy in Vietnam: Insights from implementation. *Current Issues in Language Planning, 12*(2), 225–249.

Nguyen, M. H. (2013). The curriculum for English language teacher education in Australian and Vietnamese universities. *Australian Journal of Teacher Education, 38*(11), 33–53.

Nguyen, T. H., Fehring, H., & Warren, W. (2015). EFL teaching and learning at a Vietnamese university: What do teachers say? *English Language Teaching, 8*(1), 31–43.

Nguyen, T. M. H., & Bui, T. (2016). Teachers' agency and the enactment of educational reform in Vietnam. *Current Issues in Language Planning, 17*(1), 88–105.

Nguyen, V. T., & Mai, N. K. (2015). Responses to a language policy: EFL teachers' voices. *The European Journal of Social and Behavioural Sciences, 13*(2), 1830–1841.

Nunan, D. (2003). The impact of English as a global language on educational policies and practices in the Asia-Pacific region. *TESOL Quarterly, 37*(4), 589–613.

Obaidul, H. M., & Nguyen, T. M. H. (2016). Globalization, English language policy, and teacher agency: Focus on Asia. *International Education Journal: Comparative Perspectives, 15*(1), 26–44.

Pachler, N., & Field, K. (2001). From mentor to co-tutor: Reconceptualising secondary modern foreign languages initial teacher education. *Language Learning Journal, 23*(1), 15–25.

Pasternak, M., & Bailey, K. M. (2004). Preparing nonnative English-speaking teachers: Issues of professionalism and proficiency. In L. D. Kamhi-Stein (Ed.), *Learning and teaching from experience: Perspectives on nonnative English-speaking professionals* (pp. 155–175). Ann Arbor: University of Michigan Press.

Qi, S. (2009). Globalization of English and English language policies in East Asia: A comparative perspective. *Canadian Social Science, 5*(3), 11–120.

Ricento, T. (2012). Political economy and English as a "global" language. *Critical Multilingualism Studies, 1*(1), 31–56.

Richards, J. C. (2017). Teaching English through English: Proficiency, pedagogy and performance. *RELC Journal, 48*(1), 7–30.

Rogoff, B. (2003). *The cultural nature of human development.* Oxford: Oxford University Press.

Sayer, P. (2015). "More & earlier": Neoliberalism and primary English education in Mexican public schools. *L2 Journal, 7*(3), 40–56.

Schulz, R. A. (2000). Foreign language teacher development: MLJ perspectives – 1916–1999. *Modern Language Journal, 84*(4), 495–522.

Thanh Nien. (July 10, 2013). *Pygmalion effect unlikely to propel Vietnam's English upgrade plans.* Retrieved from www.thanhniennews.com/society/pygmalioneffect-unlikely-to-propel-vietnams-english-upgrade-plans-1921.html

Thanh, N. (May 30, 2018). *Người Việt chi gần 2 tỷ USD/năm cho du học* [The Vietnamese spend nearly two billion US dollars for outbound education]. Retrieved from https://thanhnien.vn/giao-duc/nguoi-viet-chi-gan-2-ti-usdnam-cho-du-hoc-968067.html

Ton, N. N. H., & Pham, H. H. (2010). Vietnamese teachers' and students' perceptions of global English. *Language Education in Asia, 1*(1), 48–61.

Tsui, A. B. M. (2003). *Understanding expertise in teaching: Case studies of second language teachers.* Cambridge: Cambridge University Press.

van Lier, L. (2008). Agency in the classroom. In J. P. Lantolf & M. E. Poehner (Eds.), *Sociocultural theory and the teaching of languages* (pp. 163–186). London: Equinox.

Vietnam News. (March 24, 2010). *Teachers lack practical skills.* Retrieved from https://vietnamnews.vn/society/education/197964/teachers-lack-practical-skills.html#CVhWLrotJ4t2gU7F.97

Vietnam News. (January 8, 2018). *National foreign language project fails to fulfill targets.* Retrieved from https://vietnamnews.vn/society/420711/national-foreign-language-project-fails-to-fulfill-targets.html#OZTQM1GXQSbkRekc.97

VN Express. (August 8, 2017). '*Disaster*' *as Vietnam sets the bar low for future teachers.* Retrieved from https://e.vnexpress.net/news/news/disaster-as-vietnam-sets-the-bar-low-for-future-teachers-3624305.html

Wedell, M. (2008). Developing a capacity to make "English for everyone" worthwhile: Reconsidering outcomes and how to start achieving them. *International Journal of Educational Development, 28*(6), 628–639.

Wedell, M. (2011). More than just 'technology': English language teaching initiatives as complex educational changes. In H. Coleman (Ed.), *Dreams and realities: Developing countries and the English language* (pp. 275–296). London: British Council.

Wedell, M. 2009. *Planning for educational change – Putting people and their contexts first.* London: Continuum.

Young, J. W., Freeman, D., Hauck, M., Garcia Gomez, P., & Papageorgiou, S. (2014). *A design framework for the ELTeach programme assessments.* Princeton, NJ: Educational Testing Service.

Zembylas, M. (2007). Emotional ecology: The intersection of emotional knowledge and pedagogical content knowledge in teaching. *Teaching and Teacher Education, 23*, 355–367.

2 Problematising pre-service English language teacher education curriculum

Hai Ha Vu and Diana L. Dudzik

Introduction

The capacity building of English language teachers (ELTs) in Vietnam has been confronted with various issues, particularly the low language proficiency and limited pedagogical skills of many teachers, a shortage of primary ELTs in disadvantaged areas (Department of Primary Education, 2016; Hoang, 2009; Le, 2012), and a lack of professional development in the workplace (Le, 2012; Pham, 2001). Recent reforms have focused on retraining in-service English language teachers (National Foreign Language Project 2020, 2016), whereas initiatives in the pre-service sector have been limited. We argue that pre-service English language teacher education (PELTE) is among the most important factors in addressing the shortage of teachers, as well as their limited language and pedagogical competency, before these pre-service ELTs enter the workforce. Using the English Teacher Competencies Framework (ETCF), Vietnam's first subject-specific set of teacher standards, the case study in this chapter investigates a typical PELTE curriculum at a prestigious university in Vietnam. It deals with the question of PELTE quality – "What are the strengths and limitations of the current PELTE curriculum as it is mapped against the ETCF?" – in order to address the issue of building Vietnamese teachers' capacity in English language teaching.

Literature review

In order to address capacity building via PELTE, it is important to review both what capacity is to be developed and how it should be developed. The "knowledge base" of what teachers should know and be able to do (Johnson, 2009, p. 21) has evolved over time. Most significantly, there has been a recent shift from approaches whereby teachers were expected to master discrete behaviours and routines and transfer them to different contexts (Freeman & Johnson, 1998) to a sociocultural perspective. From this perspective, teacher learning is socially constructed, resulting from participating in sociocultural activities and contexts of teaching and emerging from constructing and reconstructing existing knowledge, beliefs, and practices (Waters, 2005, cited in Nguyen, 2016, p. 226). Recent literature also highlights situating teacher learning in classroom realities

(Borko, 2004; Bransford, Darling-Hammond, & LePage, 2005; Johnson, 2009) and incorporating awareness of international context and how it affects pedagogical decisions (Canagarajah, 2014; Solano-Campos, 2014).

Competency-based ELTE

In many English language teacher education (ELTE) contexts, standards or competencies have been employed to address teacher capacity building. Despite their usefulness, the employment of standards has been contested for the validity of their descriptors that characterise standards and its constrictions on teaching and learning in a "one-size-fits-all" approach (Katz & Snow, 2009). A number of studies worldwide also voice similar concerns. Hammond (2014) examined the Australian Curriculum and the National Professional Standards for Teachers and found them helpful in guiding programme design and implementation but inadequately detailed to inform classroom practices and pedagogy. She recommended that PELTE programmes should prioritise critical thinking about theory and pedagogy related to content, learning, language, and language development. DeLuca and Bellara (2013) examined the link between assessment policies, teacher competencies (standards) about assessment, and teacher education curricula and found both alignment and misalignment. Struyven and DeMeyst (2010) investigated the implementation of competency-based teacher education (CBTE) policy in Belgium, with some trainers echoing Hammond's (2014) findings that competencies were not concrete or practical enough to be applied. Additionally, the specific competencies that were implemented varied among institutions as well as among teacher educators within institutions. This may be due to the fact that the policy does not prioritise specific competencies but requires them all equally. Through the lens of a post-methods era, Murray (2009) argues that a competency-based training (CBT) approach to accreditation of vocational education in Australia is inappropriate for language teacher education. Murray's discussion assumes that competencies prescribe specific methods, procedures, and techniques, invoking a narrow view of CBT (Chappell, Gonczi, & Hager, 1995, as cited in Murray, 2009), which she calls a dangerous approach to teacher education.

However, benefits of CBTE include (1) demystifying teacher education (TE), (2) clarifying the role of institutions, (3) assuring employers about beginning teachers' knowledge and abilities, and (4) providing students with clearer goals (Whitty & Willmott, 1991, as cited in Struyven & DeMeyst, 2010). It is hence commonly agreed that competencies and standards are useful in certain ways, but it is necessary "to develop pathways that will support teachers in using standards in meaningful ways" (Katz & Snow, 2009, p. 74).

Vietnam's teacher competencies

Since 2008, ELTE in Vietnam has undertaken comprehensive reforms through the National Foreign Languages Project 2020 (NFLP, 2020), aiming to "renovate thoroughly the tasks of teaching and learning foreign language within the national education system" by 2020 (Vietnam Government, 2008, p. 1). Nearly 85% of an unprecedented budget of $US500 million was allocated for building teacher capacity. Among the initiatives was the issuance of the nation's first subject-specific teacher standards, the English Teacher Competencies Framework (ETCF). The ETCF, along with its User's Guide (MOET, 2013a), was initially disseminated through a national conference and regional workshops in 2013 and appeared in certain policy compulsory documents, but the ETCF "does not possess a legal power as strongly normative as 'Decision' and 'Circular'" (Vu, 2017).

The ETCF represents a holistic view of what teachers need to know and be able to do, including theoretical and pedagogical content knowledge, skills, and professional attitudes and values. The framework (Figure 2.1) was adapted by Dudzik (2008) from general teacher education research (Ball & Cohen, 1999; Bransford et al., 2005) and consists of five domains: subject matter, teaching, learners, professional attitudes and values, and practice and context. The in-service version, represented in the User's Guide (MOET, 2013b), emphasises practical knowledge, while the pre-service version (MOET, 2013c) is more rigorous and theoretical, as

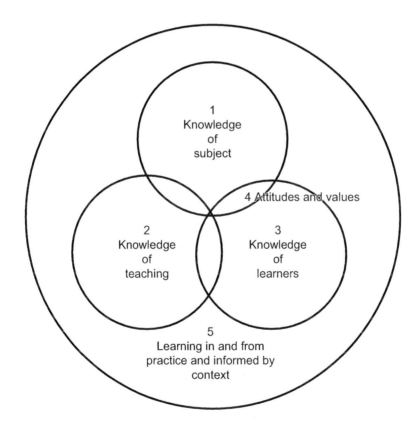

Figure 2.1 ETCF framework

Source: (Dudzik, 2008)

well as practical, and includes additional competencies. Each domain of the pre-service ETCF consists of between four and six competencies, "the levels of knowledge or skill at which teachers are expected to perform" (MOET, 2013a, p. 13). Each competency has a set of detailed performance indicators that serve as "evidences of competency" (MOET, 2013a, p. 13) in the form of can-do statements (Appendix B of this chapter).

The ETCF employs a situated framework where the cultural and educational context and the principle of learning in and from practice are foundational to all of the competencies. This situated learning (Lave & Wenger, 1991; Wenger, 1998) occurs as students participate in field experiences and as they are engaged in communities of practice among experts and novices. Petron and Uzum (2017) applied a situated learning perspective to equip general education teachers to teach content to English language learners through four field experiences with follow-up reflections and a final teaching philosophy in a methodology class, concluding that this experience of "peripheral participation in expert roles . . . as emerging teachers" (p. 68) contributed both to identity formation and expertise but should have occurred earlier in the programme to connect theory and practice. The ETCF is intended to be additive, not punitive (MOET, 2013a, p. 9) and to help identify core content and processes of teacher education and development, attending to the complex knowledge base of ELTE. However, despite this recent and multifaceted approach to capacity building, policies and funding to disseminate and implement the framework have not supported widespread adoption to date.

Approaches to capacity building

PELTE programmes need to equip teachers with both academic content and practical experience and to assist them to enter a field of work "where membership is based on entry requirements and standards" (Burns & Richards, 2009, p. 2). In Vietnam, this balance is not easy to achieve. Le (2014) describes a typical PELTE programme as "similar to Wallace's (1991) applied-science model, which relies heavily on theories delivered by experts with little or no experience teaching in the secondary school" (p. 204). This is in congruence with Hamano (2008), who also criticises the load of theoretical study with little attention to teaching methods, and Pham (2001) and Nguyen's (2013) critique of PELTE programmes in Vietnam for offering limited opportunity to develop contextual knowledge. Another challenge for PELTE in Vietnam is the low level of language proficiency among entry-level pre-service teachers. Despite entry requirements of Level B1 on the Common European Framework of Reference (CEFR), actual proficiency was "hardly B1 . . . let alone talking about their speaking and listening [skills]" (Nguyen, 2013, p. 45). As a consequence, language proficiency courses take up a considerable proportion of PELTE programmes in Vietnam.

In summary, the literature suggests that the contextualisation and synergy between professional development and practical training foregrounded in the current perceptions of ELTE as a socialisation process is yet to be achieved in

Vietnam. However, it should be noted that most of the literature reviewed so far was reported during the earlier stage of the NFLP 2020. With the introduction of the ETCF in 2013 and multiple reforms facilitated by the project recently, it is unclear whether these issues have been addressed in the current PELTE curricula and to what extent. The study presented next expects to address this research gap.

Methodology

The PELTE curriculum at one of Vietnam's premiere English TE institutions, an early adopter of the ETCF, is the object of this mixed methods case study. The programme spans four years with an annual intake of approximately 250 trainees and a total of 136 credits. An overview of the main contents covered in this programme is provided in Table 2.1. Most graduates expect to work as English language teachers at secondary schools, colleges, and universities throughout Vietnam.

The principal tools of data collection include an analysis of PELTE course syllabi ($n = 18$) and a survey of pre-service ELTs ($n = 132$), followed by interviews and focus groups with eight pre-service teachers, three teacher educators, and two PELTE programme managers ($n = 13$). The survey, conducted in English, was adapted from the ETCF Teacher Strengths and Needs Assessment (MOET, 2013a, pp. 55–61) and asked participants to rate, on a scale of 1 (lowest) to 7 (highest), the extent to which their PELTE programme had helped them to achieve the 60 performance indicators in the framework (Appendix B of this chapter). Typical interview and focus group questions for pre-service teachers (who volunteered to join by providing contact details in their questionnaire answers) included: "Why did you give item X this rating?" and "Do you agree with this rating by your peer(s)?" As a generalisation to the whole population was not an expected outcome, the survey respondents, interviewees, and focus group participants were selected based on convenience and volunteers. Student interviewees were in their final year so as to provide a more comprehensive evaluation of the PELTE programme. While the quantitative data mostly involved descriptive

Table 2.1 Main contents of the PELTE curriculum under study

Components	Number of credits
General/foundational knowledge (philosophy, informatics, second foreign language, etc.)	27
Knowledge of the broad area (geography, statistics, etc.)	6
Knowledge of the area cluster (Vietnamese culture, Vietnamese language, etc.)	8
Knowledge of the area (English linguistics, English language proficiency, English-speaking country studies and literature, etc.)	57
Knowledge of the specific area (psychology, pedagogy, assessment and testing, practicum,* etc.)	38

*3 credits

statistics analysis, the analysis of the qualitative data relied on a combination of theory-driven and data-driven code development of thematic analysis (Boyatzis, 1998). Theory-driven codes were generated from the five domains and the specific competencies of the ETCF. New codes that emerged from the data were critically examined for insights into potential omissions in the framework, yielding possible theoretical contributions from this study. Major findings are discussed here.

Findings

Analysis of course syllabi

English translations of 18 PELTE course syllabi (Appendix A) were examined and analysed in light of the ETCF. Among them, 13 were compulsory and five were electives, ten were language proficiency courses, and the remaining nine represented ELT content courses. Of the 18 syllabi analysed for this study, only two showed evidence of being explicitly aligned to the ETCF (Courses 11 and 12, Appendix A). In both syllabi, this alignment was made explicit through course objectives that were linked to specific competencies. For example, Objectives CF0, CF1, and CF2 of Course 10 were aligned with ETCF competencies 3.1, 3.2, 3.3, and 3.4 (Table 2.2). By intentionally aligning course objectives to specific ETCF competencies, the manner in which the curriculum addressed those competencies became more transparent.

The content of the 18 syllabi were also analysed to identify strengths and gaps in light of the ETCF. If 50% or more of the syllabi showed evidence of a specific competency, that competency was categorised as being "strongly" represented across the curriculum. If 25–50% of the syllabi showed evidence of a competency, it was categorised as "moderately." The rest were categorised as "weakly" represented. Across the syllabi, 14.29% of the competencies were strongly represented, 42.86% were moderately represented, and 42.86% were weakly represented (Table 2.3).

Four competencies were strongly represented across the 18 syllabi: language proficiency, knowledge of CEFR, language as a system (grammar), and professional development and lifelong learning. This finding largely represents the ten proficiency courses, which employed Competencies 1.1.a, 1.1.b, and 2, as

Table 2.2 Example of course objectives linked to ETCF (from Introduction to language teaching syllabus)

CF0	*Conceptual framework* – concepts, theories	Professional standard
CF1	and principles of ELT	1.2, 1.3, 1.6, 2.1
CF2	– *Understand* the frameworks, concepts, theories, and principles of ELT; – Use this understanding to *evaluate* the theoretical effectiveness of some approaches and methods in language teaching.	

Table 2.3 Syllabi analysis: strongly and weakly represented competencies

Strong competencies		Moderate competencies		Weak competencies	
1.1a	language proficiency	1.3	SLA	1.4	cultures
1.1b	CEFR	2.1	ELT methodology	1.5a	literary content
1.2	language system	2.2	lesson planning	1.5b	academic content
4.3	professional development and lifelong learning	2.3b	managing classroom activities	1.6	curriculum and syllabus
		2.4	Assessment	2.3a	learning environment
		2.5	Materials	2.6	technology
		3.2	learner language	3.1	learner development
		3.3	cultural values and prior learning	4.4	contributing to profession
		3.4	creativity, critical thinking, innovation	4.5	ethical teaching and testing
		4.1	Professionalism	5.1	connecting learning beyond classroom
		4.2	cooperation, collaboration, teamwork	5.3	English in SE Asia
		5.2	reflection and research	5.4	global role of English

well as assignments across the curriculum requiring student responsibility for their own learning (Competency 4.3). By contrast, 12 competencies occurred in less than 25% of the syllabi. Most competencies in Domain 5 were "weakly represented" across the syllabi. Competencies such as target language cultures (1.4), technology (2.6), and ethical teaching and testing (4.5) could have been embedded in language proficiency and ELT. While these observations might indicate weaknesses in the curriculum, caution should be taken due to the lack of detailed content (e.g., list of topics and tasks) in the translated syllabi. The syllabi analysis also revealed gaps in the ETCF. For example, the topic of teacher identity was found in several syllabi; however, there was no corresponding ETCF competency.

Survey findings

The survey (n = 132) indicates that the pre-service teachers believed the PELTE curriculum addressed all five domains codified in the ETCF. On a scale of 7.0, the mean rating for each ETCF domain was above 5.0 (SD <1.2). Examining the mean ratings for each indicator, Table 2.4 reveals that the highest-rated statements were indicators of Domains 1, 2, and 4.

Table 2.4 includes competencies from Domains 1, 2, and 4, whose indicators emphasise not only knowledge, evidenced by indicators such as "understand" and "know about" but also skills, evidenced by indicators such as "teach," "begin to apply," "collaborate," and "can use," as well as attitudes of the students for their teaching profession. However, competencies from Domain 3 and 5 are not represented but are found in Table 2.5, the lowest-rated competencies.

Considering both means and standard deviations, Tables 2.5 and 2.6 indicate that Statements 13, 57, 49, 58, and 60 (Appendix B) were given among the

Table 2.4 Highest-rated performance indicators (with the mean ratings in descending order)

Domain	Competency (see Table 2.3)	Statement number (see Appendix B)	n	m
2	2.6	32.	131	5.95
4	4.2	44.	129	5.91
2	2.6	31.	132	5.86
1	1.5a	14.	128	5.78
1	1.4	10.	131	5.73
4	4.1	43.	130	5.72
1	1.3	7.	131	5.71

Table 2.5 Lowest-rated performance indicators (with the mean ratings in ascending order)

Domain	Competency (see Table 2.4)	Statement number (See Appendix B)	n	m
1	1.5a	13.	131	4.51
5	5.3	57.	131	5.03
4	4.4	49.	131	5.18
5	5.4	60.	131	5.27
3	3.2	36.	130	5.09
5	5.3	58.	131	5.14

Table 2.6 Performance indicators with the lowest standard deviations in descending order

Domain	Competency (see Table 2.4)	Statement number (see Appendix B)	n	SD
1	1.5a	13.	131	1.561
5	5.3	57.	131	1.435
4	4.4	49.	131	1.417
5	5.4	60.	131	1.353
3	3.2	36.	130	1.32
5	5.3	58.	131	1.317

lowest ratings (5.7 < *m* < 5.96) and also the smallest standard deviations (1.3 <SD <1.6), suggesting a consensus among pre-service teachers on the weaker areas of the curriculum. Most of these competences represent Domain 5 (practice and context), specifically regarding the roles of EIL, regional issues of English in SE Asia and their ability to apply those understandings to their classrooms. This finding, also evident in the syllabi analyses, is corroborated by data from focus groups and interviews, as the following discussion demonstrates.

Interview and focus groups findings

A closer investigation into the qualitative data affirms inattention to Domain 5 and a limited connection between the curriculum and classroom and contextual realities as the main shortcoming of the programme for two main reasons. First, although various competences are addressed across the PELTE curriculum, implications for real-life classroom practices were not always made transparent to the students. For example, Statement 13 (Appendix B), the ability to "use English literature to teach language and content" (*m* = 4.51, SD = 1.56), was lowest rated out of 60 statements (Table 2.5), even though knowledge of the cultures and literatures of English-speaking countries is a stated outcome of the PELTE programme and certain focused courses (see Table 2.1). One pre-service teacher (teacher B) elaborated:

> Sometimes I take a course just to meet the credit requirements. . . . When . . . I . . . look back, I don't know what the course was about. For instance, literature . . . needs to emphasise what is most important [and] applicable to practice, rather than the teacher's following the syllabus and the course books, and then do not say how to use it in practice.

This pre-service teacher questioned the delivery of the course, which failed to foreground either the focus ("what is most important") or its relevance to real-life teaching ("how to use it in practice"). She later suggested the need for more practice and more explicit instruction regarding the application of literature in EFL teaching. The second issue highlighted was the lack of quantity and authenticity in practice:

> We only have micro-teaching in [one class] . . . to teach my own classmates. That is not very real. . . . [W]e need . . . more time for classroom observation and experiences with the real-life classrooms.
>
> (Pre-service teacher C)

> We need to gain better access to real-life teaching practices instead of focusing on lecturing and theory only . . . to develop a wider range of skills that are directly applicable to their future working experiences.
>
> (Pre-service teacher D)

Both of these students suggested the need for more practice (i.e., "more time," "wider range") and more authentic practice (i.e., "better access," "applicable," and "experiences with real-life classrooms"). One manager explained this gap:

> One issue . . . is the lack of cooperation between universities and second- ary schools, therefore there are few opportunities to approach secondary schools. [It would be better to allow students to] sit in secondary classes and reflect on what they study at university.

Synthesis of findings

In summary, the syllabi analyses, interviews, and focus groups indicate that Domains 3 (learners) and 5 (practice and context) were moderately or weakly represented in the curriculum. Some data were contradictory; for example, students rated com- petencies 1.4 (cultures), 1.5 (literary and academic content), and 2.6 (technology) among the highest strengths (Table 2.4), while these were weakly represented in the syllabi (Table 2.3). On closer examination, they reveal only partial compe- tency (Tables 2.5 and 2.6). For example, students specified that Competency 1.4 (cultures) was a strength with the statement "know about English-speaking cul- tures" (Statement 10, Appendix B) but not the ability to "include this cultural knowledge in my teaching" (Statement 11) or "use this cultural knowledge to build understanding and empathy" (Statement 12). Similarly, data were split con- cerning literary and academic content in English (Competencies 1.5a and 1.5b). Students indicated the ability to "use cultural texts (websites, songs, TV etc.) to teach language and content" (Statement 14, Appendix B) as a strength but the ability to "use English literature to teach language and content" (Statement 13) as a limitation (Tables 2.5 and 2.6). These findings corroborate student interview data suggesting that students' experience was heavy on theory and light on prac- tice. Survey data that indicates three of the five major weaker areas (Tables 2.5 and 2.6) represent Domain 5 also corroborate syllabi analysis data (Table 2.3). They were more clearly identified as major weaknesses of the PELTE curriculum by student interview data.

Discussion

Both strengths and limitations of the curriculum became evident through this research examining a prominent Vietnamese pre-service ELTE curriculum in light of a national teacher competency framework. These areas, along with sug- gested solutions for improving the curriculum, are discussed here.

Strengths and limitations

Theoretical content knowledge in competencies related to SLA theories target- ing language cultures, literary (mostly social language) content, and technol- ogy emerged as the major strength of the curriculum, indicating that pre-service teachers graduate with a solid foundation. As Livingston (2016) suggests, initial teacher education needs to provide a strong foundation for future teachers, equipping them to learn and adapt throughout their careers. The picture of a moderately comprehensive curriculum to build pre-service teacher capacity emerged, with most competencies regarding teaching (Domain 2) and learners (Domain 3) moderately represented, including theoretical content competencies such as LT (language teaching) methodology and learner language, as well as pedagogical content competencies such as lesson planning, managing classrooms, assessment, developing materials and understanding learners. Professional values and processes such as reflection, research, cooperation and collaboration, creativity, and critical thinking were also moderately represented.

However, several gaps were also identified through this research. More than 42% of the competencies were weakly represented in the syllabi, including most of Domain 5 (learning in and from practice and being informed by context). Current literature highlights the role of context in the recent conceptualisation of teacher learning as socialisation. This study also reveals a major gap between theoretical knowledge and pedagogical content knowledge evidenced by limited, decontextualised practice. Students called for "real-life" experiences that would bridge the gap between their training and the reality of teaching. The deficit in contextual knowledge (Canagarajah, 2014; Richards, 1998, 2010; Roberts, 1998; Solano-Campos, 2014) and of situated learning in real settings (Le, 2014; Nguyen, 2013) constitutes a weakness of this PELTE programme.

Suggestions for improvement

A number of strategies could be employed to maximise curricular strengths and mitigate weaknesses, which include prioritising, mapping, and embedding competencies across the curriculum; more fully employing the apprenticeship of observation; and situating teacher learning by making more connections to classroom practice.

Prioritise competencies

A number of competencies were underrepresented in the curriculum. While many of them may not warrant stand-alone courses, opportunities to embed these competencies in the existing syllabi were often missed. Examples include literature, technology, and ethical teaching and testing, with literature being most commonly cited in both qualitative and quantitative data. Professional competencies codify teacher knowledge, skills, and dispositions and can inform the rigor of teacher education content and processes (Darling-Hammond, 2016). The ETCF User's Guide (MOET, 2013a) suggests addressing priority competencies with stand-alone courses and embedding other competencies (such as soft skills, values, processes) across the curriculum, creating a more transparent, competency-based curriculum. Professional competencies employed in CBTE can help guide the content and processes of PELTE. However, policies need to prioritise competencies and support implementation, and competencies must be detailed enough to be helpful (DeLuca & Bellara, 2013; Hammond, 2014; Struyven & De Meyst, 2010). Moreover, there is a need to prioritise certain competencies to better meet the specific needs of teachers in their real-life teaching scenarios. As the PELTE curriculum in question aims to train English language teachers for many educational levels and contexts, it risks imposing a one-size-fits-all set of standards on the pre-service ELTs regardless of their career paths, teaching needs, and contexts. It hence calls for the needs to take these variations into consideration as much as possible to avoid prescribing and essentialising what teachers should know and be able to do.

Employ apprenticeship

A major gap in pre-service teachers' experience regarded preparation for the real world of language teaching. Teacher educators may think that they are modelling best practices, but these may not be explicitly apparent to teacher-learners. This lack of connection with practice and the contexts in the PELTE programme is more challenging to solve. It is here that the ETCF puts forward Lortie's (1975) "apprenticeship of observation" (p. 61), which Freeman (2016) describes as helping teacher-learners experience the teacher's point of view.

> Experiential learning is an important part of the ETCF . . . to experience the processes and activities that they are being expected to use in their classrooms . . . to not only learn about but also practice new classroom behaviors and roles.
>
> (MOET, 2013a, p. 36)

Proficiency courses are ideal for modelling new classroom behaviours, attending to the apprenticeship of observation, and providing new understandings and experiences regarding not only language but also literature, culture, academic content and connections to other subjects, and the regional and international roles and issues of teaching English.

Situate teacher learning

Situated learning, where teachers learn in and from their context, is more effective than decontextualised learning (Borko, 2004; Solano-Campos, 2014). Pre-service teacher-learning can be situated by adding authentic tasks and student work samples, classrooms case studies, and real teaching experiences paired with reflection and observation (Struyven & De Meyst, 2010) and by asking how to design authentic micro-worlds for teacher practice, scaffolding those experiences with critical feedback and coaching (Freeman, 2016). Reflective practice, "essential to teaching pre-service teachers how to make links between theory and practice" (Macknisch et al., 2017, p. 13), can be incorporated into classroom observations and field experiences that provide teaching opportunities (Farrell,

2017). Connections among novice teachers, teacher educators, and school administrators, what Farrell calls "novice-service teacher education" (2015, p. 4), can also be sought, as well as creating a course about the first teaching experience in anticipation of students' first teaching assignments (Farrell, 2015).

Limitations

Limitations of this study include its focus on the secondary education teacher preparation programme, omitting the issue cited in the introduction regarding the shortage of primary school teachers. English translations of the syllabi were analysed, not all of which were equally complete. The study would have been strengthened if it had focused on required courses rather than on some required and some electives. Additionally, interviews and surveys were conducted simultaneously with the syllabi analysis, rather than being informed by the data. Further research could investigate only the required core courses or add all electives and correlate findings with teacher–learners' perceptions. Finally, as standards alone are not sufficient for an effective ELTE programme, the interrelations between policy, curriculum, and standards could also be further problematised to "talk back" to these standards as well.

Conclusion

Pre-service teacher education programmes are foundational in building teaching capacity. Drawing on the ETCF as the analytical framework, this chapter examined a prominent PELTE curriculum in Vietnam to identify strengths and gaps. Qualitative and quantitative data were analysed to reveal two major themes. The curriculum showed a moderate alignment with the ETCF, suggesting movement towards more comprehensive preparation of pre-service teachers' capacity. However, many of these attempts seemed to fall short of the students' expectations, as there were limited connections between their education and real-life practices. Many opportunities were missed for a stronger alignment among the curriculum, syllabuses, and ETCF framework, resulting in graduates questioning their preparedness for their futures, the implications of which ripple throughout English education nationwide.

References

Ball, D. L., & Cohen, D. K. (1999). Developing practice, developing practitioners: Toward a practice-based theory of professional education. In L. Darling-Hammond & G. Sykes (Eds.), *Teaching as the learning profession: Handbook of policy and practice* (pp. 3–32). San Francisco: Jossey-Bass.

Borko, H. (2004). Professional development and teach learning: Mapping the terrain. *Educational Researcher, 33*(8), 3–15.

Boyatzis, R. E. (1998). *Transforming qualitative information: Thematic analysis and code development.* Thousand Oaks, CA: Sage Publications.

Bransford, J., Darling-Hammond, L., & LePage, P. (2005). Introduction. In J. Bransford & L. Darling-Hammond (Eds.), *Preparing teachers for a changing world: What teachers should learn and be able to do* (pp. 1–39). San Francisco: Jossey-Bass.

Burns, A., & Richards, J. C. (2009). *The Cambridge guide to second language teacher education*. Cambridge: Cambridge University Press.

Canagarajah, S. (2014). In search of a new paradigm for teaching English as an international language. *TESOL Journal*, 5(4), 767–785.

Darling-Hammond, L. (2016). Research on teaching and teacher education and its influences on policy and practice. *Educational Researcher*, 45(2), 83–91.

DeLuca, C., & Bellara, A. (2013). The current state of assessment education: Aligning policy, standards and teacher education curriculum. *Journal of Teacher Education*, 64(4), 356–372.

Department of Primary Education. (2016, January 22). *The current situation of English language teaching at primary schools and suggestions to improve the quality of English language teaching and learning for the new education programme*. Paper presented at the Conference on the recruitment and training of primary-school English language teachers to meet the demands for English language teaching today and the new course book and education programme in the future. Hanoi: Vietnam.

Dudzik, D. L. (2008). English policies, curricular reform and teacher development in multilingual, postcolonial Djibouti. *Dissertation Abstracts International*, 69, 1652.

Farrell, T. S. C. (2015). Second language teacher education: A reality check. In T. S. C. Farrell (Ed.), *International perspectives on English language teacher education* (pp. 1–15). New York: Palgrave Macmillan.

Farrell, T. S. C. (2017). Conclusion: Bridging gaps, making links and designing new spans in TESOL teacher education. In T. S. C. Farrell (Ed.), *Pre-service teacher education* (pp. 101–107). Alexandria, VA: TESOL International Association.

Freeman, D. (2016). *Educating second language teachers: The same things done differently*. Oxford: Oxford University Press.

Freeman, D., & Johnson, K. E. (1998). Reconceptualizing the knowledge-base of language teacher education. *TESOL Quarterly*, 32(3), 397–417.

Hamano, T. (2008). Educational reform and teacher education in Vietnam. *Journal of Education for Teaching: International Research and Pedagogy*, 34(4), 397–410.

Hammond, J. (2014). An Australian perspective on standards-based education, teacher knowledge, and students of English as an additional language. *TESOL Quarterly*, 48(3), 507–532.

Hoang, V. V. (2009). The current situation and issues of the teaching of English in Vietnam. *Ritsumeikan University's Institute for Teaching and Learning Journal*, 22(1), 7–18.

Johnson, K. E. (2009). *Second language teacher education: A sociocultural perspective*. New York: Routledge.

Katz, A., & Snow, M. A. (2009). Standards and second language teacher education. In A. Burns & J. C. Richards (Eds.), *The Cambridge guide to second language teacher education* (pp. 66–76). Cambridge: Cambridge University Press.

Lave, J., & Wenger, E. (1991). *Situated learning: Legitimate peripheral participation*. Cambridge: Cambridge University Press.

Le, V. C. (2012). *Form-focused instruction: Teachers' beliefs and practices: A case study of Vietnamese teachers*. Saarbrucken: Lambert Academic Publishing.

Le, V. C. (2014). Great expectations: The TESOL practicum as a professional learning experience. *TESOL Journal*, 5(2), 199–224.

Livingston, K. (2016). Teacher education's role in educational change. *European Journal of Teacher Education, 39*(1), 1–4.

Lortie, D. C. (1975). *Schoolteacher* (2nd ed.). Chicago: University of Chicago Press.

Macknisch, C., Porter-Szucs, I., Tomas, Z., Scholze, A., Slucter, C., & Kavetsky, A. (2017). Bridging theory and practice from the ground up: Reflections from a master's in TESOL program. In T. S. C. Farrell (Ed.), *Pre-service teacher education* (pp. 29–35). Alexandria, VA: TESOL International Association.

MOET. (2013a). *Competence framework for English language teachers: User's Guide.* Hanoi: Vietnam National Institute for Educational Sciences, Ministry of Education and Training.

MOET. (2013b). *Inservice English teacher competencies framework.* Retrieved from http://nfl2020forum.net/index.php/nfl2020/complete-versions

MOET. (2013c). *Pre-service English teacher competencies framework.* Retrieved from http://nfl2020forum.net/index.php/nfl2020/complete-versions

Murray, J. (2009). Teacher competencies in the post-method landscape: The limits of competency-based training in TESOL teacher education. *Prospect, 24*(1), 17–29.

National Foreign Languages Project 2020. (2016). English language teacher training within the 2020 Project. Proceedings of the Conference on Assessing and Finding Solutions to the Management and Implementation of English Language Teacher Training Activities (pp. 22-26). Hanoi, Vietnam: Ministry of Education and Training.

Nguyen, M. H. (2013). The curriculum for English language teacher education in Australian and Vietnamese universities. *Australian Journal of Teacher Education, 38*(11), 33–53.

Nguyen, M. H. (2016). Responding to the need for re-conceptualising second language teacher education: The potential of a sociocultural perspective. *International Education Studies, 9*(12), 219–231.

Petron, M., & Uzum, B. (2017). Situated learning experiences of general education teachers: Teaching content to English language learners. In Thomas Farrell (Ed.), *TESOL voices: Preservice teacher education* (pp. 67–77). Alexandria, VA: TESOL Press.

Pham, H. H. (2001). Teacher development: A real need for English departments in Vietnam. *English Teaching Forum, 39*(4).

Richards, J. C. (1998). *Beyond training: Perspectives on language teacher education.* New York: Cambridge University Press.

Richards, J. C. (2010). Competence and performance in language teaching. *RELC Journal, 41*(2), 101–122.

Roberts, J. (1998). *Language teacher education.* London: Arnold.

Solano-Campos, A. (2014). The making of an international educator: Transnationalism and non nativeness in English teaching and learning. *TESOL Journal, 5*(3), 412–443.

Struyven, K., & De Meyst, M. (2010). Competence-based teacher education: Illusion or reality? An assessment of the implementation status in Flanders from teachers' and students' points of view. *Teaching and Teacher Education, 26*, 1495–1510.

Vietnam Government. (2008). *Decision on the approval of the project entitled 'Teaching and learning foreign languages in the national education system, period 2008–2020'.* Hanoi: Prime Minister. Retrieved from http://t1.truongt36.edu.vn/chi-tiet/decision-on-the-approval-of-the-project-entitled-%E2%80%9Cteaching-and-learning-foreign-languages-in-the-national-education-system-period-2008-2020%E2%80%9D-10157.html

Vu, M. T. (2017). *Logics and politics of professionalism: The case of university English language teachers in Vietnam.* Umea, Sweden: Umea University.

Wallace, M. J. (1991). *Training foreign language teachers: A reflective approach.* Cambridge, UK: Cambridge University Press.

Wenger, E. (1998). *Communities of practice: Learning, meaning, and identity.* Cambridge: Cambridge University Press.

Appendix A

18 PELTE syllabi analysed using ETCF

Course	Type	Status
1–10. English 1A, 1B, 2A, 2B, 3A, 3B, 3C, 4A, 4B, 4C	Language proficiency	Compulsory
11. Introduction to language teaching	ELT	Compulsory
12. ESL/EFL classroom techniques	ELT	Compulsory
13. English language testing and assessment	ELT	Compulsory
14. Issues of teaching English as an international language	ELT	Elective
15. Lesson planning and material development	ELT	Elective
16. Teaching English to young learners	ELT	Elective
17. Technology in ELT	ELT	Elective
18. ESP teaching methodology	ELT	Elective

Appendix B

ETCF performance indicators used in survey

Domain	Statements: I can . . .
Domain 1. Knowledge of Language, Language Learning and Language Content and Curriculum	1. . . . use English at the level required for my teaching (C1 of CEFR). 2. . . . find opportunities to strengthen my English proficiency. 3. . . . understand the CEF/KNLNN proficiency descriptors at the levels that apply to my students. 4. . . . apply that understanding to my teaching practice. 5. . . . understand English sounds, word parts, word meanings, and word order (in general). 6. . . . teach these things at the secondary level. 7. . . . know how languages are learned. 8. . . . apply this knowledge to my own language learning. 9. . . . apply this knowledge to my teaching. 10. . . . know about English-speaking cultures. 11. . . . include this cultural knowledge in my teaching. 12. . . . use this cultural knowledge to build understanding and empathy. 13. . . . use English literature to teach language and content. 14. . . . use cultural texts (websites, songs, TV etc.) to teach language and content. 15. . . . use English academic texts to teach language and content. 16. . . . understand the English curriculum I'm required to use. 17. . . . use textbooks and required curriculum objectives when planning lessons.

Domain	Statements: I can . . .
Domain 2. Knowledge of Language Teaching	18. . . . know many strategies and techniques to integrate the 4 skills.
	19. . . . use many strategies and techniques to integrate the 4 skills.
	20. . . . use this methodology to integrate the 4 skills for authentic communication.
	21. . . . use this methodology to integrate the 4 skills to teach different kinds of learners.
	22. . . . understand what kinds of lessons, assignments and activities teach content, integrate skills, and help students learn English.
	23. . . . plan effective lessons and design assignments and activities to teach content, integrate skills and help students learn English.
	24. . . . know how to create a supportive, meaningful learning environment.
	25. . . . use the lesson plan to teach students, and give them meaningful opportunities to communicate.
	26. . . . manage classroom activities to teach students, and give them meaningful opportunities to communicate.
	27. . . . know about formative (ongoing) and summative (progress) assessment tools and techniques.
	28. . . . design and use age-appropriate assessment tools to guide my teaching and measure student progress.
	29. . . . use and adapt textbooks effectively for my teaching.
	30. . . . find and adapt materials and resources that are suitable for students' age and English level.
	31. . . . have basic computer skills and can use basic computer programmes.
	32. . . . use technology for language teaching and learning.
Domain 3. Knowledge of Language Learners	33. . . . understand learners' intellectual and emotional development.
	34. . . . know about different learning styles.
	35. . . . develop lessons that motivate different kinds of learners.
	36. . . . know about different stages of language development.
	37. . . . adapt my teaching and give feedback on students' errors in ways that are suitable to their language level.

(*Continued*)

Domain	Statements: I can . . .
	38. . . . reflect on my cultural values and learning experiences and how these affect my learning and teaching.
	39. . . . reflect on my students' cultural values and prior learning experiences and how they affect students' learning and behavior.
	40. . . . practice creativity and critical thinking in their learning and teaching.
	41. . . . help my students develop creativity and critical thinking appropriate for their age.
Domain 4. Professional Attitudes and Values in Language Teaching	42. . . . value and can promote the importance of learning English.
	43. . . . teach and behave professionally.
	44. . . . collaborate with others in teams to accomplish tasks.
	45. . . . teach students cooperation and collaboration skills.
	46. . . . learn new information about language teaching and research on my own.
	47. . . . develop teaching skills on my own.
	48. . . . find ongoing professional development opportunities.
	49. . . . contribute to the exchange of ideas in my teaching community to benefit other teachers.
	50. . . . understand the ethical issues related to language teaching and testing.
	51. . . . model ethical professional behavior.
Domain 5. Practice and Context of Language Teaching	52. . . . continue to learn about current topics that are important for English teaching.
	53. . . . connect my students' English learning to other students, classes, school, and topics.
	54. . . . practice ongoing reflection to think about my own language learning.
	55. . . . practice ongoing reflection to find answers to my teaching questions.
	56. . . . use my reflections to guide my learning and teaching.
	57. . . . understand the roles and uses of English and issues of teaching and learning English in Southeast Asia.
	58. . . . begin to apply these understandings to their lessons, assignments, materials' selection, and activities.

Domain	Statements: I can . . .
	59. . . . understand issues related to English as an international language.
	60. . . . use those understandings to inform choices of methodology, materials, content and assessment standards.

3 Risk, uncertainty, and vulnerability

Primary teachers' emotional experiences of English language policy implementation

Laura Grassick

Introduction

With the emergence of English as a global language and increased international economic trade relations, many governments have seen a need to improve the English language communicative competence of their youth. In Vietnam, this has led to the development of the National Foreign Languages 2020 Project (NFLP 2020) in which there has been a noticeable emphasis in policy on *teachers* and their role in helping to achieve the desired improvements in English language communicative competence (Bui & Nguyen, 2016; Le, Nguyen, & Burns, 2017). Policy change in relation to teachers has focused on teachers' professional standards in areas of pedagogy and English language proficiency. This has included the introduction of a new English language curriculum advocating more communicative approaches to language teaching and encouraging the use of English in the classroom by both learners and teachers, as well as a required minimum standard of English language proficiency for teachers. A similar focus on the teacher can be found in other studies of educational change (e.g., Hardman & A-Rahman, 2014; Nguyen & Bui, 2016; Zein, 2016). These studies highlight that unless attention is given to issues around teachers and their teaching quality, capacity, and language proficiency, then the likelihood of a new language or curriculum policy succeeding becomes fairly remote. Indeed, in regard to Vietnam, Bui and Nguyen (2016, p. 371) comment that:

> the fact that a great many English teachers are not sufficiently proficient to teach subjects involving English has been identified as one of the most challenging factors in current language policy implementation.

Despite the move in Vietnam (and elsewhere) to focus reform efforts on the teacher, there seems to be limited consideration of teachers' emotional experiences of educational policy change (Agudo, 2018). This may be because recognition of the people involved and how they think, feel, and respond to innovation – the emotionality of change – is often lost in top-down, rational-managerial processes of policy planning and implementation (Wedell, 2009). Yet the success (or failure) of any educational policy reform partly depends on how teachers *feel* about what they are being asked to do and the impact their emotional responses may have on how they enact change (Grassick, 2016). This chapter looks at the emotional dimension of language policy change and argues for more recognition and understanding of teachers' emotional experiences of the implementation of new pedagogy and language proficiency requirements. Using data from a previous, larger research study (Grassick, 2016), the chapter explores the feelings of a group of seven primary English language teachers as they make sense of the new requirements and changes to their professional knowledge and practice brought about by the NFLP 2020 curriculum and language policy. The data show how feelings of uncertainty and vulnerability emerge from teachers' perceptions of risk in relation to challenges to their professional selves (Kelchtermans, 2005, 2009) and changes in the contextual demands of their work. The findings highlight how a better understanding of teachers' emotions might improve the support provided for teachers during the implementation process, helping to ensure its success. The implications of the study will be relevant to policy planners, implementers, and those involved in language teacher education in Vietnam and in other contexts undergoing similar English language reforms.

Primary English language policy in Vietnam

Under the NFLP 2020, compulsory English language education has been introduced in the primary curriculum from Grade 3. This policy constitutes a significant change for primary schools. English is now considered necessary for all children across the country and no longer simply an optional subject. A new competency-based curriculum has been introduced alongside a language proficiency requirement for all English language teachers working in primary schools to reach Level B2 on the Common European Framework of References (CEFR).

For many primary teachers, the new curriculum advocates significant changes to their current classroom practice, which is often characterised by "pedagogies [that] focus predominantly on rote memorisation [and] passive learning approaches" (Le Fevre, 2015, p. 183). The move to compulsory English language education in primary schools has the added complexity of not only pedagogical change but also new knowledge in the field of teaching English to young learners (TEYL). Pre-service teacher education in primary English language teaching is a relatively new phenomenon in Vietnam offered by a few higher education institutions; therefore the majority of existing primary teachers tend to lack specific, formalised knowledge of young learner pedagogy (Nguyen, Hamid, & Renshaw, 2016). The English Teacher Competency Framework (ETCF) (NFLP 2020, 2013) provides a set of standards outlining what English language teachers need to know about teaching and learning and what they should be able to do in the classroom. The five domains include language proficiency and pedagogical skills. The framework acknowledges a need for teacher knowledge and skills to be standardised and measured, helping to ensure more equity in student learning outcomes across schools and provinces.

Alongside the new curriculum, teachers are also required to reach the B2 English language proficiency level based on CEFR or Level 4 based on the Vietnamese Language Proficiency Framework (VLPF), which was introduced in 2014 (Le et al., 2017). An initial national baseline study, which sought to investigate the current language proficiency level of English language teachers, reported that 80,000 English language teachers did not meet the language requirements as set out in the NFLP 2020 (Dudzik & Nguyen, 2013). In relation to primary English language teachers, as many as 83% were graded below the desired Level B2 (CEFR), with the majority at Level A2 (Nguyen, 2013).

Decision 1400/QD-TTg (MOET, 2008) proposed that existing teachers should be retrained in pedagogy and language skills, and a number of regional foreign language centres have been established around the country to support teacher development (Bui & Nguyen, 2016). While in-service provision can take many forms (e.g., teacher associations, school-based support), the majority of teacher support has been through workshops and courses delivered by university-level lecturers focusing on enhancing classroom pedagogy and language improvement (Bui & Nguyen, 2016; Nguyen, 2017; Tran, 2018).

Emotions and language policy implementation

Little attention has been paid to teachers' emotions in educational change research (Day & Lee, 2011; Hargreaves, 2005; Nias, 1996). Yet as Hargreaves (2005, p. 13) argues, "[T]he emotional dimension of educational change is not a frill but a fundamental improvement, and deserves increased attention." Similarly, in the field of English language education, teacher emotion has rarely been researched or reported on (Benesch, 2017; White, 2018). However, its importance is gaining ground with an increasing number of studies (e.g., Agudo, 2018; Cowie, 2011; Nguyen, 2018; Xu, 2013) that accentuate the integral part emotions play in the professional lives of English language teachers and in the implementation of English language policy change.

Teacher emotion has been traditionally viewed as an individual experience linked to cognition and psychology. More recently, research has shown how teachers' emotions are situated in social and relational dimensions, meaning that they are shaped by (and also shape) the interactions teachers may have with people and structures within an educational setting at both the macro- and micro-levels (Lasky, 2005; Liu, 2016; Zembylas, 2010, 2011). While government time and effort is usually focused on macro-level policies and plans, it is at the micro-level (and through the relationships and interactions at that level) that policy takes shape. However, many policymakers and planners seem unaware that it is the lived experiences of implementers at the micro-level that is crucial to the final outcomes of any educational change (Fullan, 2007).

This study focuses on teachers situated at the micro-level of national policy change. It frames teachers' emotional experiences of educational change within concepts of vulnerability and risk. Risk can be defined as an action or event that someone perceives to be risky because it might involve a loss of something they value or involve a failure to act as they perceive others would expect them to (Le Fevre, 2015, p. 57). In the context of Vietnam, both the new curriculum and the language proficiency requirement are likely be perceived as risky endeavours for teachers. These policy changes come with personal and professional costs and benefits that a teacher needs to weigh up and consider within the micro-level reality of their school and classroom context. Feelings of uncertainty and vulnerability can accompany risk. Van Veen and Sleegers (2006, p. 86) see vulnerability emanating from "what [teachers] have at stake in the current context of reform and changing definitions of their work." They suggest that a teacher's professional self and the contextual demands of an education reform have a strong influence on how they might feel about the changes.

Influence of professional self on teachers' emotions

Professional self refers to how teachers view themselves and their job – how they are perceived by others, and the related issues of normativity (Kelchtermans, 2009, pp. 261–262). Underpinning "professional self" are teachers' previous educational experiences and knowledge, beliefs and values. Reform often involves changes to the educational norms, values, and behaviours expected of teachers. In many contexts, including Vietnam, recommended classroom pedagogies imply more interactive or learner-centred approaches where L2 language use in the classroom is unpredictable and creative and where the teacher may have a less dominant role (Le & Do, 2012; Nguyen, 2012). A new curriculum that challenges teachers' beliefs is asking teachers to question not only their previous teaching knowledge and experience but also their current beliefs and values and what they do in the classroom. This can create a sense of vulnerability, since conventional perceptions of a "good teacher" may no longer be relevant (Hu, 2002). Such changes may remove teachers' feelings of stability and security and create perceptions of risk as they grapple with the new situational demands of the job and what is at stake for them. Teachers may feel that their professional self is being questioned by different stakeholders such as parents, school leaders, and the wider society (Gao, 2008). The considerable public scrutiny of English language teachers' capacity in the initial stages of the implementation of the NFLP 2020 is likely to have threatened teachers' professional selves.

Influence of context on teachers' emotions

Whether teachers have opportunities to collaborate and learn with and from others is likely to influence how they feel about a changing professional environment. Thus, teachers' feelings about change implementation may be mediated by the kind of support provision they receive. Research studies have indicated that without culturally and contextually appropriate professional development, teachers may struggle to make sense of a new policy or curriculum (Uztosun, 2018; Wedell &

Grassick, 2018; Zein, 2016), increasing their feelings of uncertainty and vulnerability. In a rush to meet implementation deadlines, training courses can often become a tick-box exercise rather than providing development opportunities designed to meet the real needs of teachers (Yan, 2018). Such training provision may fail to recognise the risks that an innovation might mean for teachers' professional selves.

Teachers' emotional responses to change can also emanate from their "positionality" (Goodson, 2014) or their perceived level of agency within the reform process. In their study of teacher agency and educational reform in Vietnam, Nguyen and Bui (2016) argue that teacher agency is crucial to the implementation of meaningful change. In many change implementation contexts, teachers tend to be seen by policymakers and planners as compliant followers of policy (Lee & Yin, 2011; Yin, Lee, & Wang, 2014) with few established formal communication mechanisms to allow teachers to voice their concerns or feelings about the changes that are happening to them and around them. Rather than creating feelings of enthusiasm in embracing new knowledge and ways of teaching and learning, this lack of agency can lead to indifference and feelings of compulsion in having to follow national policy (Lee & Yin, 2011).

This chapter responds to the call by researchers for more focus on emotionality in educational change (Agudo, 2018; Uitto, Jokikokko, & Estola, 2015; Xu, 2013) by exploring the following research questions:

- How do teachers feel about the new primary English language curriculum?
- How do teachers feel about the language proficiency requirements?
- How are their feelings related to challenges to their professional self and the contextual demands they are faced with in the implementation process?

The study

The participants

The seven teachers in this study were selected because of their role as key teachers in the initial implementation phase of the NFLP 2020 starting from 2011/2012. The teachers work in state primary schools in both urban and semi-rural districts within a major urban province. Brief profiles of the teachers are given in Table 3.1.

Table 3.1 Profile of the participants

Teacher (pseudonym)	Mai	Lien	Thanh	Chi	Bao	Nhung	Chau
Male/female	Female	Female	Male	Female	Female	Female	Female
Teaching experience	14 years	12 years	16 years	9 years	6 years	10 years	18 years
Location of school	Urban district	Rural district	Urban district	Rural district	Urban district	Urban district	Urban district

The teachers were initially approached through their District Office of Education and Training. I explained the details of the research to them and gained their consent. All the participants signed a consent form that set out their role, gave assurances about issues of anonymity and confidentiality, and explained how their data would be used. All documentation given to the participants and gatekeepers was provided in both English and Vietnamese. The interviews were conducted in English following the wishes of the participants. The group interviews included an interpreter.

Data collection

Data were collected through a series of three qualitative semi-structured interviews over four months in 2014. The first semi-structured interview lasted 40–50 minutes and focused on teachers' general feelings about the current reform and their role in the implementation process. The second interview, conducted a few weeks later, probed more deeply into the complexity of their feelings voiced in the first interview in relation to the new language policy. This interview lasted around one hour. The third interview was conducted as a group interview. It aimed to clarify and verify emergent data and to explore further the teachers' collective perceptions of their experiences of reform implementation. All the interviews were audio-recorded and transcribed. Where L1 was used, the transcripts were then translated and checked by Vietnamese colleagues. I was conscious that knowledge of my previous involvement in English language teaching in Vietnam and in the initial stages of the NFLP 2020 might influence how the participants responded to me and the kind of experiences, thoughts, and feelings they chose to share or to leave unsaid. I tried to alleviate this by developing a relationship with the participants through the interviews and by ensuring mutual understanding of the conversations through summarising parts of what I had heard and asking participants to confirm their understanding.

Data analysis

Once transcribed and translated, the interview transcripts were analysed and organised through NVivo software using a thematic analysis approach (Braun & Clarke, 2013). This involved initial descriptive coding related to the research questions and then more inductive and interpretative coding related to emotions, experiences, and contextual demands across the participant data set. The initial stages of analysis were discussed with the teachers through the questioning in the second and third interviews, which allowed for adjustments of the coding. The participants were given the interview transcripts in both English and Vietnamese, and any inaccuracies reported were changed. The final data analysis was shared with a colleague working in a similar research area. They were able to confirm that my interpretations of the data reflected the voices of the participants.

Findings and discussion

Perceptions of risk to teachers' professional selves

The NFLP 2020 and the repositioning of English in the primary school curriculum has brought about more intense scrutiny of the competence and capacity of primary English language teachers around normative issues of what constitutes a good teacher in terms of their pedagogical practices and language level. The introduction of the NFLP 2020 and the new curriculum policy appears to have done little to alter colleagues' perceptions of primary English and teachers, partly because, as Bao (INT2) put it:

> Maths and Vietnamese classes are taught in a different way where the students only sit and they don't need to talk like in an English class . . . so we often get complaints about the noise and my children out of their seats.

The perceptions of others, as reported by the teachers, seemed to create feelings of uncertainty about what was expected of them and their own ability as English language teachers. Indeed, several participants commented that English and English teachers were not viewed seriously by colleagues. This is exemplified by Lien:

> I hope that after 2020 our life will be more comfortable in terms of the viewpoint from other colleagues. . . . [M]any teachers say that English is just a short break for children to relax after Maths and Vietnamese. So they think that the English teacher is not as important or have important roles as other teachers. I feel rather sad about it because we are all teachers. We have the same salary, but they look down at us? I don't like it.
>
> (Lien. INT1)

This tension with colleagues' expectations and a new pedagogical approach is a source of worry for many of the teachers, particularly because they were also grappling with *how* to implement the necessary changes into their classroom practice. Indeed, adopting a new teaching approach was no easy matter. Lien's comments that follow exemplify teachers' anxiety about the communicative requirements of the new curriculum and how this might be done in large classes with young children and in ways that constitute a significant shift from current classroom practices and behaviours.

> I'm very nervous because the curriculum is different from what we used to do. The approach is speaking and listening, while we teach the children the grammar, . . . so I feel very nervous. How, by what way could children reach it? So nervous . . . and worried.
>
> (Lien. INT2)

The new curriculum and pedagogy requires that teachers adopt more communicative practice activities in their lessons. However, the dilemma for teachers was how to do this within the syllabus time frame since communicative activities tend to be more time-consuming. Similar temporal tensions are reported by Chen and Day (2015) in their account of teachers in China grappling with national educational reform. These time constraints seemed to create a lot of emotional burden, as Nhung remarked:

> I feel stressed because it's too difficult and little time. . . . When I meet a lesson I feel worried; how can I follow everything to finish the first semester? It's nearly the end of first semester but we haven't finished 10 lessons, so we worry.
>
> (Nhung. INT2)

The feelings of anxiety and uncertainty seemed to stem from teachers' desire to "be professional" and to follow the new curriculum requirements, while also dealing with conflicting messages emanating from colleagues, temporal constraints, and the perception of risk associated with accountability. In the following extract, Nhung expresses her worries about being blamed by others for not being able to cover the whole syllabus. Trying to implement a communicative pedagogy was particularly risky for Nhung because repercussions would come from secondary school teachers of perceived higher status. This fits other studies (e.g., Wang, 2011) where teachers felt obliged to continue with the teaching methods they were familiar with because they posed the least possible risk to their professional selves.

> I am worried, very worried because . . . if we don't teach carefully in time and all the units . . . when for example I teach Grade 4 next year another teacher will teach Grade 5. If they don't study carefully in Grade 4, so it's difficult to study Grade 5 and the other teacher will complain.
>
> (Nhung. INT2)

Perceptions of risk were also associated with the B2 requirement. Teachers expressed uncertainty and anxiety about not being able to achieve the desired level.

> [I]f I cannot get the B2 I think the way they [principal and parents] look at me will be different.
>
> (Bao. INT1)

> I mean many teachers are afraid of being sacked if they don't get B2 . . . and me I'm so worried, what if I fail?
>
> (Lien. INT1)

These interview excerpts reflect the situation in Vietnam described in other studies. For example, citing Phan (2016) and Nguyen and Thanh (2015), Le et al. (2017) report that many teachers are under pressure to reach the required language proficiency standards, with the threat that otherwise they might lose their jobs. While this pressure may partly explain the improved language proficiency levels of teachers tested in 2014/2015 (Le et al. 2017), it is probably not conducive to a sustainable approach to educational change and teacher change.

Some of the teachers had attended a B2 language course and gained a certificate showing their B2 proficiency level. However, it is interesting that they still had doubts about their English language ability, as Chi (INT1) points out: "[A]lthough I have B2 I always consider that I am under B2 level. . . . [M]y speaking skill is bad. . . . I don't believe myself." Even with the achievement of B2, some of the teachers still appeared to have little credibility as English language teachers in the eyes of others, and as one teacher remarked, "[Y]ou know many people say that if a teacher is good at speaking English, they will not teach at primary schools" (Thanh. INT1). Indeed, there seemed to be some scepticism about the benefits teachers have gained by reaching the language proficiency requirements at official levels within the education system. In a meeting I attended, a local official stated that "teachers are not any better even though they have the B2 certificate." Similar perceptions about the language proficiency requirement were reported by Tran (2018). The self-perceptions and perceptions of others related to teachers' capacity mentioned so far have highlighted the threats to teachers' professional selves and the concomitant feelings of vulnerability.

The influence of support provision on teacher emotion

All the participants felt that the support they had received to help them with the new pedagogical and language proficiency requirements was insufficient and lacked relevance to their classroom and school realities. This fits Chen and Day's (2015) research, which shows that while policymakers and other stakeholders have high expectations of teachers during reform implementation, they do not always provide the kind of support required to help teachers meet those expectations. As in this study, teachers are very often left to muddle along as best they can.

The teachers had attended a three-month methodology and language course organised by local universities as part of the NFLP 2020's teacher capacity building plan. While the teachers expressed enjoyment with the language proficiency course because it "improves my English" (Bao. INT2), they felt confused as to what new language skills were required to teach the new curriculum. The teachers reported that the language proficiency courses were based on adaptations of IELTS and TOEFL tests and involved learning language items that, when contextualised, were set in an academic English context. This appeared to be contrary to the more practical language classroom use that the participants believed they needed. Mai's words, which follow, highlight her uncertainty about the relevance of the B2 requirement for her classroom teaching context where the language she uses on a daily basis with her primary-aged students in the classroom is "simple English" (Mai. INT1). She felt that an understanding of young learner pedagogy is more useful particularly because this is an area that she had had no prior training in.

> I think is this B2 good or not good? Or important or not important? Because teaching for young learners we don't need a lot of English knowledge . . . some specialist in MOET said that if teacher can't get B2, they can't teach anymore. But it is not necessary because for primary teachers I think the more important thing is teaching methodologies, especially teaching children. . . . [Y]ou know many teachers who have been teaching for 20 years, that means they got the knowledge with the old teaching method. I think the traditional teachers "say" and the students "listen and repeat" but now it's [the new methodology].
>
> (Mai. GroupINT)

Mai's view is shared by some of the other participants:

> [I]t's hard to teach children, young learners. Some teachers they don't have B2 [certificate] but they teach very well, perfectly. They have some more experience. I think it's [methodology] important.
>
> (Thanh. INT1)

> [O]ur English is good enough to teach the primary students and the methodology is very important, yeah. Some teachers they come from the university and they cannot teach primary students.
>
> (Bao. INT2)

Of interest is that these comments seem to contradict the teachers' reports of the beneficial outcomes of achieving a B2 Level of proficiency, suggesting the dynamic nature of teacher emotions. For example, many teachers felt it was important to have a good level of English language proficiency, particularly with the focus on compulsory English in the primary school curriculum. In addition, they recognised that poor language skills would lead to a loss of face in classes where many of the students attend extra lessons in private language institutes and may even have a higher level of proficiency than the teacher. As Chau remarked:

> [S]ome teachers don't get B2, I think they don't know how to teach the children with their knowledge. English is important . . . and many of my students can speak English very well and if I can't speak English or don't know a word they say "oh," and I feel terrible, embarrassed!
>
> (Chau. INT1)

So while there was a general recognition of the usefulness of B2, the underlying tensions and anxiety that the teachers felt about the language proficiency course and requirements were related to the actual implementation and the perceived relevance to their own classroom realities. In this context, the teachers tended to view the course as an administrative obligation rather than seeing it as part of longer-term professional development. As Lien commented:

> I just wanted to pass B2 so I'm not sacked! So it's about the test format and how I can pass. . . . I don't think academic language is easy and how can it help my primary students? I just look at the test questions and try to pass.
>
> (Lien. GroupINT)

This raises questions about standards for language teacher proficiency and the extent to which the desired improvements achieved through these B2 language courses really address the needs of teachers and the wider concern of teachers' language use in the classroom – critical issues that Le et al. (2017) have also highlighted.

The teachers reported similar anxieties regarding the methodology component of the three-month course. There seemed to be a heavy focus on theoretical knowledge and little practical relevance to the classroom contexts of the primary teachers.

> [T]o be honest they didn't help me much. . . . [T]hey introduce me to things that I think we cannot achieve. . . . I think it is a waste of time to sit listening to something that isn't applicable to my teaching.
>
> (Chau. INT2)

This may have been because the professional development facilitators were university lecturers who had little knowledge or understanding of either young learner pedagogy or the classroom context – a situation also raised by Bui and Nguyen (2016). All the teachers felt a sense of frustration about the university teachers' lack of understanding of the primary teaching context, as Mai's remarks indicate:

> University trainers don't know about primary students, they teach adults and so they lecture and know methodology for older students . . . quite different, not suitable for my primary children.
>
> (Mai. GroupINT)

This limited relevance and applicability to local contexts was also evident in the lack of in-school follow-up. Teachers seemed to have very few opportunities to experiment with new pedagogy and activities in their actual classroom settings, opportunities that might lessen teachers' perceptions of risk and feelings of vulnerability.

The data discussed so far highlight the "contextual confusion" (Grassick & Wedell, 2018) experienced by the teachers in terms of the mismatch between the intended policies and the local realities at the micro-level. This seems to be particularly true of policy reforms that have been "borrowed" from other contexts and countries (Tan & Reyes, 2016), with little thought to the "contextual fit" of the "receiving" nation or of the implementers who may struggle to make sense of it.

The influence of collaborative learning opportunities on teacher emotion

Once the formal training courses had come to an end, the teachers returned to their schools. The majority of them expressed a sense of isolation since each was the only English teacher working in their school. This meant there were few opportunities for peer collaboration and learning in schools and no encouragement for teachers to try out and reflect on the new teaching practices. This isolation appeared to increase teachers' uncertainties about whether they were doing "the right thing" in the classroom and seemed to negate the initial support that the teachers had received. Bui and Nguyen (2016) suggest that EFL teachers in Vietnam are unfamiliar with the idea of peer learning and with the collegiality involved in reflection and sharing professional experiences. However, building familiarity by providing space for collaboration at the school level would help teachers to feel empowered as implementers of the NFLP 2020 and perhaps help to shape and move policies in a context-appropriate direction.

The feeling of isolation for the teachers in this study also extended to the limited opportunities the teachers had to use and practise their English.

> As a teacher, I have to improve my skills, but it is quite constrained without a communicative environment. . . . [A]fter the course ended, we came back to our normal teaching, just me and my students, and my English skills did not seem to be as good as before, in the absence of communicative situations.
>
> (Chi. GroupINT)

The teachers' feeling of isolation was exacerbated by the lack of available support from other colleagues. In addition to having no peers to turn to, they were also unable to seek support from those above them. Indeed, in all the research schools, "the principal or the vice principal and the other teachers in the school they don't know English" (Bao. INT2). Consequently, teachers felt they had been left on their own to make sense of the changes. As Bao points out:

> [T]eachers in Maths and Vietnamese frequently have many opportunities for professional development. It could be the case the vice-principal specialises in Maths and Vietnamese, so he or she can give lots of support to teachers in these subjects. For English . . . class visits and observation by senior mentors are rare, and professional development is only occasional.
>
> (Bao. GroupINT)

Feeling unsupported and isolated seemed to do little to allay the uncertainties and anxieties the teachers had about the new curriculum and language policy and suggests a school context that was more likely to encourage continuity than change. This is concomitant with Fullan's (2007) argument that collaboration as a tool for successful implementation must surely outweigh teacher isolation.

The influence of agency on teacher emotion

Teachers' sense of isolation also relates to their lack of involvement in the planning and reviewing of the NFLP 2020. While the teachers' commented on the importance of English and the necessity of the NFLP 2020, they appeared to know little detail of the planned curriculum policy outcomes and how it would affect them beyond attending training courses. As Nhung stated:

> We have to get B2, but what if we forget . . . what happens after many years? Other subject teachers don't need to spend so much time and hard work, but what do we get? I don't know about our salary if it changes or we get promotion, I don't know. I feel so tired about everything.
>
> (Nhung. GroupINT)

Teachers' also expressed feelings of frustration and resignation about not being heard by those above them. They were keen to provide feedback on their experiences of implementing the new curriculum policy, but there seemed to be no mechanisms in place to do this. Some of the teachers were able to attend meetings with their district level-MOET representatives to voice their concerns about the new curriculum; however, these appeared to be merely gestures rather than meaningful opportunities for being listened to.

> [H]e (district level official] always says "please raise your hand, please say," but nothing will be changed. He can't change anything.
>
> (Lien. GroupINT)

This suggests that teachers emotions were bound up in experiences of power and powerlessness over their professional decision making (Hargreaves, 2001, p. 1072). The fact that few of the teachers insights into implementation reached those of influence higher up the system had emotional significance for the teachers because the policy implementation process affected them directly. The teachers were expected to have the kind of agency in the classroom that would enable them to facilitate an open, creative, and unpredictable learning process, as the ETCF states (NFLP 2020, 2013, p. 8):

> The vision . . . is to build the professional English teaching beyond the level of technicians or teaching machines . . . to practising teachers with "adaptive expertise."

However, the agency through which teachers might achieve "adaptive expertise" seemed to be restricted by the nature of support provision, the temporal constraints, by the opportunities to be involved in shaping the NFLP 2020 in local contexts, and ultimately by the feelings of uncertainty and vulnerability that this created along with the risks to their professional selves.

Conclusion and implications

This chapter provides an account of the role that teachers' emotions play in the understanding and enactment of language policy reform. The findings highlight the dilemmas teachers faced in grappling with the new curriculum and language proficiency requirements. Their anxieties and uncertainties emanated from their need to balance the existing normative conceptions of a good teacher with the changes implied by the policy directives of the NFLP 2020. At the same time, teachers were receiving conflicting messages from the context around them regarding a rigid syllabus and time frame, expectations of others, and the relevance of what they were being asked to do. This contextual confusion threatened teachers' professional self and created feelings of vulnerability, consistent with the research findings of studies carried out by Le Fevre (2015) and van Veen and Sleegers (2006). The mismatch between the rational push towards improved teacher standards and the reality of local contexts also related to teachers' feelings of being supported (or not). Teachers wanted to make changes but felt frustrated and inadequately prepared due to the (ir)relevance of the methodology and language training courses, in terms of both the content and the university lecturers' understanding of primary classroom realties. While tensions, uncertainties, and ambiguities are a normal part of an educational reform process (Fullan, 2007), teachers still need support to be able to cope with the emotionality of change. They need space and time to make sense of change both at the individual and the social levels and should be afforded collaborative opportunities to reflect on, adapt, and share new classroom practices. Many of the teachers' emotional responses to policy change came from a "crisis of positionality" (Goodson, 2014). This implies that teachers' limited agency, their understanding of change as simply following a new policy, and their inability to voice their concerns or opinions have led to feelings of uncertainty and vulnerability and lowered perceptions of professional self (Kelchtermans, 2005, 2009; van Veen & Sleegers, 2006).

A number of suggestions for language policy implementation in Vietnam and elsewhere are proposed:

- Greater understanding is required of what a new language policy means for teachers in terms of the contextual challenges it may bring and the time and effort required before any significant changes are visible in teachers' classrooms or in student learning outcomes.
- Greater recognition is needed of the kind of support appropriate for not only teachers but also teacher educators, so they have more awareness and knowledge of the classroom contexts in which teachers work. This would help to address some of the "contextual confusion" mentioned in the chapter.

- If policy change is to be sustainable, teacher support needs to be school based to allow for ongoing reflection and peer collaboration. Teacher support also needs to recognise the emotionality of change to help teachers cope with threats to their professional selves. More thought should be given to teachers' professional standards over time – how these might be maintained and the emotional costs to the teacher.
- It is crucial that policymakers consider the involvement of teachers at all stages of planning and implementation. Teachers might then feel a sense of ownership and inclusion and make better sense of what they are being asked to do differently. The development of communication channels would allow teachers' voices (and hence feelings) to be heard and factored into implementation review.

Although this is a small-scale study, it has attempted to bring attention to the emotionality of educational change so that those involved in policy planning and implementation, in Vietnam and elsewhere, might recognise that educational change is "socially complex" (Fullan, 2007): it involves people and what they think, feel, and do.

References

Agudo, M. (Ed.). (2018). *Emotions in second language teaching.* New York: Springer.

Benesch, S. (2017). *Emotions and English language teaching.* New York: Routledge.

Braun, V., & Clarke, V. (2013). *Successful qualitative research.* Washington, DC: Sage Publications.

Bui, T., & Nguyen, H. (2016). Standardizing English for educational and socio-economic betterment: A critical analysis of English language policy reforms in Vietnam. In A. Kirkpatrick & R. Sussex (Eds.), *English language education policy in Asia* (pp. 363–388). London: Springer.

Chen, J., & Day, C. (2015). Tensions and dilemmas for teachers responding to system wide change. In Q. Gu (Ed.), *The work and lives of teachers in China* (pp. 3–22). London: Routledge.

Cowie, N. (2011). Emotions that experienced English as a Foreign Language (EFL) teachers feel about their students, colleagues and their work. *Teaching and Teacher Education, 27,* 235–242.

Day, C., & Lee, J. C.-K. (2011). Emotions and educational change: Five key questions. In C. Day & J. C.-K. Lee (Eds.), *New understandings of teacher's work: Emotions and educational change* (p. 1). New York: Springer.

Dudzik, D., & Nguyen, N. (2013). *Vietnam's English teacher competencies framework: Policies, context, basis and design.* Paper presented at the teacher competency frameworks: Developing excellence in teaching, Kuala Lumpur, Malaysia.

Fullan, M. (2007). *The new meaning of educational change.* New York: Teachers' College Press.

Gao, X. (2008). Teachers' professional vulnerability and cultural tradition: A Chinese paradox. *Teaching and Teacher Education, 24,* 154–165.

Goodson, I. (2014). Context, curriculum and professional knowledge. *History of Education, 43,* 768–776.

Grassick, L. 2016. *Complexity, connections and sense-making: Stakeholder experiences of primary English language curriculum change in one province in Vietnam*. Unpublished PhD thesis, Leeds, University of Leeds.

Grassick, L., & Wedell, M. (2018). Temporal dissonance, contextual confusion and risk: Learning from the experiences of teachers living with curriculum change. In M. Wedell & L. Grassick (Eds.), *International perspectives on teachers living with curriculum change* (pp. 247–271). London: Palgrave Macmillan.

Hardman, J., & A-Rahman, N. (2014). Teachers and the implementation of a new English curriculum in Malaysia. *Language, Culture and Curriculum, 27*(3), 260–277.

Hargreaves, A. (2001). Emotional geographies of teaching. *Teachers College Record, 103*(6), 1056–1080.

Hargreaves, A. (2004). Inclusive and exclusive educational change: Emotional response of teachers and implications for leadership. *School Leadership and Management, 24*(3), 287–309.

Hargreaves, A. (2005). Educational change takes ages: Life, career and generational factors in teachers' emotional responses to educational change. *Teaching and Teacher Education, 21*, 967–983.

Hu, G. (2002). Potential cultural resistance of pedagogical imports: The case of communicative language teaching in China. *Language, Culture and Curriculum, 15*(2), 93–105.

Kelchtermans, G. (2005). Teachers' emotions in educational reforms: Self-understanding, vulnerable commitment and micropolitical literacy. *Teaching and Teacher Education, 21*(8), 995–1006.

Kelchtermans, G. (2009). Who am I in how I teach is the message: Self-understanding, vulnerability and reflection. *Teacher and Teaching: Theory and Practice, 15*(2), 257–272.

Lasky, S. (2005). A sociocultural approach to understanding teacher identity, agency and professional vulnerability in a context of secondary school reform. *Teaching and Teacher Education, 21*, 899–916.

Le, M., Nguyen, T. M. H., & Burns, A. (2017). Teacher language proficiency and reform of English language education in Vietnam, 2008–2020. In D. Freeman & L. LeDrean (Eds.), *Developing classroom English competence: Learning from the Vietnam experience* (pp. 19–33). Phnom Phen: IDP Australia.

Le, V. C., & Do, T. (2012). Teacher preparation for primary school English education: A case of Vietnam. In B. Spolsky & Y.-I. Moon (Eds.), *Primary school English-language education in Asia* (pp. 106–128). New York: Routledge.

Lee, J., C.-K., & Yin, H.-B. (2011). Teachers' emotions and professional identity in curriculum reform: A Chinese perspective. *The Journal of Educational Change, 12*, 25–46.

Le Fevre, D. M. (2015). Barriers to implementing pedagogical change: The role of teachers' perceptions of risk. *Teaching and Teacher Education, 38*, 56–64.

Liu, Y. (2016). The emotional geographies of language teaching. *Teacher Development, 20*(4), 482–497.

MOET. (2008). *Approval of the Project entitled 'teaching and learning foreign languages in the national education system, Period 2008–2020'*. Decree 1400. Hanoi: The NFLP 2020.

NFLP 2020. (2013). *Competency framework for English language teachers*. Hanoi: Vietnam Institute of Education Sciences.

Nguyen, H. T. M. (2012). Primary English language education policy in Vietnam: Insights from implementation. In R. B. Baldauf, Jr., R. B. Kaplaan, N. M.

Kamwangamalu, & P. Bryant (Eds.), *Language planning in primary schools in Asia* (pp. 121–147). New York: Routledge.

Nguyen, H. T. M. (2017). *Model of mentoring in language teacher education*. Cham, Switzerland: Springer.

Nguyen, H. T. M., & Bui, T. (2016). Teachers' agency and the enactment of educational reform in Vietnam. *Current Issues in Language Planning, 17*(1), 88–105.

Nguyen, L., Hamid, M., & Renshaw, P. (2016). English in the primary classroom in Vietnam: Students' lived experiences and their social and policy implications. *Current Issues in Language Planning, 17*(2), 191–214.

Nguyen, M. H. (2018). ESL teachers' emotional experiences, responses and challenges in professional relationships with the school community: Implications for teacher education. In M. Agudo (Ed.), *Emotions in second language teaching* (pp. 243–259). New York: Springer.

Nguyen, N. (2013). *National foreign languages 2020 project*. Presentation at Higher Engineering Education Alliance Conference. Cần Thơ, Vietnam: Can Tho University.

Nguyen, T., & Thanh, B. (2015). *Chương trình tiếng Anh theo đề án: Thiếu giáo viên đạt chuẩn* [The NFLP2020: Lack of qualified teachers]. Thanhnien. Retrieved from http://thanhnien.vn/giaoduc/chuong-trinh-tieng-anh-theo-de-an-thieu-giao-vien-datchuan-614540.htmlNias, J. (1996.) Thinking about feeling: The emotions of teaching. *Cambridge Journal of Education, 26*(3), 293–306.

Phan, T. (2016). *Dạy ngoại ngữ không chuẩn, thà không dạy còn hơn* [It is better to stop if standard requirements are not met]. Saigon Online. Retrieved from http://www.sggp.org.vn/giaoduc/2016/9/433835/

Tan, C., & Reyes, V. (2016). Curriculum reform and education policy borrowing in China: Towards a hybrid model of teaching. In C. Chou & J. Spangler (Eds.), *Chinese education models in a global age* (pp. 37–49). Singapore: Springer.

Tran, L. (2018). Meeting the demands of ELT innovation: Teachers' linguistic and pedagogic challenge, In M. Wedell & L. Grassick (Eds.), *International perspectives on teachers living with curriculum change* (pp. 83–203). London: Palgrave Macmillan.

Uitto, M., Jokikokko, K., & Estola, E. (2015). Virtual special issue in teachers and emotions. *Teaching and Teacher Education, 50*, 124–135.

Uztosun, M. S. (2018). In-service teacher education in Turkey: English language teachers' perspectives. *Professional Development in Education, 44*(4), 557–569.

van Veen, K., & Sleegers, P. (2006). How does it feel? Teachers' emotions in a context of change. *Journal of Curriculum Studies, 38*(1), 85–111.

Wang, D. (2011). The dilemma of time: Student-centred teaching in the rural classroom in China. *Teaching and Teacher Education, 27*, 157–164.

Wedell, M. (2009). *Planning for educational change*. London: Continuum International Publishing Group.

Wedell, M., & Grassick, L. (Eds.). (2018). *International perspectives on teachers living with curriculum change*. London: Palgrave Macmillan.

White, C. (2018). The emotional turn in applied linguistics and TESOL: Significance, challenges and prospects. In M. Agudo (Ed.), *Emotions in second language teaching* (pp. 19–35). New York: Springer.

Xu, Y. (2013). Language teacher emotion in relationships: A multiple case study. In X. Zhu & K. Zeichner (Eds.), *Preparing teachers for the 21st century* (pp. 371–393). New York: Springer.

Yan, C. (2018). Balancing change and tradition: A Chinese English teacher's experiences of curriculum reform. In M. Wedell & L. Grassick (Eds.), *International perspectives on teachers living with curriculum change* (pp. 61–83). London: Palgrave Macmillan.

Yin, H., Lee, C-K. J., & Wang, W. (2014). Dilemmas of leading national curriculum reform in a global era: A Chinese perspective. *Educational Management, Administration and Leadership, 42*(2), 293–311.

Zein, S. (2016). Factors affecting the professional development of elementary teachers. *Professional Development in Education, 42*(3), 423–440.

Zembylas, M. (2010). Teacher emotions in the context of educational reforms. In A. Hargreaves, A. Lieberman, M. Fullan, & D. Hopkins (Eds.), *Second international handbook of educational change* (pp. 221–236). Cham, Switzerland: Springer International Handbooks of Education.

Zembylas, M. (2011). Teaching and teacher emotions: A post-structural perspective. In C. Day and J. K. Lee (Eds.), *New understandings of teacher's work: Emotions and educational change* (pp. 31–43). New York: Springer.

4 Exploring teacher learning in mandatory in-service training courses

Challenges ahead

Le Van Canh

Introduction

In-service training (INSET), despite its critiques, remains the most common approach to professional development for second language teachers, particularly in developing countries. However, the current knowledge about what teachers learn (or do not learn) in traditional professional development activities such as top-down mandatory INSET is both limited and fragmented. The challenge is greater when the cause-and-effect, linear relationship between in-service training and teacher change has been questioned (Kubanyiova, 2012). This reality calls for the need to research teacher learning as a complex system rather than as an event (Opfer & Pedder, 2011) in order to explain what teachers learn, why they learn it, and under what conditions. These insights are significant in making mandatory INSET more effective to teachers' professional growth because they help us to understand the nature of teacher learning in the INSET context. I will begin the chapter with a literature review on INSET as a model of professional development for language teachers. Then I will present some of the findings of my study on the professional knowledge that Vietnamese EFL teachers acquired in several national top-down and mandatory INSET courses targeted at improving teachers' English proficiency and pedagogical competencies as well as how that knowledge influences their instructional practices. I will conclude the chapter with the argument that mandatory top-down INSET should, for many compelling reasons, continue to serve as one of the leading approaches to professional development for EFL teachers but needs to be restructured to respond to the complexity of teacher learning.

The impact of in-service teacher training

Unlike the bottom-up approach to teacher development that empowers teachers to change their instructional practice in the ways they believe are contextually appropriate (Freeman & Johnson, 1998), INSET is a top-down change process for teachers within a particular educational system, which requires teachers to transfer the prescribed innovative instructional strategies into their classroom irrespective of local contexts (Fullan, 2007). As a result, teachers have often found the prepackaged information presented by university-based teacher educators with little knowledge of local conditions irrelevant and boring, though it was occasionally amusing (Corcoran, 1995; Little, 1994). Smylie (1989) pointed out that although most INSET programmes were accompanied by evaluations – typically consisting of filling out a form about what was enjoyable – efforts to measure what teachers learned had not been part of typical evaluation fare.

In comparison with the research body of second language pre-service teacher education, the literature on INSET is considerably smaller in spite of recent expansion (e.g., Borg, 2011; Freeman, 1993; Waters, 2006; Wichadee, 2011). There are three foci in this research agenda: (1) impact of INSET on teachers' transformation of their existing beliefs about language learning and teaching, which Freeman (1993) refers to as "renaming experience" (Borg, 2011; Freeman, 1993; Lamb, 1995); (2) impact of INSET on teachers' "reconstructing practice," to use Freeman's (1993) term; and (3) impact of INSET on teachers' cognitive change or changes in beliefs leading to behavioural change or changes in classroom practice (Kubanyiova, 2012; Sansom, 2017; Uysal, 2012). An exceptional study reported by Golombek and Johnson (2004) showed that teachers' emotion functions as a catalyst for the teachers' professional growth. These findings are aligned with the recent theoretical perspectives on teacher learning such as the socio-cognitivism (Atkinson, 2011; Bastone, 2010) and complexity theory (Kiss, 2012; Larsen-Freeman & Cameron, 2008). These perspectives highlight the interconnectedness of mind, body, and the world as a nested system in which teacher learning is embedded.

The review of the literature on INSET reveals three major limitations. First, much of the reported research was undertaken by the teacher educators on their own programmes and classes in which participation in the programme was voluntary rather than mandatory, but rarely were issues of dual researcher/teacher educator roles discussed (Grossman, 2005). This limitation raises ethical concerns, as well as the validity of data generated this way (Silverman, 2001; Smylie, 1989), especially when data were elicited as part of course participants' formal assessment. Secondly, research on INSET for language teachers, especially large-scale after-course research conducted by independent researchers, remains scant. As Tarrou, Opdal, and Holmesland (1999) stress, conducting systematic after-course evaluations is an important first step towards the improvement of the current INSET programmes and the design of more effective future INSET activities. Lastly, the process-product approach adopted in the documented research body has masked the complexity of teacher learning in INSET courses, thereby failing to provide insights into how teacher learning is embedded in their lived experiences, learning contexts, and working conditions. As a result, we need more theorising to enhance the impact of INSET as an approach to professional development for second language teachers. This research, which was conducted in Vietnamese settings, is a step towards that goal.

Since the aim of this research was to explore how teacher learning emerges in the mandatory INSET context, the research design was based on the constructivist grounded theory method (Charmaz, 2006). Grounded theory is appropriate when the research aim is to understand the process rather than to verify an existing theory (Lingard, Albert, & Levinson, 2008). This research approach enables the researcher to enter the teacher participants' lives to see it from the inside, eventually illuminating their "unobtainable views" (Charmaz, 2006, p. 24) that outsiders usually assume about the world. These unobtainable views include teachers' feelings, emotions, and actions regarding their learning in the INSET context.

The research context

In Vietnam, the dominant discourse in teacher development supports the view that training equates improvements in teaching that lead to improvements in learning and learners' academic attainment. The standard INSET model is based on the assumption that teachers lack fundamental subject-matter knowledge and pedagogical competencies. Therefore, INSET has always been a government-funded means of remedying those deficits and mandated annually during the summer time with minimal follow-up support.

The recent development of National Foreign Languages 2020 Project, which is targeted at the improvement of Vietnamese citizens' English proficiency, places a great emphasis on teachers' competence through mandatory top-down INSET courses (Le, 2015). The INSET courses under this investigation were designed and delivered by commissioned universities to lift practising teachers' English proficiency to the nationally required level benchmarked in the CEFR (Common European Framework of Reference)-based National Framework of Foreign Language Proficiency and to upgrade their teaching skills. The language improvement course was designed to be delivered within 100 class periods (50 minutes each), whereas the teaching methodology course was to be completed within 50 class periods face to face. The courses were delivered in ten weeks from June to mid-August, 2017. All teacher educators in charge of delivering the course were young lecturers with fewer than ten years of teaching experience at the tertiary level from the commissioned universities, and many of whom did not have adequate knowledge of the world of real English language classrooms where the participant-teachers were working.

Research questions

This study was undertaken in an attempt to explore how the interaction of a variety of elements in the educational ecology influences teachers' sense-making of the input provided in top-down, mandatory INSET courses. Such understanding may provide a foundation for further empirical work towards better conceptualisation of teacher learning in INSET courses. With that purpose in mind, the researcher sought answers to the following questions:

1   How do practising teachers make sense of the input from the top-down mandatory INSET courses? And what contributes to their sense-making of the provided input?

2   How does their sense-making of the INSET input reshape their teaching practices?
3   What challenges should be addressed so that top-down mandatory INSET can have significant impact on teachers and students in their classroom?

Participants

For this study, 101 teachers (28 primary school; 32 lower secondary school; and 41 upper secondary school), accounting for approximately 13% of the total INSET participants in 2017 working in 11 provinces throughout Vietnam, were selected randomly in a draw from the list of participants provided by the National Foreign Language Project (commonly known as NFLP 2020 or Project 2020) Managing Board, which manages all INSET programmes for English-language teachers. All had completed either the 50-hour INSET course on teaching methodology or a 120-hour course on language improvement mandated by the Ministry of Education and Training. Therefore, the participants were those with the relevant information to share. Their teaching experience ranged from four to 15 years. The list of the chosen participants was provided to the relevant provincial specialist, who informed the selected participants of the purpose of the research and invited them to a school arranged by the specialist as scheduled. The specialist accompanied me to the field but was not involved in either the interviews or observations.

Methods of data collection

The research was conducted intensively from October 30, 2017 through December 5, 2017, three months after the training courses were completed. As the constructivist-grounded theory approach (Charmaz, 2006) requires thick description, rich data for the study were obtained through qualitative focus group interviews and classroom observation. These two methods of data collection help to uncover the intrinsic dynamics of the individual teacher–learner relationship including their lived experience, cognition, emotion, relationship with other teacher-learners and teacher educators in the course, as well as the pedagogical and sociopolitical context (Larsen-Freeman & Cameron, 2008). In order to collect the data for the study, I went on field trips to 11 provinces, representing Vietnam's different geographical and socio-economic areas: mountainous, urban, plain, coastal, economically developed and economically underdeveloped. Permission for entry into schools or research sites was granted by the Project 2020 authorities. I stayed two days in each province, visiting primary, lower secondary, and upper secondary schools.

Qualitative focus group interviews (Dörnyei, 2007) were used to generate data. While all the focus group interviews were formal and prearranged, they were characterised by high levels of rapport because the rooms allowed for privacy, and all the research participants had been well informed of the purpose of my research, which was partly to help them make their voices heard. Also, they all knew that I did not have any role in the INSET courses, and some of them knew very well about me from various local professional conferences and seminars in which they participated. During the interviews, my role was just a "moderator," who was to raise issues for discussion and to elicit the participants' opinions (see the Appendix for this chapter for the focus group interview protocol), as well as to make sure that all members of the group had a chance to express their views (Dörnyei, 2007). Each of the 11 visited provinces had one group, whose size varied ranging from seven to 12 teachers, and each session lasted approximately two hours. The research participants were also informed that the discussions were audio-recorded, and the working language could either be English or Vietnamese, but English was never used except for some intrasentential code-switching.

Responses to the interview questions overlapped, and answers to some questions were volunteered in advance as participants expanded their initial points. So responses were like a continuous dialogue rather than a series of discrete questions. Issues related to the practicality of the course content, and the personal difficulties in completing the course were most explicitly addressed.

In addition to the interviews, an unstructured classroom observation method was adopted to get direct access to what was actually happening in the classroom in an attempt to supplement the data gathered in the focus group interviews (Dörnyei, 2007). In all cases, the observed teacher, who was nominated by the provincial specialist, was the one teaching either in the school where the focus group interview was arranged or in a nearby school to save travelling time. As a result, the observed teacher was informed well in advance; yet teaching followed the regular syllabus with real students. A total of 53 teachers (17 primary school; 15 lower secondary school; 21 upper secondary school) working in 11 surveyed provinces were observed. Each teacher was observed once. The observed lessons were also audio-recorded, and I, as the researcher, took notes of the critical incidents in the lesson while observing. I did not use any predetermined criteria for observation because I planned to allow the data to emerge from the natural setting. What I did while observing teachers teaching was to make field notes of what the audio-recording failed to capture such as the seating arrangement, class-size, and the physical condition of the classroom. The classroom observation procedure was the same in all observed classes. Before the observation, I met and had a short talk with the teacher in an attempt to establish some rapport. When the bell rang signaling the start of the lesson, I followed the teacher into the classroom and took a seat at the back of the classroom.

Data analysis

A four-stage analytical procedure of qualitative research involving data coding, developing themes, organising codes and themes, and defining and describing the findings and interpretation (Marshall & Rossman, 1989) were adopted in this study. For the trustworthiness of the study (validation and reliability of the research), the researcher and a research assistant in the university, who had earned a doctoral degree in applied linguistics from an Australian university, coded one focus group interview independently. Then, code lists of the researcher and those of the research assistant were compared using the inter-rater reliability formula recommended by Miles and Huberman (1994). The inter-rater reliability score for the data analysis of the teacher focus group interview was 0.83, which is acceptable. Then other interviews were coded by only the researcher himself.

For observational data, I listened through all the audio-recorded lessons with a focus on the instructional strategies the teacher used and the teacher–student and student–student interactions, then transcribed the meaningful lesson extracts, the ones that helped me to answer my research questions. Then I used the observation notes to interpret the data.

Findings

Interaction between classroom experience and individual learning orientation

Teachers' classroom experiences, or the practical knowledge teachers co-constructed with their students over time in a particular situation of practice, shaped what they learned in the INSET courses. Most of the teachers' uptake was related to the very basic language teaching techniques that satisfied their immediate classroom needs.

A good many of the primary school teachers said that they had learned how to make the lessons more interesting to their young learners with techniques like "singing while pointing to parts of the body" or other games such as "lucky number," "slap the board," or "crossword puzzles," which were not in the coursebook. They also said that before the course they often presented grammar though "sentence patterns," but now they used chants instead. One primary school teacher also acknowledged that the more she learnt, the more she realised that her pronunciation and speaking skills were "problematic" and that the course helped her to improve these areas, which gave her "more confidence in speaking English in teaching." Some lower secondary school teachers reported that the course helped them to revise and to expand their vocabulary, while for others the course made them aware that it was unnecessary to teach everything in the coursebook or that the lesson plan should indicate distinctive steps to be followed in one lesson. For example, one upper secondary school teacher said:

> I teach in the countryside where I don't have the opportunity to practice speaking English. After the course I feel more confident in speaking English in the classroom. I have also learned how to use connectors to make my writing more coherent. I had forgotten many English words but now I had chance to revise them. I also picked up some English idioms that I can teach my students to use in writing, for example, "shopping is my cup of tea."
>
> (Lower secondary school teacher in Quang Binh)

Apart from some basic teaching techniques that are characterised as surface-learning, the significant uptake of the course input was limited. The single reason a great majority of the teachers provided was that the course input was so theoretical and decontextualised:

> I want to emphasize that we are keen to learn but trainers need to know what we need. It is really hard work to attend the course, but we benefited too little in return. 80% of the course content was familiar to us, not much new knowledge except for how to use games in teaching. We wish to learn something more practical, something we can use in our classrooms. We had to travel quite a long way to the training venue but we were disappointed about the course content. The trainers did not know anything about our students; they did not know anything about our classes. So when we asked them for suggestions on how to deal with problems we encountered regularly in the classroom (e.g., students' vocabulary is so limited; students are unmotivated) they failed to give specific advice. They just advised us to share our experience among ourselves but the trouble is we did not have that experience, I mean the experience in dealing with those common problems effectively.
>
> (Upper secondary school teacher in Phu Tho)

It is the experiences of working with large, multi-level classes and unmotivated learners in input-poor environments that blocked the intake from the course. One upper secondary school teacher from Dong Thap province said frankly:

> I have to teach multi-level classes. There are students who are absolutely illiterate in English. After the lesson, they put their textbook and notebook in their school bag, never open it at home. As many as 30–40% of the students in my class know nothing about English after so many years learning the language. What I was taught in the course was of no practical use. The trainers know very little about our contexts. Their students in the university are different. Without knowing about our contexts how can they help us solve our own problems?

This is echoed by another teacher from an upper secondary school in Nghe An province:

> The training course is useful in that it helped teachers to develop their knowledge of English, improve their English proficiency and knowledge of teaching English but that knowledge is not helpful to our teaching. In my class, of the 45 students only a few are interested in learning English. The trouble is their English declines over time. The training course failed to help me to deal with the situation. Reflecting on the training course I realized that what I needed was not provided. The content is not grounded in my teaching reality. Although I gained some knowledge about teaching, I am unable to use the new knowledge in my teaching. I wished I could have learned the way to develop my students to use English for communication.

Teachers from a mountainous area said that the technology component was useless and a waste of time to them because the technology infrastructure was not in existence in their area. One teacher even questioned why they were introduced to the technology-mediated techniques while what they had wished for years was just an audio-recorder for teaching listening skills.

Interaction between the physical and emotional states and uptake

Emotional and physical fatigue arising from the INSET learning experience considerably affected teachers' motivation for learning. While attendance was mandatory, no teacher was released from work to attend the training courses because the school had to finish the syllabus according to the prescribed teaching schedule. Teachers had to teach from Monday through Friday at their school, and they had to attend the training courses every Saturday and Sunday for two months. Because the training courses were formal, teachers in each province had to gather together in one training venue. To get to the training venue, teachers had to travel either by motorbike or coach every training day. It was either unaffordable or impossible for them to stay overnight because of either the cost or family responsibilities. Although none of the teachers was explicit, I know that weekends, for them, are the time for private tutoring for extra income. This means attendance of mandatory training courses incurred a financial loss. Although a few teachers complained that the courses were not long enough for them to internalise the great amount of the input, a good, many of them claimed that the courses were unnecessarily lengthy and the scheduling was inappropriate, making them feel physically and emotionally exhausted. For these teachers, course attendance became stressful for them. A teacher in Yen Bai province claimed:

> We had to attend the course during the weekend while we had to teach the whole week. We were physically worn out by the week end and could not learn much. Doing two things: teaching and taking the training course at the same time is unbearably exhausting to us. The trainers gave much home reading, but in the evening after finishing the house work, my mind didn't work and my eyes closed. You know one teacher in my class fainted in the bathroom. Luckily, someone found her lying unconscious there and took her to the nearby hospital in time.

Another upper secondary school teacher from Dong Thap province also raised this issue:

> The course is good giving us opportunities to learn from each other and to learn from university lecturers. After 21 years teaching, it was the first time I had the opportunity to upgrade my knowledge and teaching skills. I was so excited at first. However, after eight weekends travelling to and from the training venue while I had to teach the whole week every week, I was really exhausted. The pressure was so great and we felt stressed with six hours in

the training room a day. We had to quit our personal interests to attend the course but we were not satisfied with what we gained. It was so stressful to us if you know how far we had to travel every weekend. Some of us you know had to travel 100km every day while we do not have money for lodging.

In the interviews a great majority of the teachers explicitly expressed their negative feelings about the pressure of improving their English proficiency for certification (i.e., to achieve the required proficiency benchmark). They said that they felt humiliated rather than excited attending the INSET course because they had the impression that others looked at them as if they were underqualified teachers. They also added that what they had gained in terms of language improvement would soon go away because they never used the kind of language they had been trained to use in their work.

Observational data

All the observed lessons revealed some common issues: teachers tried to apply some basic teaching techniques, largely games and the use of PowerPoints, without understanding the underlying rationale of those techniques. Teachers tended to use pointless activities that took up valuable class time in the name of fun and engagement. Although teachers said in the interviews that, after completing the INSET courses, they became more confident in adapting the coursebook to the students, this was not supported by the observational data. Due to limited space, the following are just few lesson extracts to illustrate my point.

The first extract is from the taught lesson to grade 12 students. It is a writing lesson in which students are to practise writing a letter of request in English. The coursebook presents a short text introducing the ten best universities in the word, and the task is that students have to write a letter requesting for information they want to have before applying to that university.

1	Teacher:	You are going to watch a video clip [about ten world-class universities]. Try to remember the information and then answer my questions.
2	Teacher:	[played the video clip on her computer and the students watched it on the projector screen]
3	Teacher:	[when the video show is over] Tell me what can you see in the video?
4	Students:	Tall building green grass
5	Teacher:	[echoing the students] Tall building green grass – what else?
6	Student :	Rivers
7	Teacher:	[pointing to another picture] Is the computer room new?
8	Student :	[silent]
9	Teacher:	Rivers and a lot of students, right.

10	Teacher:	[Write the names of the ten universities in the video clip on board.]
11	Teacher:	[pointed to the list of the universities] There are a lot of choices here. If you study abroad which university would you choose and why. For example Cambridge university, do you know Cambridge?
12	Teacher:	What do you need to know?
13	Student 1:	Curriculum
14	Student 2:	Tuition fee
15	Student 3:	Scholarship
16	Teacher:	Do you want to know where to stay – it's accommodation? What about exams?
17	Teacher:	If you want to know all this information, what [how] can you know?
18	Student:	Google
19	Student :	I'll send an email
20	Teacher:	Ok you have to write a letter to them
21	Teacher:	Today I'll help you to write a letter of request. Open your book please.

Then the teacher explained the new words in the sample letter before showing the jumbled version of this letter on the projector screen, and asked the students to renumber the sentences in the right order. Following this was the teacher's presentation of the structure of a letter of request to the students. Finally, the students were put into groups and wrote a letter of request using the prompts given (the task is in the coursebook).

While the video clip has nothing to do with the task of writing a letter of request, the teacher spent approximately one-third of the 45-minute class period on it. This probably evidenced the teacher' uptake of using technology in teaching English from the INSET course. After the lesson ended, there was no guarantee that the students were able to write a simple letter of request in English.

The next extract is from a listening lesson taught to grade 6. The lesson focus is on the structures "Shall we . . . ?" and "Let's . . . ." to be used for making suggestions. The teacher began the lesson by showing a self-edited video clip on some places of interest in Vietnam and eliciting the students by asking the question, "What can you see in the picture?" before asking the students to listen to the audio transcript.

The teacher checked sentence by sentence with individual students she nominated, giving the correct answer when necessary without telling the students why. It is possible that the teacher had learned that prediction was an effective listening strategy that students needed to learn. To develop students' ability to predict the upcoming information, teachers need to activate the students' schema to decide in advance what aspects of the text to concentrate on, rather than doing a jigsaw exercise like the one quoted in the preceding lesson extract.

1 Teacher: Before listening I'd like to you to guess the content of the lesson.
2 Teacher: [wrote six sentences from the listening text in the wrong order, then asked individual students to go to the board and number of the sentences in the order they think they appear in the listening text, each student numbering one sentence]
3 Teacher: Open your book. Listen and check your prediction. [played the audio transcript]
4 Teacher: [played the audio transcript again] Let's listen the second time.
5 Teacher: Now check your prediction. What number first?

Discussion

Findings from this study provide additional empirical evidence of the complexity of teacher learning and sheds more light on both how teachers learn in INSET courses and the conditions that support and promote this learning. These findings lend support to Avalos's (2011, p. 10) assertion:

> Teacher professional learning is a complex process, which requires cognitive and emotional involvement of teachers individually and collectively, the capacity and willingness to examine where each one stands in terms of convictions and beliefs and the perusal and enactment of appropriate alternatives for improvement or change. All this occurs in particular educational policy environments or school cultures, some of which are more appropriate and conducive to learning than others.

As indicated in this study, learning in INSET courses is not a linear process (Kiss, 2012) but of multicausal nature. Teachers in this study did not attend the courses voluntarily: instead, their attendance was mandatory. The timing and the scheduling were not appropriate to them because they had to teach all week and then spend their weekends attending the course. Very few of them viewed participation in the courses as a privilege in their professional growth, even though the courses were aimed to improve both their subject matter knowledge and pedagogical content knowledge. On the contrary, INSET was, in the minds of the teachers, not an opportunity for professional growth but an additional demand on their time, a financial loss, a cause of physical exhaustion, and thus a painful experience. The interaction and intersection of all these factors created the "nested" network that shapes a teacher's individual orientation to learning, which, in turn, impacts teachers' uptake.

The findings of this study are aligned with the studies by scholars who maintain that emotions, feelings, and bodies are intricately nested, thereby triggering different thought processes that can either facilitate or hinder learning (Ferryok, 2010; Golombek & Doran, 2014; Kiss, 2012; Kubanyiova, 2012; Kubanyiova & Feryok, 2015). As indicated in this study, teachers' emotional and physiological fatigue and financial losses constituted teachers' negative feelings about the

INSET courses, which negatively affected their uptake. They had to travel a long way to and from the training venue for eight consecutive weekends because they were not released from regular teaching. They had to pay the travel expenses incurred from attending the INSET course from their basic salaries. In addition, because of their attendance, they missed out on the extra income they should have earned from their private tutorials (Kubanyiova, 2012) or their second jobs. The INSET courses were delivered June–August, the three hottest summer months in most of Vietnam. Getting up early every morning and travelling in the terrible summer heat by motorbike or low-quality public transportation had actually exhausted the teachers before they arrived at the training venues, which were large halls to accommodate 50–70 participants. These halls were not air-conditioned but ventilated with ceiling fans.

In addition, attending the INSET course on language improvement made them feel that they were unqualified teachers. The teachers in this study experienced physiological and emotional exhaustion as they were unable to engage meaning-fully with the input from the INSET courses. In their emotionally depleted state, they were unlikely to learn, i.e., to reorganise their experiential knowledge in light of the propositional knowledge provided in the INSET courses. As a result, focusing merely on INSET content, strategies, and outcomes disengages teachers who are emotionally driven by a sense of professional and moral meaning.

The observational data in this study lend further support to the view that learn-ing "is not the straightforward appropriation of skills and knowledge from the outside in" (Johnson, 2006, p. 238). Teachers in this study tended to fall back on their familiar practices in which teachers told the students to go through all the exercises (largely closed ones) in the coursebook. It seemed that they were satisfied if they felt things had gone well in every 45-minute slot, unaware that once they left, students' performance was limited only to the exercises that had been covered. Although the students were asked to do group work, the group tasks were not appropriate (for example, writing down the answers to compre-hension questions or forms-focused exercises on the large sheet of paper to show to the teacher), and in all cases, only one or two students were working while others were just looking on. In addition to the class size of 35–45 students being seated on fixed desks, there was a great variation in students' English proficiency. In many grade 12 classes were students who even had to struggle reading aloud simple sentences in the coursebook, let alone using English meaningfully. In my short talks with the teachers before observation, I was informed that there were students who were either poor at reading and writing Vietnamese or unmoti-vated to study all school subjects in every school, every class. Some teachers were unable to hide the physical fatigue on their faces as a result of the heavy workload both inside the school and at home because a great number of them were of the childbearing and childcaring age. This calls for the redefinition of INSET goals, which are teachers' understanding of the complex relationships among content, context, learners, and pedagogy, and their competence in using that understand-ing to develop contextually-appropriate and context-specific teaching strategies, rather than the transmission of outsiders' prepackaged knowledge.

Directions for the future INSET

In professionally deprived contexts like Vietnam, teachers have not been adequately trained because of the hasty decision to make English mandatory for everyone. After graduation, they have to work in isolation with minimum support for professional development from the education system. Teachers often find themselves having to cope with large classes of unmotivated students in poorly equipped schools. They also have to experience high stress, anxiety, and frustration to produce high rates of passes at the standardised examinations while their monthly salaries are minimal. Unsurprisingly, their motivation towards professional growth is low. Under such circumstances, the knowledge that teachers co-construct with their students and other teachers in their communities of practices (Wenger, 1998) throughout their professional lives stays unquestioned for many years and gives rise to their inertia, cognitive dissonance, or personal resistance to learning. As a result, mandatory INSET is crucial, but it has to be restructured to make it more instrumental to teachers' (re)constructing knowledge and understanding of themselves and their learners. Since the knowledge and theoretical insights teachers gain from INSET courses makes sense only with the wisdom born of their teaching experience before and after their attendance at INSET courses and the comfort born of their love for knowledge, the approach to INSET that addresses the deficits of teachers' fundamental knowledge has to be contested. This approach may, at best, make teachers more knowledgeable but no more effective in their follow-up instructional practices. As revealed in this study, there was a great variation in the way each individual teacher made sense of the knowledge they received from INSET. This is because teacher knowledge is multi-faceted and their sense-making of the external knowledge is shaped by the interaction between the external knowledge and the personal knowledge they developed from their lived experience. Therefore, INSET should be reconceptualised in order to produce "reflective teachers, in a process which involves socio-cognitive demands to introspect and collaborate with others, and which acknowledges previous learning and life experience as a starting point for new learning" (Wright, 2010, p. 267). As Freeman (2016) has recently suggested, language teacher education should be "a bridge that serves to link what is known in the field with what is done in the classroom, and it does so through the individuals whom we educate as teachers" (p. 9). Simply mandating attendance at top-down INSET courses will not bring about the intake that leads to significant reconceptualisation of classroom practices on the part of the participant-teachers. What is needed for enhancing teacher capacity for successful implementation of the ELT initiative in Vietnam and in other similar contexts is a strong leadership that can orchestrate the interaction between top-down control and bottom-up autonomy (Wedell, 2009).

While teaching is principled, learning to teach is not only complex and "self-organizing" (Kiss, 2012), lifelong, and "adaptive to the ecosocial environment" (Atkinson, Churchill, Nishino, & Okada, 2018, p. 489) but also emotionally driven. This view poses the challenge of how to align top-down change with emerging bottom-up change in a "nested" ecological system in which different elements (emotion, embodied cognition, motivation, identity, agency and action) are interconnected and relational. Unfortunately, teachers' emotional and affective responses to INSET tends to be ignored by policymakers, course developers, and teacher educators who view learning simply as the mental process of accumulating decontextualised information, unaffected by teachers' emotional state. According to Bullough (2009), emotions send messages about our identity, such as "what sort of person we are, to our identity, and so are intertwined within them are our hopes, expectations, and desire" (p. 36). In other words, our emotions not only frame our perceptions of the world and our identity but also drive our actions. Therefore, emotion is complex and multi-componential, comprising elements such as appraisal, physiological change, subjective experience, emotional expressions, and action tendencies (Sutton & Wheatley, 2003). Thus, the nexus of teacher cognition, teacher emotion, and teacher behaviour should be thoughtfully considered in developing both INSET policies and approaches so that teachers are both supported and challenged to move through situations of increasing demand or responsibility and to cope happily with the resulting challenges, such as the impact of INSET. Put another way, it is essential that ecological conditions that offer in-service teachers both access to others with greater expertise or agents of change and incentives for engaging in collaboration be created through a careful orchestration of bottom-up and top-down professional development strategies supported by a strong leadership. That orchestration is to scaffold teachers to "connect their ways of knowing to theory, both emic and etic, through modes of engagement that lead to praxis" (Johnson, 2006, p. 242).

Conclusions

The study provides an answer to the question of why teacher learning does or does not occur in the mandatory INSET courses. It shows the complexity of teacher learning and calls for new reorientation of INSET to enhance its impact on teachers' performance, and thereby learners' learning, particularly in professionally deprived contexts. I argue that the mandatory INSET should remain as a dominant approach to professional development for teachers, given the reality that teachers in these EFL contexts have limited exposure to innovative theories and models of teaching, which fails to enable them to reconstruct their personal practical knowledge. However, for the enhancement of its impact on teachers' classroom performance, mandatory INSET should be supported with locally appropriate teacher policy that intrinsically motivates every individual teacher to become a lifelong learner who is eager to find novel ways of providing the best possible learning experience for the learners in their classes. Apart from that, unless the unpredictability and uniqueness of learning outcomes and the professional autonomy of teachers are acknowledged, encouraged, and officially endorsed, the goal of INSET and other professional development strategies, which is teachers' engagement in and with professional growth in an attempt to reconstruct their teaching practices, will remain unfulfilled.

As Kubanyiova (2018, p. 2) has noted, the task of language teacher education in the age of increasing ambiguity and unpredictability should involve:

> educating "responsive meaning makers in the world": teachers who do not shy away from the politics of the social worlds in which their practices are located, but who are, at the same time, committed to growing their capacity of "knowing what to do" in the particular moment of an educational encounter.

This perspective is commensurable with Vietnamese learning culture, which is deeply rooted in the Buddhist philosophy. It views knowledge as holistic and embodied, rather than abstract. As a result, for most of the Vietnamese, learning occurs as the result of the dynamic interaction among the individual learner's body, cognition and emotion while she or he is actively practicing what is being learned. In order for INSET courses to exercise their impact on teachers' professional competence and instructional practice, it is critical to detail the ways in which teachers' emotion, cognition, and activity interact in a complex and dynamic way, leading to teachers' renegotiation of their identities through the enrichment of their professional lives with newly acquired abilities and insights.

References

Atkinson, D. (2011). A sociocognitive approach to second language acquisition. In D. Atkinson (Ed.), *Alternative approaches to second language acquisition* (pp. 143–166). London: Routledge.

Atkinson, D., Churchill, E., Nishino, T., & Okada, H. (2018). Language learning great and small: Environmental support structures and learning opportunities in a sociocognitive approach to second language acquisition/teaching. *Modern Language Journal, 102*(3), 471–493.

Avalos, B. (2011). Teacher professional development in teaching and teacher education over ten years. *Teaching and Teacher Education, 27*(1), 10–20.

Bastone, E. (2010). *Sociocognitive perspectives on language use and language learning.* Oxford: Oxford University Press.

Borg, S. (2011). The impact of in-service teacher education on language teachers' beliefs. *System, 39*(3), 370–380.

Bullough, R. V. (2009). Seeking eudaimonia: The emotions in learning to teach and to mentor. In A. P. Schutz & M. Zembylas (Eds.), *Advances in teacher emotion research: The impact on teachers' lives* (pp. 33–53). New York: Springer.

Charmaz, K. (2006). *Constructing grounded theory: A practical guide through qualitative analysis.* Los Angeles, CA: Sage Publications.

Corcoran, T. C. (1995). *Transforming professional development for teachers: A guide for state policymakers.* Washington, DC: National Governors' Association.

Dörnyei, Z. (2007). *Research methods in applied linguistics.* Oxford: Oxford University Press.

Ferryok, A. (2010). Language teacher cognitions: Complex dynamic systems? *System, 38*(2), 272–279.

Freeman, D. (1993). Renaming experience/reconstructing practice: Developing new understanding of teaching. *Teaching and Teacher Education, 9*(5–6), 485–497.

Freeman, D. (2016). *Educating second language teachers.* Oxford: Oxford University Press.

Freeman, D., & Johnson, K. E. (1998). Reconceptualizing the knowledge-base of language teacher education. *TESOL Quarterly, 32*(3), 397–417.

Fullan, M. (2007). *The new meaning of educational change* (4th ed.). New York: Teachers' College Press.

Golombek, P., & Doran, M. (2014). Unifying cognition, emotion, and activity in language teacher professional development. *Teaching and Teacher Education, 39*, 102–111.

Golombek, P. R., & Johnson, K. E. (2004). Narrative inquiry as a mediational space: Examining emotional and cognitive dissonance in second language teachers' development. *Teachers and Teaching: Theory and Practice, 10*, 307–327.

Grossman, P. L. (2005). Research on pedagogical approaches in teacher education. In M. Cochran-Smith & K. M. Zeichner (Eds.), *Studying teacher education: The report of the AERA panel on research and teacher education* (pp. 425–476). Mahwah, NJ: Lawrence Erlbaum.

Johnson, K. E. (2006). The sociocultural turn and its challenges for second language teacher education. *TESOL Quarterly, 40*(1), 235–257.

Kiss, T. (2012). The complexity of teacher learning: Reflection as a complex dynamic system. *Journal of Interdisciplinary Research in Education, 2*(1), 17–35.

Kubanyiova, M. (2012). *Teacher development in action: Understanding language teachers' conceptual change.* Basingstoke: Palgrave Macmillan.

Kubanyiova, M. (2018). *Language teacher education in the age of ambiguity: Educating responsive meaning makers in the world.* Language teacher research (Early online), 1–11.

Kubanyiova, M., & Feryok, A. (2015). Language teacher cognition in applied linguistics research: Revisiting the territory, redrawing the boundaries, reclaiming the relevance. *Modern Language Journal, 99*(3), 435–449.

Lamb, M. (1995). The consequences of INSET. *ELT Journal, 49*(1), 72–80.

Larsen-Freeman, D., & Cameron, L. (2008). *Complex systems and applied linguistics.* Oxford: Oxford University Press.

Le, V. C. (2015). English language education innovation for the Vietnamese secondary school: The project 2020. In B. Spolsky & K. Sung (Eds.), *Secondary school English education in Asia* (pp. 182–200). London: Routledge.

Lingard, L., Albert, M., & Levinson, W. (2008). Grounded theory, mixed methods, and action research. *BMJ* (online), *337*(a567), 459–461.

Little, J. W. (1994). Teachers' professional development in a climate of educational reform. *Educational Evaluation and Policy Analysis, 11*(2), 165–179.

Marshall, C., & Rossman, G. B. (1989). *Designing qualitative research.* London: Sage Publications.

Miles, M. B., & Huberman, A. M. (1994). *Qualitative data analysis* (2nd ed.). Thousand Oaks, CA: Sage Publications.

Opfer, V. D., & Pedder, D. (2011). Conceptualizing teacher professional learning. *Review of Educational Research, 81*(3), 376–407.

Sansom, D. W. (2017). Reinvention of classroom practice innovations. *ELT Journal, 71*(4), 423–432.

Silverman, D. (2001). *Interpreting qualitative data: Methods for analyzing talk, text and interaction* (2nd ed.). London: Sage Publications.

Smylie, M. A. (1989). Teachers' views of the effectiveness of sources of learning to teach. *Elementary School Journal, 89*(5), 543–558.

Sutton, R. E., & Wheatley, K. E. (2003). Teachers' emotions and teaching: A review of the literature and directions for future research. *Educational Psychology Review, 15*(4), 327–358.

Tarrou, A. H., Opdal, L. R., & Holmesland, I. S. (1999). Improving teacher education through evaluation: An analysis of four Norwegian case studies. *European Journal of Teacher Education, 22*(2–3), 135–157.

Uysal, H. H. (2012). Evaluation of an in-service training program for primary-school language teachers in Turkey. *Australian Journal of Teacher Education, 37*(7), 14–28.

Waters, A. (2006). Facilitating follow-up in ELT INSET. *Language Teaching Research, 10*(1), 32–52.

Wedell, M. (2009). *Planning for educational change: Putting people and their context first*. London: Continuum.

Wenger, E. (1998). *Communities of practice: Learning, meaning, and identity*. Cambridge: Cambridge University Press.

Wichadee, S. (2011). Professional development: A path to success for EFL teachers. *Contemporary Issues in Education Research, 4*(5), 13–24.

Wright, T. (2010). Second language teacher education: Review of recent research on practice. *Language Teaching, 43*(3), 259–296.

Appendix
Focus group interview protocol

1 What were your general feelings about the course?
2 How far did the course conform to your expectations? What did you find most satisfactory/least satisfactory about the course?
3 How useful did you find the course content to your teaching?
4 What parts of the course did you find most practical to your teaching?
5 What parts of the course caused you to rethink your teaching practice?
6 What parts of the course did you find least practical to your teaching? Why did you think so?
7 How did you feel about the logistics of the course, e.g., the scheduling, the organisation of the course, the materials, etc.?
8 What personal difficulties did you encounter while completing the course?
9 How helpful did you find the trainers' expertise and approach to course delivery?
10 If there are similar courses in the future, but they are not mandatory, will you attend them? Why do you think so?

5 Teachers' professional learning in the context of language education reforms

Hoa Thi Mai Nguyen, Tram Do Quynh Phan, and Manh Duc Le

Introduction

Developing teachers' professional learning is essential for improving the learning outcomes of students. This is of ultimate importance to enhance the quality of education. The field of research on teacher professional learning is relatively young, but recent years have witnessed a growing body of teacher learning research (Borko, 2004). While consensus exists about the value and importance of teacher professional learning, the current literature fails to explain exactly how changes in educational policy impact professional learning and how teachers develop their professional learning within their school context. Specifically, further research is needed to widen our understanding of EFL teachers' professional learning in the context of educational changes in Asian countries like Vietnam.

In Vietnam, teachers' professional development (PD) is widely recognised as an important component in the field of language education in Vietnam, especially as National Foreign Language Project 2020 (NFLP 2020) has been undertaken nationwide in recent years. MOET considers PD a backbone for the success of educational language reform (MOET, 2016). Bui and Nguyen (2016) also highlighted the needs of PD within Project 2020's implementation as a vehicle to foster teachers' self-directed learning in ways that benefit student learning. However, teacher professional development has been a matter of great concern not only to educational leaders, educators, and teachers but also to the whole community, as the quality and quantity of English teachers in Vietnam are widely seen as problematic (Le & Do, 2012; Nguyen, 2011; Nguyen, Nguyen, Nguyen, & Nguyen, 2017; Nguyen, 2017; Nunan, 2003). This depressing fact has heightened the need for a drastic renovation in English language education in general and for English teacher professional development in particular. However, little is known about how teachers have experienced professional learning at their schools, whether there are changes in teacher professional learning practices, and, if so, how much these changes have impacted upon their professional learning. In addition, language teacher development is an emerging area that receives insufficient attention in the context of Vietnam (Nguyen, 2017; Pham, 2001). Without firm research-based evidence, it is hard to ensure the quality of professional learning activities.

Teachers' professional development (PD) and professional learning (PL)

For language teachers, professional development is understood as a range of activities to improve and enhance language proficiency as well as other teaching skills, especially within the current educational reform (Richards & Farrell, 2005). In their book, they have listed a number of PD activities, such as workshops, self-monitoring, teacher-support groups, keeping a teaching journal, peer observations, teaching portfolios, case analyses, peer coaching, team teaching, and action research. These activities move on a continuum, from being individual on one side to being collaborative on the other. An impressive body of research on teacher professional development has so far been conducted in language education. Most of the studies have focused on the current situation of language teacher professional development, the benefits of teacher professional development, different models of PD, or the challenges encountered by teachers in participating in professional development activities. However, the literature on teachers' PD tends to focus on a top-down approach and on teachers' perceptions of PD benefits and constraints, and it very often ignores teachers' needs and interests. The concept of professional learning is under-theorised. To effectively implement language policy, Liddicoat and Baldauf (2008) have recently called for closer examination of the role of teacher professional development at the grass roots level in different contexts. More empirical studies from a wider range of contexts including Vietnam are needed to further understand teachers' professional learning in language policy implementation.

A search of the relevant literature in language education in Vietnam has revealed that the topic of teacher professional development is an emerging research area in this context of change. The current PD literature in Vietnam has focused on a number of aspects. Firstly, a cluster of studies have explored teachers' experiences of different language teacher PD activities (Mai & Ocriciano, 2017; Nguyen, 2017; Phan, 2017). As PD initiatives in Vietnam have a top-down approach run by the authorities (MOET, or DOET), PD activities tend to occur in preselected places with structured content (Nguyen, 2017; Nguyen & Mai, 2018; Pham, 2001). To disseminate PD activities, different models have been employed, such as the cascade approach (Hamano, 2008; Hayes, 2008) and the train-the-trainer model (Vu & Pham, 2014). PD activities take many forms, such as summer school, qualification upgrading, demonstration lesson training, and in-school training (Hamano, 2008; Hayes, 2008; Le & Yeo, 2016; Nguyen, 2017; Saito, Khong, & Tsukui, 2012). Nevertheless, these models have been criticised as ineffective because of time, funds, and human resources (Nguyen & Mai, 2018). Teachers have to periodically relocate to predetermined venues for a series of PD workshops, which turn out to be ineffective in resolving teachers' situated pedagogical problems due to the ignorance of teachers' specific needs and their school environments (Nguyen & Mai, 2018).

Even when teachers participate in some PD sessions, it may be argued that these activities are unlikely to advance teachers' pedagogical knowledge and skills. Le and Yeo (2016), in particular, reported that one PD workshop programme they analysed contained 15 modules on primary English teaching methodology but was intended to last only 3 weeks with 10 hours of training a day. The quality of this type of PD was a concern in their study. In addition, PD content has been described as theory-based, formal, and irrelevant to teachers' needs (Hamano, 2008; Hayes, 2008; Le & Barnard, 2009; Le & Yeo, 2016; Nguyen, 2017). Recent research has also shown that English teachers in Vietnam are resistant to applying what they have been trained in PD sessions because of their preferences for familiar teaching techniques and insufficient support from principals and teaching resources (Hayes, 2008; Le & Barnard, 2009; Le & Yeo, 2016).

In order to support this process through professional development activities, it is of crucial importance to understand how the teacher learning process occurs and how PL is conceptualised. Teacher professional learning is known as complex and highly contextually situated (Borko, 2004; Johnson & Golombek, 2011). Much literature in the field of teacher professional development has focused on investigating the impact of specific models or programmes in isolation from the complex teaching and learning environment and teachers' needs at the schools in which they work. This reflects the common understanding of the notion of teacher development over the years. However, this concept has changed. Recent literature calls for research on teacher learning in which the professional learning process is not seen as separate, distinct processes but rather is embedded in the complex teaching and learning environment in which teachers live. As Cole (2012) argued, teacher professional learning is viewed as "the formal and informal learning experiences undertaken by teachers and school leaders that improve their individual professional practice and the school's collective effectiveness as measured by improved student engagement and learning outcomes" (p. 4).

Although much research has been conducted on teacher professional development in language education, there seems to be a lack of studies that have conceptualised the teachers' professional learning in their own contexts, particularly the interplay of various personal and contextual factors that influence their professional learning experience. This highlights the need for more research with a more rigid theory to be carried out in this area in the context of Vietnam.

Using activity theory to conceptualise teacher professional learning

The current study investigated teacher professional learning under the perspective of Vygotskian sociocultural theory. Vygotskian sociocultural theorists conceptualised human mental functioning, in this case teacher professional learning, as being socially distributed and mediated by culturally, historically, and socially developed tools within which subjects live, learn, and work (Engeström, 1987; Grossman, Smagorinsky, & Valencia, 1999; Johnson & Golombek, 2011; Wertsch, 1993). As Engeström put it, "The individual could no longer be understood without his or her cultural means; the society could no longer be understood without the agency of individuals who use and produce artifacts" (Engeström, 2001, p. 134).

Activity Theory originated from Lev Vygotsky (1978)'s revolutionary idea of *mediated action*, Vygotsky's idea of cultural mediation of actions, which is graphically illustrated as the triad of subject, object, and mediating artifact (Engeström,

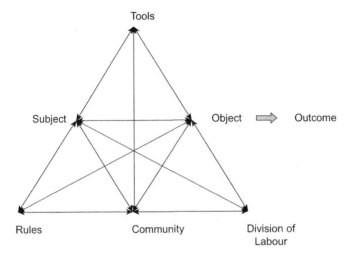

Figure 5.1 The structure of human activity

Source: (Engeström, 1987, p. 78)

2001; Thorne, 2004). It was further developed by Leont'ev, who proposed that individual or group actions embedded in the activity systems must be understood as collective and social (Leont'ev, 1981). Engeström (1987) introduced the ideas of community, rules and outcomes (see Figure 5.1).

Rules refers to any formal or informal norms and conventions that place affordances as well as constraints on the actions and interactions within the activity system (Engeström, 1987). The *community* refers to other individuals and/or subgroups who share the general object of the activity. The *division of labour* refers to how tasks are divided among the community (Grossman et al., 1999; Yamagata-Lynch, 2003).

In this paper, we focus on the second generation of CHAT, due to the focus on understanding human activity (teachers' professional learning) within a complex social context (schools). It "allows for a focus at the level of individual teacher practices but also at the broader organisation level" (Murphy & Rodriguez-Manzanares, 2008, p. 444). Thus, we conceptualise the teachers' professional learning as an interrelated activity within systems regulated by an objective that aims to achieve an intended outcome (becoming a better teacher).

Research methodology

A qualitative case study approach was employed for the current study because it is compatible with the theoretical framework and the nature of the phenomenon under research, which explores teacher professional learning amid change – a highly complex phenomenon in real contexts.

Data were generated through a number of strategies including documents, classroom observations, and interviews. Documents were teaching materials,

ELT training documents, teacher evaluations, school policy, DOET/BOET policies and instructions. The participant teachers were involved in initial interviews, post-lesson interviews and final interviews, focusing on how they perceived the NFLP 2020 generally (e.g., the teacher standard requirements, the new curriculum) and their professional learning specifically (e.g., training courses/workshops, their learning activities). Semi-structured interviews that were conducted in Vietnamese were also held with other participants, such as lead teachers of ELT groups, school principals, DOET/MOET supervisors. The focus was on their perception of the national language project and their management with regard to teacher professional learning in that particular context. The current chapter reports the data on their professional learning experience.

For data analysis, a constant comparative method (Strauss & Corbin, 1998) was employed for code identification, thematic analysis and identifying findings. For identifying activity systems, the comprehensive eight-step procedure suggested by Yamagata-Lynch (2010) was used in this study.

Findings

The findings are structured according to different components of the teacher professional learning activity in the light of activity theory, as illustrated in Figure 5.2.

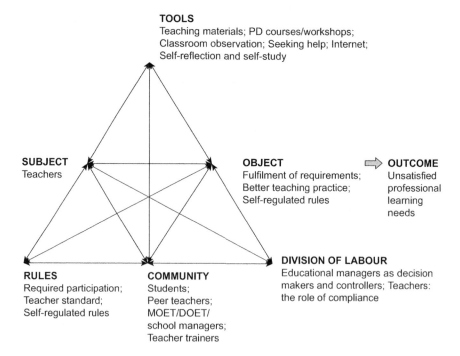

TOOLS
Teaching materials; PD courses/workshops;
Classroom observation; Seeking help; Internet;
Self-reflection and self-study

SUBJECT
Teachers

OBJECT
Fulfilment of requirements;
Better teaching practice;
Self-regulated rules

OUTCOME
Unsatisfied
professional
learning
needs

RULES
Required participation;
Teacher standard;
Self-regulated rules

COMMUNITY
Students;
Peer teachers;
MOET/DOET/
school managers;
Teacher trainers

DIVISION OF LABOUR
Educational managers as decision
makers and controllers; Teachers:
the role of compliance

Figure 5.2 The activity system of teacher professional learning

Source: (after Engeström, 1987)

The participant teachers as subjects of the activity system

The participants of this activity were the four English teachers at Vietnamese urban schools who were selected to implement the pilot curriculum. The teachers were considered to be "key teachers" who had competence in English language and English language teaching. All of the participants were female with teaching experience ranging from 5 to 24 years.

Objects of the professional learning activity system

According to activity theory, the object is the "problem space" at which the activity is oriented and that is transformed into outcomes through the mediation of external and internal physical and/or symbolic tools (Engeström, 1993, p. 67). Data show that the objects of the participant teachers' professional learning activities were varied. The first common object was to fulfil the requirements of attendance, especially of the PD training courses and workshops organised by the MOET, DOET, or BOET and to obtain the required certificates. As Nga said, "[M]y name is on the list. So I just go. . . . It's a requirement" (Nga). The teachers believed that participation in the PD could help them to obtain the required certificates, especially the mandated language proficiency ones. Most of the opinions were to be "safe," "to get it done," or "not being tortured this way or that way" (Nga, Nhung, Tam, Thanh). However, according to the teachers, the mandated standards of language proficiency have been poorly introduced by MOET and DOET. Different institutions taught, assessed, and awarded the certificate in different ways. Participants found it confusing and misleading when setting goals for their learning activity. One teacher shared:

> Yes, the requirement is C1. In fact, getting C1 is not easy. Some teachers were assessed to be at B2. They have to upgrade to C1. . . . But now DOET said "B2 is still ok, not necessarily C1." DOET instructions are very confusing.
>
> (Nhung)

Table 5.1 Socio-demographic characteristics of the participants

Characteristic	Participants			
	Nga	*Nhung*	*Tam*	*Thanh*
Gender	Female	Female	Female	Female
Degree	Degree	Master	Degree	Degree
Age (years)	41	49	27	35
Teaching experience (years)	18	24	5	7
Language proficiency	C1	C1	C1	B2
Grades	10, 11, 12	10, 11, 12	3 and 5	4 and 5
Textbooks	Tieng Anh 10,11, 12	Tieng Anh 10, 11, 12	UK English Program, Tieng Anh 5	Tieng Anh 4, 5

The second common object of the teachers' professional learning engagement in this study was to "teach better," which meant delivering the lessons in "more interesting" and "more appropriate" ways for their students using the new textbooks (Tam, Nga, Nhung). For teaching effectively, they aimed at improving their background knowledge, especially knowledge of English language and language skills so that they could teach English through English. They especially aimed at finding ways to teach the "new parts" (Nhung, Thanh) and undertake assessment of students' language use and learning outcomes (Tam), especially assessment of student performance in out-of-class activities (Nhung). They also sought to fulfil their learning needs of how to assess students' speaking and writing skills. Thanh consistently expressed her desire for more PD activities: "I believe that PD is important for me. It's never enough. If I don't regularly refresh my knowledge and skills, they will become outdated. I expect to maintain continuous PD activities." Although the teachers aimed at fulfilling the requirements, the main purposes of their professional learning were more closely connected to their daily teaching practice with the new textbook series.

The third object of the teacher professional learning activity was to become more self-regulated in their professional activities . After failing the language proficiency assessment and attending the language proficiency upgrade course, Nhung said, "I have to study, study hard. To show that I'm not worse than those who passed [the assessment]. To show that I'm not bad at all" (Nhung). A similar goal was found in teachers' efforts in applying new teaching equipment, in investing more time and effort in demonstration lessons or their teaching practice. For example, Nga said she invested more time and effort in making the demonstration lessons "more interesting, with more activities, more for demonstration" (Nga). Or Nhung recounted her efforts in using the language lab room with multiple functions that had not been used by her colleagues. She said "we are trained but no one could use [to teach]. . . . Only me, who finds a way to use. . . . I think it's only me who teach this way [using multimedia language lab]" (Nhung). The goal of recognition seeking was also well illustrated in the efforts to maintain the award of "Excellent teacher of the city." As one teacher shared, "I have been considered as an excellent teacher of the city so I always try to learn to improve my teaching practice" (Thanh).

The tools in the teacher professional learning activity systems

The first important and available tools in the professional learning activity system were the teaching materials, specifically the textbooks. All four teachers shared that the textbook was important. It changed the way teachers and students taught and learnt. The new textbooks with updated topics, teaching methodology and new information, were reported to activate the participant teachers' thinking and learning. Using the new books, teachers needed to find different ways to update the knowledge and think critically by themselves, as Nhung reported:

I have more knowledge when using this series. . . . Before teaching, I have to read, to search extensively on the Internet. For example, Gandhi's statement "Be the change you wish to see in the world. . . . Literal meaning is easy but figurative meaning is difficult. Or "think global, act local." I had to search tremendously on the internet but no one explained. I had to ask others.

Besides the updated topics, the new teaching methodology embedded in the textbook activities, especially the project-based ones, created both tensions and affordances for the teachers' learning activity. They felt motivated when seeing students' progress in language skills, especially confidence in speaking (Nga). The teachers reported that they had struggled in applying this new methodology to students with low language proficiency. When implementing the project-based tasks, they had difficulty in oral assessment, classroom management during students' presentations, and grouping students. This situation encouraged them to learn more about the methodology by themselves and to ask their colleagues for ideas.

The teachers held different views on the degree of the teacher books' usefulness to their teaching practice. Some found the teacher books were helpful with "relatively clear procedures" (Nga). They were used as "a frame" or "tools" for teachers to build ideas for designing their own teaching activities (Tam). To motivate students, they tended to change some activities in the textbooks to make it "a little bit different, strange, and fun" (Nga) and make it more appropriate to a particular group of students (Thanh). However, the teacher books provided limited support related to the content or explanation of teaching methodology (Nhung).

The second set of tools that contributed to the participants' learning were the PD courses and workshops organised by the MOET, DOET, and BOET, such as workshops for textbook change and competency-based assessment. Referring to these activities, the teachers expressed more negative than positive attitudes. They showed their disappointment that these workshops "were just on the surface, not very useful" (Tam) and were "completely ineffective, just for fun" and "nothing new" (Nhung). The PD training courses that supported the teachers to a certain extent were the language proficiency upgrading courses for those who failed the language proficiency assessment. Being "irritated" when being "assessed inappropriately" (Nhung), they found these to be opportunities to sharpen their "blunt" language skills, especially speaking skills, with "foreigners" as instructors (Nga). They stated benefits such as, "I think my speaking skill is better, maybe I'm more confident in using English in class" (Nga), or "I learnt many interesting idioms such as 'know something inside out' or 'know you like the back of my hand'" (Nhung). However, Nhung shared that she rarely used the new language knowledge she obtained from the course because her students' language proficiency was much lower. Despite the quality, opportunities for PD activities were limited and unequally available to all teachers. As one teacher expressed, "I'm not properly trained to teach this book . . . Possibly because I am not a permanent teacher, so I was not chosen to do some training about the book" (Thanh).

The third learning tool the teachers reported was peer classroom observation. All four teachers experienced learning benefits from peer classroom observation. For example, Nga shared she could learn from peer comments because "maybe we don't see but observers can see better" (Nga). However, they said that they were rarely peer observed. The class observations occurred only when supervisors/inspectors were coming to the school and/or they needed to submit the documents to the principal (Nhung). In addition, in those observed lessons, which managers often attended, the teachers in charge often chose to teach the "easy" lessons for "demonstration" to avoid poor evaluation (Thanh). Their peer teachers tended to give "good, good comments" because "who would badly evaluate others?" (Nhung). Therefore, learning opportunities were limited for the observers; however, most of the participant teachers believed that they had learnt better from observing their colleagues teaching similar lessons in school.

Another tool mediating the teachers' learning was to seek help from colleagues. However, this tool was used more through personal networks than teacher meetings or well structured PL activities. The content of a two-hour meeting every two weeks of the ELT section was mainly for administrative work rather than for professional activities (Nga, Nhung, Thanh). In addition, a less collaborative community among teachers hindered the opportunities to learn. As shared by a teacher who failed to seek learning opportunities from her colleagues:

> [T]hey don't share professionally, even when I asked what they learnt from the workshop, they just said "oh god, nothing, only time-wasting." The workshop could be useless to them individually. But I think it may be useful, but they don't want to share or don't know how to.
>
> (Thanh)

Professional chats often informally happened "during breaks, when designing tests or marking exams together or after classroom observation" (Nhung). The circle of sharing was more between peer teachers who were friends rather than with all colleagues (Nhung, Nga).

Another important learning tool the teachers frequently mentioned was the Internet. They frequently relied on the Internet to upgrade their background and language knowledge, practice their language skills, seek answers to difficult textbook tasks, teaching materials, or teaching aids. The Internet seemed to be the first source the teachers sought help from when they had difficulties in teaching, as some of them shared: "[L]ook for teaching materials on the Internet, like a video clip. Sometimes, I also search for a demo lesson . . . search the forums for teaching procedures" (Tam) and "Many demo lessons on Youtube are good. I also imitate" (Nga). They confessed that Internet searching took them a lot of time and effort. However, they frequently could not find the answers to their questions even after "extensively" searching (Nga, Nhung, Tam).

The last important and dominant tool in teacher learning activity frequently mentioned was the process of self-reflection and self-study. They stated that they self-reflected through the process of their peer classroom observation, lesson planning, and their teaching practice. For example, one teacher shared:

> Peer observation at district level, I evaluate, there've been many times I find it very effective because I've learnt a lot about teaching methodology, about the strengths and weaknesses of others. From the weaknesses, I myself draw the lessons for my teaching practice.
>
> (Thanh)

Describing the most important learning source, a teacher shared:

> I read, observe, and think. Think. Draw a lesson. For example, this year I use this activity. If it doesn't work, next time I'll change. What's good, I'll note down. It's more successful with this way. It's important to read and consider if the activities are ok. If they're appropriate [for students]. It's a process.
>
> (Nga)

The community in the activity system of teacher professional learning

The important community involved in the learning activity of these teachers was that comprised of their students, peer teachers of English and other subjects, and educational managers, especially lead teachers. Students created the main push for teacher learning. As Nga stated, "[S]tudents were better so I had to change myself" (Nga). Thanh shared:

> Many times, when students could not understand the lessons because of too many new words, grammatical points, I found myself something like impotent. I keep wondering, a lot. I must ask for workshop attendance, or classroom observation or do something to improve, to find more appropriate methods for my students.

Students' learning needs created higher motivation for teachers to learn. The teachers' motivation for constant learning stemmed from their desire to deliver more effective lessons for their students. Other community members were their peer teachers and team leaders who had impact on the teachers' learning to some degree. Nhung confessed, "Wen I am teaching, for example about global warming, fossil fuels. I don't know. I have to ask chemistry teachers such as how fossils are made, greenhouse effect, etc. . . . . I also need to ask history teachers." They sometimes shared information, difficulties, and confusions; sought information; and learnt from their peers who were also implementing the pilot curriculum, especially from the lead teacher (Nga, Tam). Under such conditions, they devoted themselves to making lessons interesting, with much investment in gathering resources and preparing activities for their students. For example, Thanh was inspired about teaching pronunciation. Her interest came from her observations that many of her colleagues found it challenging to teach. Therefore, she decided to challenge herself by voluntarily presenting a demonstration on this language aspect at her school and invested time into locating resources and activities for it. Her dedication finally brought success, and she is now well known for teaching pronunciation in the region.

Parental involvement also appeared to place pressures on these teachers to invest their time and energy into teaching methods. In interviews, Tam stated that the school enabled parents to communicate with the school leaders through email. Therefore, parents would send their feedback on their children's learning progress to the school leaders who might then question the teachers for further information. In such a working context, Tam felt "very pressured and competitive" because she had to strive to maintain good-quality teaching (Tam). She further explained that she aimed to "create a good professional reputation" among students, parents, and school leaders.

Rules in the activity system of the teacher professional learning

The rules regulating their PL activities included formal rules from the upper levels of management and their self-regulated rules. The formal rules tended to force teachers to learn rather than motivate them. Most of the teachers said that they had to participate in PD workshops and training courses to achieve the teacher language standards. According to the English Teacher Competency Framework (ETCF), they were also required to obtain the mandated levels of language proficiency, at least B2 for primary and lower secondary school teachers and C1 for upper secondary school teachers. As mentioned, this requirement was confusing. The teachers were also required to participate in other PD activities such as teaching demo lessons, classroom observation, teacher meetings of the ELT section (once every two weeks), or doing research. The upper secondary school teachers, for example, were required to give at least four demo lessons and observe at least 18 lessons per year. They were not then given opportunities to reflect on their own practice and choose to attend the PL relevant to their needs and their teaching context. This formal rule tended to force teachers to learn rather than to motivate them.

Besides the requirements from the upper levels of management, the learning activities of participant teachers were mediated by the teachers' self-regulated rules including investment of time and effort and even money. In order to have learning opportunities, the preceding teacher had to spend more time, effort, and money on teaching the new curriculum. The following is an example:

> The vice principal assigned me to teach this class because he likes to give me a [learning] opportunity. If teaching year 1, 2, 3, I may forget my knowledge. Teaching the new MOET curriculum, with that content, I'll not forget mine. Maybe I may have difficulty for the first year, but in the second or third year, I'll overcome, and find out the appropriate methods for my own

students. It takes time to accumulate [teaching aids], to ask from colleagues. For the first classes, I have to make an impression with students, so I have to invest more. We have to use our own money.

(Tam)

Division of labour in the activity system of teacher professional learning

The division of labour within the community between teachers and school, DOET, MOET, and administrators was hierarchical, where teachers were expected to follow the instructions of upper levels of management. Managers had responsibilities to send teachers to PD activities and to check their completion. Teachers were expected to obtain necessary knowledge and skills for realising the curriculum's goals. When being asked whether teachers were properly supported professionally, principal A (province A) confirmed: "[T]eachers have been trained! If there were training courses organised by DOET and MOET, our school always sent them there in turn." In addition, they were expected to be active in information sharing or seeking PD activities to upgrade their knowledge and pedagogical skills. However, as previously discussed, the time pressure for administration work as well as a less collaborative culture limited the opportunities for sharing. As Thanh pointed out, in the teacher meetings where teachers were expected to develop professionally, "[W]e hardly discuss our teaching. When no-one asks. No-body asks and of course no-one responds." Predominantly, teachers tended to undertake their learning activities in isolation. As Tam shared, "I just learn around 20%–50% from my ELT group. Mainly I learn by myself." When being asked what support Nga expected to have, she responded, "What support? You have to do it yourself."

It seems the division of labour between teachers and educational managers showed limited support for teachers' professional learning. The communication between the two groups tended to be monologic transmitting from the upper level to the lower level. The intentions of the managers were not clarified and properly understood. The voices of the teachers were marginalised.

Outcome

Mediated by different tools, the professional learning needs of the teachers were still unsatisfied. Their learning often occurred in isolation. The teachers found ways to fulfil their needs personally rather than seeking formal ways through management levels; however, they were not always successful. Therefore, they felt a lack of confidence in their implementation. As Thanh shared about her teaching with the new textbook:

I find problems in all parts. I don't feel confident in any parts because I'm not trained, not supported from the textbook designers and teacher books. I get stuck and keep wondering in every part. Because at the end of each class, students only grab the knowledge of that lesson but aren't able to use the language they've learnt in other lessons. I think my teaching is more failure rather than success.

(Thanh)

Although the NFLP 2020 had spent a great amount of money on teacher professional development, it seems the teachers' learning needs were generally not satisfied. The teacher learning activity happened more in isolation with little support.

Discussion

The aim of this paper is to explore the professional learning system of a group of teachers in a specific context in Vietnam. The findings were analysed from the perspective of activity theory to provide a comprehensive picture of teacher learning. The different components of activity theory were identified to raise critically important issues to be considered to further understand the current situation of teachers' professional learning and to enhance the effectiveness of PL activities.

Three issues related to the object of the teacher professional learning were the fulfillment of the requirements such as PD activity attendance and certificates, better teaching practice, and the self-regulated object of recognition seeking from peer teachers. The first goal of their PL seems to be very common in many contexts where the teachers have to fulfil their PL requirements. This top-down approach may encounter some resistance from the teachers; however, it can be seen as the first step in developing their professional practice in response to the changes in the English curriculum. The finding also provides ample evidence to show the lack of communication and consistency in the adoption of the English Teacher Competency Framework (ETCF) in enhancing teachers' language competence from the MOET and DOET. The adoption of this framework in PL for teachers is still in its infancy and has experienced some barriers such as lack of communication and consistency. This supports Nguyen and Hamid's (2015) research, which showed the failure of the adoption of this framework in addressing some critical issues in the practice of teaching and learning the language in the country of Vietnam

The findings from this study showed the NFLP 2020 has created relatively positive impacts on the teachers' motivation to enhance their professional learning. Teachers still have a strong desire for "true" professional learning and are in real need of PD for their effective teaching. The impact of new reforms has triggered the teachers' motivation to learn to enhance their teaching practice in order to keep up with the changes and to enhance the quality of learning for their students. The new requirements, as well as the new curriculum, have created learning opportunities for teachers. This is contrary to previous studies, which have doubted the impact of the NFLP 2020 (Hayes, 2008; Le & Barnard, 2009; Le & Yeo, 2016).

Data also show that the teachers considered the language proficiency upgrading activities as opportunities for practising their English language skills and building confidence in English use. However, the teachers found limited impact of the PD activities on their teaching practice. In other words, these predetermined PD activities did not satisfy the teachers' learning needs. Similar to previous studies (Chinh, Le, Tran, & Nguyen, 2014; Hamano, 2008; Hayes, 2008; Le & Nguyen, 2012; Nguyen, 2011), it was found that one-off professional development activities were not successful in creating changes in teaching practice. This evidence possibly calls for a bottom-up PD approach rather than that from imposed policy mandates. Teacher development does not exist in a vacuum but is situated in a particular context, with particular people who have particular needs, purposes, and goals (Kumaravadivelu, 2001; Le & Nguyen, 2012). Hence it is both inappropriate and impractical to provide the same training content to teachers from different working contexts. It also implies that the voices of teachers should be heard, as they have agency to resist the PD activities if they find them inapplicable to their teaching responsibilities at the workplace. In addition, in relation to the policymaking process, top-down policymakers should be aware of the regional differences and the need to empower and provide teachers across the regions with sufficient professional support and resources when the policy is transferred and translated into classrooms (Nguyen & Bui, 2016). They should take account of teachers' inner worlds to foster their positive agency. Hargreaves (1997) also has suggested that teachers' professional learning should address issues of interest to teachers and not issues raised by others. It is assumed that English primary teachers would promote their agency if they gain confidence in making use of contextual constraints. This agency can be exercised at both the individual and the collective levels. At an individual level, the teacher can enact their agency to plan their learning goals and to direct, regulate, and responsibly manage their learning (Pyhältö, Pietarinen, & Soini, 2014, 2015). At the collective level, they are empowered to learn through others: considering others as a learning resource or working cooperatively with others for shared learning. This emphasises the role of schools in supporting them to be agentive agents for their own learning and the learning of others.

It can be seen from the findings that the mandated textbook as the new tool created a big impact on the process of teacher professional learning. The new tool with new ideas such as developing critical thinking and project-based teaching, which were not familiar to the teachers, had sparked their professional learning activity. The teachers attempted to update their background knowledge, as well as teaching skills, in order to better plan and deliver the lessons to suit their students' current learning needs. The teacher book should be designed in a way that supports teachers' professional learning. The book is not only for student learning but should also be for teacher learning. It should provide, for example, the underlying principles of design, resources for further reading, and space for reflections so that teachers can be thoughtful decision makers and reflective practitioners (Ball & Cohen,1996; Davis & Krajcik, 2005; Farrell, 2007).

The study shows that the teachers used other tools to achieve their learning object such as peer classroom observation, seeking support from colleagues, self-study and self-reflection, and the Internet. The finding shows that they used the Internet very often to look for more information to enhance their teaching practice. Although the teachers commonly used the Internet, their professional learning was not always satisfied. Therefore, there should be training and constant support through the provision of e-learning and teaching resources, as well as web navigation skills stemming from the teachers' learning needs.

The teachers said peer classroom observation could be a potential tool to support their learning from peers, as could self-reflection. However, peer observation was often carried out in the form of teacher evaluation; therefore, they tended to cope with such observations rather than consider them as learning opportunities. For real and effective learning to happen, peer classroom observation and peer collaboration should be organised in a way that teachers feel free from the anxiety of losing face and free from being formally. The school should become a learning organisation for teachers where they feel free from these obstacles. It is well documented that the school is the unit or centre of change (Fullan, 2007) and that school culture is the essence of sustained success (Hattie, 2012). This emphasises the need to incorporate a number of in-school models of PD that foster teachers' collaboration, observation, and reflection. To promote their professional learning, there should be ongoing activities such peer observation, mentoring, peer mentoring, critical friends group, instructional rounds, and action research, all of which creates opportunities for teachers to collaborate, reflect, investigate, and seek ways to improve their practice with the support of others. These activities would help practically link teacher learning and student learning.

Conclusion

Language teachers play a fundamental role in implementing the changes in language learning and language policy. Many scholars have portrayed teachers' crucial role in educational change. Priority should be placed on providing quality teacher education and professional development programs to help teachers to implement reforms (Le & Nguyen, 2012; Nguyen, 2017).

Professional learning may be undervalued in Vietnam as a result of teachers' perceptions of the necessity for certificates or awards to satisfy administrative requirements (Le & Yeo, 2016) rather than for learning that springs from their inner motivation and needs. The current study calls for radical changes in teachers' professional development. The notion of teacher professional development should move beyond the concept of learning in one-off workshops, lectures, or seminars. It is more effective and desirable if it is collaborative, context relevant, and based on teachers' needs and desires (Le & Nguyen, 2012; Nguyen, 2017; Timperley, 2011). The use of activity theory can be used as a map for designing teachers' professional learning. From the preceding analysis viewed from the perspective of activity theory, the PL activity needs to address:

- The need to identify the teachers' needs and objectives for their PL.
- The need to empower the teachers by providing more opportunity to negotiate and have shared visions and a plan for their own PL.
- The need to be sensitive to the issue of context, which is compounded by certain rules in the system.
- The need to empower schools to build a collaborative learning community at school where all the PL activities aim to enhance students' learning and the effectiveness of the school.
- The need to provide teachers with appropriate tools to mediate their own PL activities.

Although the study shows a comprehensive picture of teachers' professional learning at their local schools, the finding cannot be generalized, but they may be relatable to similar contexts. The study calls for larger-scale studies in other contexts.

References

Ball, D. L., & Cohen, D. K. (1996). Reform by the book: What is or might be: The role of curriculum materials in teacher learning and instructional reform? *Educational Researcher*, *25*(9), 6–8.

Borko, H. (2004). Professional development and teacher learning: Mapping the terrain. *Educational Researcher*, *33*(8), 3–15.

Bui, T. T. N., & Nguyen, H. T. M. (2016). Standardizing English for educational and socio-economic betterment? A critical analysis of English language policy reforms. In R. Kirkpatrick (Ed.), *English education policy in Asia*. Cham, Switzerland: Springer.

Chinh, N. D., Le, T. L., Tran, Q. H., & Nguyen, T. H. (2014). Inequality of access to English language learning in primary education in Vietnam. In H. Zhang, P. W. K. Chan, & C. Boyle (Eds.), *Equality in education* (pp. 139–153). Rotterdam: SensePublishers.

Cole, P. (2012). *Linking effective professional learning with effective teaching practice*. Melbourne: Australian Institute for Teachers and School Leadership.

Davis, E. A., & Krajcik, J. S. (2005). Designing educative curriculum materials to promote teacher learning. *Educational Researcher*, *34*(3), 3–14.

Engeström, Y. (1987). *Learning by expanding: An activity-theoretical approach to developmental research*. Helsinki: Orienta-Konsultit.

Engeström, Y. (1993). Developmental studies of work as a testbench of activity theory: The case of primary care medical practice. In S. Chaiklin & J. Lave (Eds.), *Understanding practice: Perspectives on activity and context* (pp. 64–103). Cambridge: Cambridge University Press.

Engeström, Y. (2001). Expansive learning at work: Toward an activity theoretical reconceptualization. *Journal of Education and Work*, *14*(1), 133–156.

Farrell, T. S. C. (2007). *Reflective language teaching: From research to practice*. London: Continuum.

Fullan, M. (2007). *The new meaning of educational change*. New York: Teachers College Press.

Grossman, P. L., Smagorinsky, P., & Valencia, S. (1999). Appropriating tools for teaching English: A theoretical framework for research on learning to teach. *American Journal of Education, 108*(1), 1–29.

Hamano, T. (2008). Educational reform and teacher education in Vietnam. *Journal of Education for Teaching, 34*(4), 397–410.

Hargreaves, A. (1997). From reform to renewal: A new deal for a new age. In A. Hargreaves & B. Evans (Eds.), *Beyond educational reform: Bringing teachers back in* (pp. 105–125). Buckingham: Open University Press.

Hattie, J. (2012). *Visible learning for teachers: Maximizing impact on learning.* London: Routledge.

Hayes, D. (2008). *Primary English language teaching in Vietnam.* Paper presented at the Primary Innovations, Regional Seminar, Bangkok.

Johnson, K. E., & Golombek, P. R. (2011). A sociocultural theoretical perspective on teacher professional development. In K. E. Johnson & P. R. Golombek (Eds.), *Research on second language teacher education: A sociocultural perspective on professional development.* London: Routledge.

Kumaravadivelu, B. (2001). Toward a postmethod pedagogy. *TESOL Quarterly, 35*(4), 537–560.

Le, P. H. H., & Yeo, M. (2016). Evaluating in-service training of primary English teachers: A case study in Central Vietnam. *The Asian EFL Journal Quarterly, 18*(1), 34–51.

Le, V. C., & Barnard, R. (2009). Curricular innovation behind closed classroom doors: A Vietnamese case study. *Prospect, 24*(2), 20–33.

Le, V. C., & Do, T. M. C. (2012). Teacher preparation for primary school English education: A case of Vietnam. In B. Spolsky & Y. Moon (Eds.), *Primary school English education in Asia* (pp. 106–128). New York: Routledge.

Le, V. C., & Nguyen, T. T. M. (2012). Teacher learning within school context: An econological perspective. *Indonesian Journal of Applied Linguistics, 2*(1), 53–68.

Leont'ev, A. N. (1981). *Problems of the development of mind.* Moscow, Russia: Progressive Publishers.

Liddicoat, A. J., & Baldauf, R. B. (2008). *Language planning in local contexts: Agents, contexts and interactions.* Clevedon: Multilingual Matters.

Mai, T., & Ocriciano, M. (2017). Investigating the influence of webinar participation on professional development of English language teachers in rural Vietnam. *Language Education in Asia, 8*(1), 48–66. http://dx.doi.org/10.5746/LEiA/17/V8/I1/A04/Mai_Ocriciano

MOET. (2016). *Hội nghị trực tuyến về triển khai giai đoạn 2016–2020, định hướng đến năm 2025 của Đề án Ngoại Ngữ Quốc Gia 2020* [Online conference on the implementation of Vietnam's National Foreign Languages 2020 Project in the period 2016–2020, orienting to 2025]. Retrieved from https://dean2020.edu.vn/vi/news/Tin-tuc/hoi-nghi-truc-tuyen-trien-khai-giai-doan-2016-2020-dinh-huong-den-nam-2025-cua-de-an-ngoai-ngu-quoc-gia-2020-386.html

Murphy, E., & Rodriguez-Manzanares, M. A. (2008). Using activity theory and its principle of contradictions to guide research in educational technology. *Australasian Journal of Education Technology, 24*, 442–447.

NFLP 2020. (2016). *Đề án "Dạy và học ngoại ngữ trong hệ thống giáo dục quốc dân giai đoạn 2008–2020" Kết quả giai đoạn 2011–2015 và kế hoạch triển khai giai đoạn 2016–2020.* Paper presented at the The NFPL 2020 – Reviewing outcomes 2011–2015 and planning strategies 2016–2020, Hanoi.

Nguyen, H. T. M. (2011). Primary English language education policy in Vietnam: Insights from implementation. *Current Issues in Language Planning, 12*(2), 225–249.

Nguyen, H. T. M. (2017). *Model of mentoring in language teacher education.* Cham, Switzerland: Springer.

Nguyen, H. T. M., & Bui, T. (2016). Teachers' agency and the enactment of educational reform in Vietnam. *Current Issues in Language Planning, 17*(1), 88–105.

Nguyen, H. T. M., Nguyen, T. H., Nguyen, V. H., & Nguyen, T. T. T. (2017). Local challenges to global needs in English language education in Vietnam: The perspective of language policy and planning. In C. S. K. Chua et al. (Eds.), *Un(intended) language planning in a globalising world: Multiple levels of players at work* (pp. 214–233). Warsaw, Poland: De Gruyter Open.

Nguyen, V. H., & Hamid, M. O. (2015). Educational policy borrowing in a globalized world: A case study of common European framework of reference for languages in a Vietnamese university. *English Teaching: Practice & Critique, 14*(1), 60–74.

Nguyen, V. T., & Mai, N. K. (2018). Professional development as part of English education initiatives in the ASEAN. In K. Hashimoto & V. T. Nguyen (Eds.), *Professional development of English language teachers in Asia: Lessons from Japan and Vietnam* (pp. 11–25). New York: Routledge.

Nunan, D. (2003). The impact of English as a global language on educational policies and practices in the Asia-Pacific Region. *TESOL Quarterly, 37*(4), 589–613.

Pham, H. H. (2001). Teacher development : A real need for English departments in Vietnam. *English Teaching Forum, 39*(4).

Phan, Q. N. (2017). *Professional learning communities: Learning sites for primary school English language teachers in Vietnam.* Doctoral dissertation, Sydney University of Technology, Sydney, Australia. Retrieved from https://opus.lib.uts.edu.au/bitstream/10453/120201/2/02whole.pdf

Pyhältö, K., Pietarinen, J., & Soini, T. (2014). Comprehensive school teachers' professional agency in large-scale educational change. *Journal of Educational Change, 15*(3), 303–325.

Pyhältö, K., Pietarinen, J., & Soini, T. (2015). Teachers' professional agency and learning – from adaption to active modification in the teacher community. *Teachers and Teaching, 21*(7), 811–830.

Richards, J., & Farrell, T. (2005). *Professional development for language teachers: Strategies for teacher learning.* Cambridge: Cambridge University Press.

Saito, E., Khong, T. D. H., & Tsukui, A. (2012). Why is school reform sustained even after a project? A case study of Bac Giang Province, Vietnam. *Journal of Educational Change, 13*(2), 259–287.

Strauss, A. L., & Corbin, J. (1998). *Basics of qualitative research: Techniques and procedures for developing grounded theory* (2nd ed.). Thousand Oaks, CA: Sage Publications.

Thorne, S. (2004). Cultural historical activity theory and the object of innovation. In K. van Esch & O. St. John (Eds.), *New insights into foreign language learning and teaching* (pp. 51–70). Frankfurt: Peter Lang.

Timperley, H. (2011). *Realizing the power of professional learning.* Maidenhead, UK: Open University Press.

Vu, M. T., & Pham, T. T. T. (2014). Training of trainers for primary English teachers in Vietnam: Stakeholder evaluation. *The Journal of Asia TEFL, 11*(4), 89–108.

Vygotsky, L. S. (1978). *Mind and society: The development of higher mental processes.* Cambridge, MA: Harvard University Press.

Wertsch, J. V. (1993). *Voices of the mind: A sociocultural approach to mediated action.* Cambridge, MA: Harvard University Press.

Yamagata-Lynch, L. C. (2003). Using activity theory as an analytic lens for examining technology professional development in schools. *Mind, Culture, and Activity, 10*(2), 100–119.

Yamagata-Lynch, L. C. (2010). *Activity systems analysis methods: Understanding complex learning environments.* New York: Springer.

6 Leveraging teaching knowledge to develop teachers' classroom English

Working at scale

Donald Freeman and Anne Katz

Introduction: challenges in improving teachers' classroom English

As national education systems around the world incorporate English as a core component in their primary and secondary curricula, increasing numbers of teachers within those systems are being required to provide English language instruction (Graddol, 1997, 2006). In many settings however, teachers do not have sufficient command of English to be able to address these new instructional demands. Government reforms designed to strengthen teachers' English proficiency for use in classroom teaching have been widely implemented, but often with little success (Wedell, 2011). In many national education systems, this policy goal is expressed as increasing teachers' ability *to teach English in English* or simply *to teach in English*. To enact this goal, ministries have relied on developing teachers' general English proficiency to improve their classroom language competence. These language targets are usually expressed in general proficiency metrics taken from the Common European Framework Reference (CEFR), reinforcing the curricular and assessment assumptions that general English will serve teachers in classroom teaching.

Supporting improvement in teachers' use of classroom English is a complex problem. It has several facets, which we organise along three dimensions: teachers' *access* to professional development, *equity* in how these opportunities are made available, and availability and use of *resources* for providing them. Teachers' interests in and need for classroom English language is often related to national policy expectations, which then raises the *question of access* – of how to reach and support teachers who are seeking to or need to improve. The demand for training extends across diverse teaching contexts: from teachers in metropolitan areas to those working in rural areas; from teachers who teach English as a subject matter full-time to those, like primary teachers in many countries, who are now expected to incorporate English into their general instructional responsibilities. Furthermore, in national systems, such as Spain, Italy, and others, that are introducing or extending teaching subjects in English – an approach known as Content and Language Integrated Learning or CLIL (Coyle, 2007) – which is intended to foster student learning of both simultaneously – the demands for teachers to develop classroom English competence is heightened (Lopriore, 2018).

The demand for access introduces *questions of equity* in which professional development opportunities are available to which teachers. Prevailing systems of providing professional development, although well intentioned, can be inherently inequitable. Most reforms rely on familiar models that depend on some form of face-to-face input. This training is then often extended through a cascade design in which the participants, who have received the initial training, pass on what they have learned to their peers. These face-to-face plus cascade designs are bound to create iniquities, however. Face-to-face sessions cannot accommodate large numbers of teachers, and the sites are geographically clustered, making it difficult for some teachers to participate. Thus, some teachers will have the opportunity to experience the original training, while others – often those in more remote areas – can participate only through the cascade. This means of making training available introduces questions of how to provide access to equivalent professional development opportunities across varying contexts.

A further dimension to this challenge of equitable distribution of access to professional development will improve teachers' classroom English. The teachers working in schools and communities that are less accessible, often due to geographical location or economic need, have greater need for support, which can then compound the challenge. This question of how to address teachers' different needs raises issues of how financial and pedagogical resources are used within national educational systems.

Even with the aspirational goal of supporting all teachers, and in spite of well intentioned planning, most national education systems find it challenging to distribute financial and pedagogical resources equitably. Schools in rural areas can be disadvantaged; better prepared teachers are usually concentrated in certain communities. The human and technological infrastructures for providing professional development opportunities are often unevenly distributed. All of these resourcing challenges can lead to what Rigney (2010) called the "Matthew effect," in which early access to opportunities leads to further opportunities, thus building advantages for some while disadvantaging others. In the case of improving instruction in national educational systems, teachers who are able to take part in professional development benefit from the opportunities, while teachers who cannot participate – often due to factors beyond their control – fall farther behind.

Reframing the challenge of scalable professional development

To increase access of ELT teachers in national systems to equitable professional development opportunities and to better use resources to support this access, we have argued that the challenge itself needed to be fundamentally reframed. Rather than seeing the problem as one of scale, which would assume that the solution simply lay in extending prevalent designs to more teachers, we took a different approach. We use Constas and Brown's (2006, p. 247) definition of "scale" as "describ[ing] efforts to implement an intervention or group of interventions across a large numbers of varied settings." It is widely understood that improving the quality of instruction through professional development introduces challenges of "scalability" (e.g., Bryk, Gomez, Grunow, & LeMahieu, 2016; Educational Development Center, 2011), of providing that professional development to large, geographically dispersed numbers of teachers. Given this framing, it is not surprising that most approaches define scale in quantitative terms. As Coburn (2003, p. 3) observed, "Definitions of scale have traditionally restricted [the] scope, focusing on the expanding number of [teachers and] schools reached by a reform." "Such definitions," she continues, "mask the complex challenges of reaching out broadly while simultaneously cultivating the depth of change necessary to support and sustain consequential change." These efforts often encounter problems in reaching – and influencing the thinking and the classroom practice of – teachers across a variety of teaching situations (Schneider & McDonald, 2006).

In our work, we have understood "scale" somewhat differently. We see the problems of scale as the ways in which educational systems and providers address the breadth of need and demand to prepare and support teachers across diverse contexts with varying access to teaching resources (Freeman, Katz, Burns, LeDrean, & Hauck, 2013). This definition elaborates four critical aspects of scale: (1) the breadth of need and demand (2) in reaching teachers who are (3) teaching in diverse contexts and locations and with (4) varying resources and support. In some senses, our working definition of scale does not differ fundamentally from the conventional ones just mentioned. We, too, are concerned with reaching numbers of teachers who do not have access and who have not been served by professional development as currently provided. However, rather than concentrating on how professional development is provided, our definition takes the teachers' situations and perspectives as a starting point and emphasises how they can participate in the opportunities they are offered.

The four aspects of scale outlined here – the need and demand; accessibility; diversity of teaching contexts; and varying resources and support – translate into specific challenges in designing and providing scalable professional development opportunities in ELT. We summarise the central challenge of scale in ELT professional development as follows: to design and to implement opportunities for teachers to learn that are equitable for the national teaching force, meaning these professional development opportunities are accessible to any teacher who wants or needs to participate. Equitable access does not guarantee the outcomes will be the same for every participating teacher. Access simply provides opportunities to learn; how participants use those opportunities, what they learn from them, is a matter of individual agency, a point to which we return later in this chapter.

To address this framing of the challenge of scale in ELT requires a rethinking of content and participation as the building blocks of reform and professional development. We need to re-examine how we conceptualise English as the *content* in these professional development efforts and how we design meaningful opportunities for teachers to *participate* in learning it, opportunities that are equally accessible and that can lead to documented results for all teachers. We argue – and our work has shown (e.g., Freeman et al., 2013) – that the content of professional development can be rethought so that teachers can use what they know and are already doing to build their classroom English competence. Using what teachers know how to do as the basis for strengthening their classroom language achieves several ends. The approach encourages participants to make immediate connections with what they do in their classroom. The learning process is symbiotic: as teachers are refining or modifying these classroom practices by using English rather than the national language, to carry them out, they report they are teaching differently (Freeman, 2017). This immediate connection helps to build participants' professional confidence, as they see their own teaching reflect the discourse of global ELT. This combination of making immediate connections and building professional confidence in doing so recasts how teachers participate in and learn through the professional development. We refer to this approach as "leveraging" the content to successfully extend participation in and thus learning from these scalable professional development opportunities. In the next section, we turn to the specifics of how teachers' classroom knowledge is leveraged.

A leveraged approach to content and participation

Rethinking the content: a framework for the language of classroom teaching

Rethinking content entails rethinking how language is defined. In classes that teach English for general English proficiency, learning objectives centre on the component systems that make up the structure of the language. Learners – whether school students or teachers in language courses – study the features of these systems, such as grammatical structures, pronunciation, and discourse genres. Non-specialised content topics that are presumed to be relevant to large swathes of learners, such as favourite movies and things to do on the weekend, are selected and used in lessons so that learners can practice newly learned language forms.

From this smorgasbord of content, learners are meant to encounter, learn, and thus put together the particular language they need or are interested in. In classes for groups of learners with varying personal interests and aims in learning English, an approach that focuses on content topics of general interest can be viable and even sensible. However, for learners with clear professional goals, like teachers who know what they need to learn, the approach is less useful. As one primary school teacher who, as part of a national reform, had been placed in such a general English course to learn the classroom language needed to teach in English remarked, "I may be dead by the time I learn enough English to properly do my job . . . . the job I am already doing and quite well."

We argue for an alternative way of conceptualising English competence that begins by examining how language operates within specific contexts of use. This approach, known as Language for Specific Purposes (LSP), starts from the specific language used for doing particular actions in a specific context. For those who are learning a language with particular aims or uses in mind, this approach tailors instruction to their learning needs. In applying this use-based approach to defining the language content that teachers need to learn, an international expert panel, co-sponsored by National Geographic Learning and Educational Testing Service, developed the English-for-Teaching framework (see Freeman, Katz, Garcia Gomez, & Burns, 2015). The framework builds on the notion of contextualised language, organising the content to be learned around the specific language that teachers use in teaching. In this way, the framework captures the English teacher's need for carrying out the day-to-day instructional tasks of the classroom.

The goal of the English-for-Teaching framework was to develop a scalable pro-gramme that would equip large numbers of teachers with English language skills they could use to teach English *in* English. Using an LSP approach to define the language aims, the English-for-Teaching framework identified specialised language through which teachers carry out predictable instructional routines in their class-rooms. To collect this language, data were drawn from several sources, including a task analysis of classroom practices, a review of ten national curricula to identify the kinds of classroom language teachers would need to enact various learning activities, and an examination of classroom language data collected in several countries involved in the project (see Young et al., 2014). From analyses of these complex data, three functional areas of language-for-teaching were developed: managing the classroom, understanding and communicating lesson content, and assessing students and giving feedback.

The three language areas of English-for-Teaching, shown as A, B, and C in Figure 6.1, enact interconnecting pedagogical functions that operate within the classroom. (We note that, while the focus is on English language classrooms specifically, the framework can be applied to the language used in teaching most classroom subjects.)

Each language area is connected to a specific domain of teaching knowledge that in effect "drives" a particular type of classroom language. *Situated use* (Figure 6.1, lower left) reflects the methodological knowledge that teachers draw on as they interact with students to shape learning experiences. *Content* (lower right) represents teachers' knowledge of the national curriculum, which serves as the basis for their classroom lessons. These two domains of teaching knowledge provide the basis for choosing specific language structures from the broad range of possibilities in *language knowledge* (top). Teachers' *situated use* of classroom English is mediated by their *language knowledge*, which in effect circumscribes how they implement lessons to present, practice, and assess the *content*.

The language that teachers need to control in order to teach in English is organised by the particular teaching tasks they do. For example, in *managing the classroom*, teachers use language knowledge to interact with students to carry out various pedagogical routines and tasks in the situated context of the class-room. In *understanding and communicating lesson content*, teachers use their language knowledge and knowledge of relevant content from the national cur-riculum to develop lessons. In *assessing students and providing feedback*, teachers

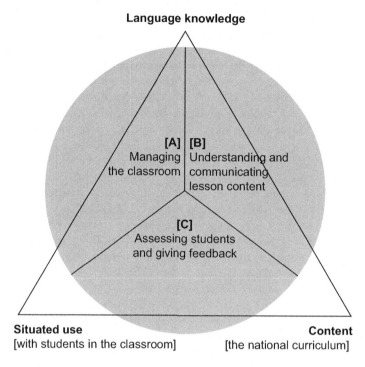

Language knowledge

[A] **[B]**
Managing | Understanding and
the classroom | communicating
lesson content

[C]
Assessing students
and giving feedback

Situated use
[with students in the classroom]

Content
[the national curriculum]

Figure 6.1 The English-for-Teaching Framework (Freeman et al., 2015)

use language knowledge to provide information to their students about their learning progress towards national curriculum targets. Table 6.1 gives examples of classroom tasks in each of the three functional areas and English language exemplars connected to these sample tasks.

In building teachers' classroom language resources, the prevalent argument has been that teaching is an unstructured knowledge domain in which teachers' actions are highly contingent on who, what, and where they are teaching. The only way then to address the nature of the work, the argument goes, is to equip teachers with the breadth of language they will need, and general proficiency training is seen as the best means to this end. While there is some logic in this approach, it misses the fact that practising teachers supported by most ELT reforms already know how to carry out instruction; what they need are the English language resources to enact their instruction in English. Rather than tackling the breadth of the unstructured knowledge of classroom teaching, the LSP approach focuses on a small set of exemplars that can be used to carry out the particular classroom task. These exemplars are clearly not all the possible language the teacher could use in the situation, nor are they necessarily the "best" if such could be established. The exemplars provide teachers with the linguistic

Table 6.1 English-for-Teaching – functional areas, sample classroom tasks, and language exemplars (Educational Testing Service & National Geographic Learning, 2011)

Functional area	Classroom routine Teacher task	Language exemplars
Managing the classroom	1. Making announcements	• *There will be a test tomorrow. Remember to review the new vocabulary.*
	2. Moving from one activity to another	• *Now we are going to check your homework.*
	3. Encouraging participation by asking students to carry out a classroom task	• *Who wants to help pass out these worksheets?*
Understanding and communicating lesson content	4. Giving instructions for a listening activity	• *Underline the words you hear in the story.*
	5. Explaining how to carry out an activity	• *Let me explain the first step.*
	6. Giving examples as a guide	• *Please listen carefully to the example.*
Assessing students and giving feedback	7. Assessing student performances during an activity	• *Your response does not use the past tense correctly.*
		• *Great. Your answer is correct.*
	8. Encouraging self-correction.	• *Something is missing. Try again.*

tools that enable them to perform these predictable tasks and interactions with students in English.

The first element in rethinking the challenge of scalable ELT professional development is centred on rethinking how the content is defined. By providing a defined set of English resources that map onto their classroom practices, these language tools help teachers to leverage their pedagogical knowledge to develop classroom English language skills and become confident in what they are doing.

Redesigning participation: building teacher agency in professional development

The second element focused on rethinking how teachers could gain access to the content. As we have argued, the challenge of scale is to provide equitable access for those who want or need to participate, meaning that everyone has the same opportunity to learn the content. Online, rather than face-to-face training, seemed the most feasible way to meet this challenge. Online delivery of training programmes has surged in popularity in the past decade, with the promise of cost-effective and equitable means of providing professional development to large numbers of teachers in both urban and rural settings. In this sense, it addresses conventional notions of scalable training by allowing participants with Internet access the flexibility to study course content at their convenience and wherever they are located. However, research on effective online learning for teachers suggests that additional aspects of online courses are critical for creating high-quality educational training programmes. Effective online teacher preparation courses share three features: course content that is relevant and applicable to the classroom, sustained practice of what is being learned, and monitored learning and feedback on that learning (McCrory, Putnam, & Jansen, 2008; Murray, 2012; Penuel, Fishman, Yamaguchi, & Gallagher, 2007). In designing the online learning platform to deliver the *English-for-Teaching* professional development course, we addressed these three features, which we elaborate here.

Relevant content. As explained, the course content is based on the functional language of the classroom as presented in the English-for-Teaching framework. In this way, the language structures and vocabulary presented in each lesson are directly related to the regular tasks that teachers enact in their classrooms, tasks such as explaining a grammar point, directing students to turn in their homework, or encouraging students to participate. The language is introduced within a lesson sequence, not as stand-alone vocabulary or discourse units. As a result, teachers meet the language within the particular classroom routine as it is used in instruction. This connection renders the content directly relevant and useable so that participants can begin implementing these English language skills immediately with their students.

At the end of the *English-for-Teaching* course, teachers sit for an assessment to document their learning. Unlike other English language tests, the *English-for-Teaching* assessment derives from the same design blueprint as the course content and format. The assessment employs the same kinds of task types and language selections found in the instructional materials and thus represents the work teachers engage in on a daily basis.

Sustained practice. The online delivery of the *English-for-Teaching* course supports self-paced access to the content, giving participants the flexibility to determine when and how long they will study. Three key features guide this self-access and promote participation. At the start of the course, participants do a self-assessment of the course content, which then provides them with an individualised Path of Learning. This initial self-assessment asks participants to rate their confidence in using classroom English in carrying out the various classroom tasks across the three domains – managing the classroom, understanding and communicating lesson content, and assessing students and giving feedback. The resulting Path of Learning helps them determine how to spend their time in the course based on the classroom language topics they feel they already know and can use. This initial assessment provides a sort of baseline against which participants can see their own progress. They know, however, that all the course content will be part of be part of the final course assessment and that they are therefore responsible for it.

The initial self-assessment and final course assessment frame the self-access design of the course. Participating teachers know what they are responsible for learning in the course, and they can decide how to fit the course into their work and personal lives rather than being asked to follow a predetermined course schedule. The individualised nature of this approach also means that teachers can study as much or as little as they decide they need for their own learning. The course includes multiple opportunities for practice across various types of oral and written tasks. It allows participants to review and repeat practice activities until they are satisfied with their performance.

These elements of initial self- and final course assessment, of individualised learning pathways through the course, and of open-ended possibilities to practice the content all contribute to participants' sustained engagement in their own learning. At the core of this design, then, is the concept of teacher agency, which Wyatt (2018, p. 196) defines as follows:

> [T]eacher agency . . . describes teachers' efforts to make choices within a host of contexts: in establishing and maintaining relationships with learners and colleagues, in engaging with new curricular requirements and assessment practices, . . . in participating in on-going professional development opportunities and . . . workplace initiatives, [and] in adapting . . . to the diverse requirements of their working contexts.

Through implementations with over 24,000 teachers in 25 countries, engagement has also been facilitated through a variety of supports. These range from face-to-face events such as workshops, meetings, and informal get-togethers to asynchronous connections via social media messaging systems (What'sApp, Facebook, and QQ, among others). Some of these support structures are regularly scheduled while others are periodic, depending on participants' needs and expectations for implementation. As diverse as these particular participation structures are, they share certain features. They encourage deeper teacher involvement in the learning process, often through collective problem solving or question answering. They provide a means to monitor and thus strengthen individual teacher's participation. They help participants to articulate and build connections with their classroom teaching. And they offer a social environment that combines professional and personal interactions.

Participants use these virtual environments, which are frequently self-generated, to process their learning experiences. The aim is not to reteach material that has already been presented in the online course. As forms of professional support, these systems create a socio-technical exoskeleton that facilitates practice and extension of the online learning experience. This distinction – between access to the online platform that provides all participants with the opportunity to practice and to learn the course content and the social exoskeleton of virtual (and to a lesser extent face-to-face) support – is critical to building and maintaining participating teachers' sense of agency and control over their own professional learning.

Monitored participation and feedback: Participation and performance in the course can be monitored both by teachers themselves and by programme coordinators. As they move through the course, teachers receive feedback through self-check tasks within and at the end of each of the learning units. From this information, they can make decisions about their progress and about whether to review and practice specific areas of the content or to continue on to the next unit. Within the course, the online platform uses speech-recognition software that provides teachers with immediate feedback on their oral production. As with the written tasks, participants can practice orally as much or as little as they would like. These multiple opportunities for feedback help them to develop a clearer understanding of what they are learning and to build their confidence in the classroom language they have mastered.

The back end of the online *English-for-Teaching* platform gives training coordinators information about which activities participants have completed, how much time they have spent on each course topic, as well as performance information on the various tasks. This level of information helps these coordinators to monitor teacher progress through the course and to plan for supplemental professional development activities as needed.

Taken together, these features that are built into the *English-for-Teaching* online platform go well beyond conventional designs for online course delivery. Quite literally echoing Wyatt, the participation is designed to help teachers "make choices within a host of contexts . . . in [these] on-going professional development opportunities," which supports their sense of agency and contributes to the effectiveness of the overall learning experience. By building on content that is closely aligned with classroom practice and that has immediate applicability for interacting with students, by using participation structures that encourage individualised learning pathways, by providing feedback that clarifies participants' performance in terms of learning aims, the *English-for-Teaching* course is designed to leverage what participating teachers know. This engagement serves to develop their professional confidence in what they do in the classroom.

Operationalising the framework in the course: three examples

In this section, we illustrate how the *English-for-Teaching* framework and course has been implemented to address local needs and contexts, with three examples drawn from distinct settings in Saudi Arabia, Vietnam, and India. Table 6.2 provides a snapshot of the similarities and differences across sites. Commentaries by key individuals involved in each implementation highlight differences and offer insights into comparable positive outcomes.

Implementation organised centrally: Saudi Arabia

Within the context of a national action plan to reconfigure the Kingdom of Saudi Arabia's economic and development sectors, the Ministry of Education identified a need for the professional up-skilling of teachers to contribute to the plan's goals. Improving English language skills was one component of the education plan. Mr. Abdulrahman Al-Furaih, head of the English Language Department for the Ministry of Education, describes the context for the reform project, the selection and piloting of the ELTeach programme, which included the *English-for-Teaching* course and another course focusing on teaching methodology.

Table 6.2 Three implementations of the *English-for-Teaching* course: a comparative snapshot

	Saudi Arabia	Vietnam	India
Scope and management of the implementation	*Organised centrally* through Ministry of Education	*Organised regionally* through Departments of Education and Training (DOETs)	*Organised sectorally* through a funded project to support ELT madrassahs
Supports for participants' learning	*WhatsApp* groups; MOE organised help desks to support online access	Via email or text to their designated coordinator who provides support	*WhatsApp* groups; Online and monthly workshops
Number of teachers	500	8,000	120

Commentary
Mr. Abdulrahman Al-Furaih
Head of the English Language Department
Ministry of Education

The Kingdom of Saudi Arabia is a relatively young country and the education system has developed rapidly since the 1950s. There are currently close to six million students studying in Ministry of Education schools; elementary, intermediate, and secondary across 46 educational directorates. The education system is predominantly centralized and employs 600,000 teachers in 35,000 schools throughout the Kingdom. The Ministry of Education provides professional development programmes for teachers in the areas of English language proficiency and pedagogy. It realizes that educational improvement . . . is key for the Kingdom [in] achieving the goals and aspirations defined in both the *National Transformation Programme 2020* and the *Saudi Vision 2030*.

In 2012 the Ministry of Education conducted a pilot of the recently released *ELTeach* programme. The pilot programme was deemed to be a success by all stakeholders and a roll-out in 15 educational directorates of both [the] *English-for-Teaching* and the [teaching methodology] *Professional Knowledge for ELT* was organized. The Ministry of Education emphasised planning and preparation to ensure maximum benefit . . . in [these] professional development programmes. [To this end], Ministry of Education supervisors were trained to administer and monitor courses.

Additional pre-implementation initiatives included: [developing] selection criteria for teachers to participate in the courses; [defining] roles and responsibilities of Ministry of Education supervisors; [forming] *WhatsApp* groups to provide ongoing support to participants; [creating] a central supervisors' group as well as directorate-specific groups through which to communicate and offer help to participants. In addition, a communication plan was developed to foster professional learning communities among participants and to encourage self-reflection and sharing in the *WhatsApp* groups. These forward thinking and pro-active measures resulted in a smooth start to the programme and excellent participation and completion rates and results.

One of the constants with professional development programmes is the goal of skill transfer from those participating in programmes to their colleagues. Feedback from the field during the courses was collected to support teachers and supervisors during and after the programmes. Two of these innovative tools included monthly reports for supervisors to complete to monitor progress and feedback from the field, and surveys conducted during the programme to respond to teachers' needs and also to determine how these programmes were benefiting them and their students. The feedback received through these tools demonstrated teachers participating in the programmes had more confidence to use English as the language of instruction. Teachers gained a range of innovative learning and teaching pedagogies to engage their students and they reported students enjoyed their classes more.

Implementation organised regionally: Vietnam

Like Saudi Arabia, Vietnam has been undergoing a national reform effort more particularly focused on improving the quality of foreign language education. In contrast to the centralised system in Saudi Arabia, teacher professional development in Vietnam is delegated regionally to local Departments of Education and Training and provided by universities throughout the country. In the following commentary, Dr. Pham Thi Hong Nhung, associate professor and director of the Language Teacher Development Center at Huế University of Foreign Languages, Vietnam, describes how the *English-for-Teaching* course was introduced as part of a larger professional development plan to increase teachers' English language proficiency. She reports on the impact of the *English-for-Teaching* course on teachers and their classrooms.

Commentary
Dr. Pham Thi Hong Nhung
Associate Professor and Director of the Language Teacher
Development Center
Huế University of Foreign Languages

Together with the launch of the national project "*Teaching and Learning Foreign Language in the Public-Sector Educational System for the 2008–2020 Period*," the Vietnamese Ministry of Education and Training (MOET) provided classroom English training for successive cohorts of teachers across 10 regions in Vietnam. Teachers of different levels of general English proficiency from the CEFR B1 to C1 from primary, lower secondary school, and high schools were selected by local Departments of Education and Training (DOETs). They were sent to authorised university-based institutes to be trained in classroom English proficiency through the *English-for-Teaching* course. The course allowed the MOET and the DOETs to quickly develop teachers' classroom English proficiency directly, thus improving the teaching process in the Vietnamese context. The goal was to address a common lack of qualified English language teachers because the proficiency standards for teachers are high, compared with their current level of proficiency. *English-for-Teaching* training has been used as a strategic response to the pressing need to have an adequate supply of teachers for a large-scale implementation of the pilot national English language education curriculum, planned to be formalised in 2019.

Research has shown that in Vietnam although in-service teachers across different levels of proficiency from CEFR B1 to C1 appreciated both general English proficiency training and the *English-for-Teaching* training, they found classroom English training more relevant and practical to their teaching context (Freeman & LeDrean, 2017). Pham (2017) has shown that the *English-for-Teaching* training was reported by teachers in her study to have brought about change in their use of classroom language. This then created positive changes in students' behavior that, in turn, changed the teachers' attitudes and beliefs about the nature of classroom language and professional development. The in-service teachers investigated also showed that when the resources are limited and do not allow the provision of both sets of training, they preferred the *English-for-Teaching* training because it was highly relevant, could be sustained in the classroom, made achieving classroom English proficiency feasible, and had an observable impact on students' behavior as well as on their own confidence in using English to teach English.

Implementation organised for a particular educational sector: India

In a programme sponsored by the Regional English Language Office of the United States Embassy in India, teachers at madrassahs, Islamic schools often connected with mosques, in several Indian states were enrolled in the *English-for-Teaching* course to help them develop their English language skills. World Learning, a non-governmental organisation, was contracted to deliver the course, and Ms. Lois Scott-Conley, Education Advisor in Curriculum and Training for World Learning, administered the project. In the commentary that follows, she describes how the *English-for-Teaching* course was implemented and its reported impact on participating teachers.

Commentary
Ms. Lois Scott-Conley
Education Advisor in Curriculum and Training
World Learning

Teachers in madrassahs in India have long taught English in traditional classes focusing on English structures and general content vocabulary, using Urdu as the medium of instruction. As part of a Career Development Programme sponsored by the US Embassy's Regional English Language Office, a new approach for teacher professional development was adopted. By selecting *English-for-Teaching* for the training course, the first innovation was to engage teachers in a programme that focused on helping them learn English they could use in the classroom. The second was to construct an approach to professional development that offered a blended Training of Trainers model across 30 cohorts of trainers and teachers. Each cohort consisted of a "Trainer" and a cohort of participants who were teachers in their training communities. Trainers participated in a five-day Training-of-Trainers workshop. To support teachers as they moved through the *English-for-Teaching* course materials, trainers provided technical help, encouragement, and discussion online and delivered monthly workshops to review and practice the material they were learning in *English-for-Teaching*. Trainers and teachers then participated in a final conference during which they synthesised what they had learned, shared how they were using it, and prepared "cascading" teacher training workshops to share their learning with colleagues.

World Learning provided cascading support to both trainers and teachers. Via *WhatsApp*, World Learning staff coached trainers in providing technical support, sharing progress reports, creating workshop reflections, incorporating schedule reminders, and delivering encouragement.

Teachers across cohorts reported positive results as a result of this training. 98% of the teachers at the final conference felt their confidence had improved in using English in their classes. As one teacher noted, "I feel my classroom language had got much better." Teachers also reported that by modeling more spoken English, their students were speaking more English. Not surprisingly, 92% of the teachers said their students had improved their understanding of spoken English. 86% of teachers said that their students have told them that their teacher's speaking in English is helping them learn. In a development that echoes the cascading model in this implementation, 86% of participating teachers mentioned that they have also shared with other teachers what they have learned.

Closing: a different view of scalable professional learning opportunities

This chapter has proposed modifying how we think about the problem of scale in professional development. Scalable reforms have generally been defined as those that can reach large numbers of teachers across diverse teaching circumstances. In the particular case of reforms in English language teaching intended to improve teachers' command and use of English in their classrooms, the vast majority of initiatives have depended on conventional definitions of the language content to be learned and on common ways of implementing training in that content. The former has generally been defined in terms of general English proficiency, in the logical – though largely untested – assumption that the better the teacher's command of general English, the better the classroom teaching. The latter – ways of training teachers in general proficiency content – have usually resorted to face-to-face delivery that is sometimes then meant to cascade from teachers who have received the direct training to those who have not.

There are two fundamental flaws in this conventional view of content and participation in scalable reforms that aim to develop teachers' use of English in classroom teaching. First, in focusing the content on general English proficiency, teachers' fluency in the language is assumed *de facto* to represent their competence in teaching it (Freeman, 2016). Command of general language is taken as a necessary – though perhaps not sufficient – condition for a teacher to teach English in English. Second, these reforms assume that face-to-face delivery through conventional forms of instruction are effective means of organising teachers' participation. When teachers are treated as ordinary students in an English language classroom in order to become "better" teachers, their agency as learners and their professional knowledge as teachers are overlooked, if not neutralised, and the power of choosing how to participate in learning the content is defused.

We argue that both teachers' agency and their professional knowledge can – and should be – engaged in these efforts for improvement to be successful and lasting. When the content is redefined as the classroom English used in teaching, and when participation in learning that content is organised in a monitored, supported, self-accessed training design, teachers' knowledge of classroom practice and their agency are leveraged with good results. This leveraging brings to bear a different view of scale in these reforms. Scalability is no longer a matter of "reaching large numbers of teachers" as previously defined. Instead, scale becomes a matter of designing equitable access to professional learning opportunities for teachers across diverse contexts and with varying resources. The "diverse teaching circumstances" in which participants work can provide the backbone for their learning. Teachers' knowledge of what they do in their classrooms daily with their students scaffolds their learning of classroom English. Taken together, this redefinition of content and participation has the potential to leverage what teachers know and do to create more equitable, resource-efficient access to professional development, which supports effective, durable improvements in classroom English teaching.

References

Bryk, T., Gomez, L., Grunow, A., & LeMahieu, P. (2016). *Learning to improve: How America's schools can get better at getting better*. Cambridge, MA: Harvard Education Press.

Coburn, C. E. (2003). Rethinking scale: Moving beyond numbers to deep and lasting change. *Educational Researcher, 32*(6), 3–12.

Constas, M., & Brown, K. (2006). Toward a programme of research on scale-up: Analytical requirements and theoretical possibilities. In B. Schneider & S. McDonald (Eds.), *Scale-up in education* (Vol. I, pp. 19–36). Lanham, MD: Rowman & Littlefield.

Coyle, D. (2007). Content and language integrated learning: Towards a connected research agenda for CLIL pedagogies. *International Journal of Bilingual Education and Bilingualism, 10*(5), 543–562.

Educational Development Center. (2011). *Scaling innovation: A preliminary review of the literature.* Newton, MA: National Center for Scaling Up Effective Practice.

Educational Testing Service & National Geographic Learning. (2011). *ELTeach: English-for-teaching.* Boston: National Geographic Learning.

Freeman, A., Katz, P., Garcia Gomez, A., & Burns, A. (2015). English-for-teaching: Rethinking teacher language proficiency for the classroom. *English Language Teaching Journal, 69*(2), 129–139.

Freeman, D. (2016). *Educating second language teachers: The same things done differently.* Oxford: Oxford University Press.

Freeman, D. (2017). The case for teachers' classroom English proficiency. *Regional English Language Journal, 48*(1), 1–12.

Freeman, D., Katz, A., Burns, A., LeDrean, L., & Hauck, M. (2013). *The ELTeach programme global implementation report.* Boston: National Geographic Learning.

Freeman, D., & LeDrean, L. (Eds.). (2017). *Developing classroom English competence: The Vietnam experience.* Language Teaching in Asia Monograph. Phnom Penh, Cambodia: International Development Programme (Australia).

Graddol, D. (1997). *The future of English.* Milton Keynes, UK: British Council.

Graddol, D. (2006). *English next.* Milton Keynes, UK: British Council.

Lopriore, L. (2018). *Reframing teaching knowledge in content and language integrated learning: A European perspective.* Language Teaching Research (published online).

McCrory, R., Putnam, R., & Jansen, A. (2008). Interaction in online courses for teacher education: Subject matter and pedagogy. *Journal of Technology and Teacher Education, 16*(2), 155–180.

Murray, D. (2012). *A case for online English language teacher education.* Monterey, CA: TIRF (The International Research Foundation for English Language Education).

Penuel, W. R., Fishman, B. J., Yamaguchi, R., & Gallagher, L. P. (2007). What makes professional development effective? Strategies that foster curriculum implementation. *American Educational Research Journal, 44*(4), 921–958.

Pham, N. (2017). *English-for-teaching* Training: Initial impact on in-service EFL teachers' classroom discourse: A case study. In D. Freeman & L. LeDrean (Eds.), *Developing classroom English competence: Learning from the Vietnam experience* (pp. 72–83). Phnom Penh: IDP Education.

Rigney, D. (2010). *The Matthew effect: How advantage begets further advantage.* New York: Columbia University Press.

Schneider, B., & McDonald, S. (Eds.). (2006). *Scale-up in education.* Lanham, MD: Rowman & Littlefield.

Wedell, M. (2011). More than just 'technology': English language teaching initiatives as complex educational changes. In H. Coleman (Ed.), *Dreams and realities: Developing countries and the English language* (pp. 275–296). London: British Council.

Wyatt, C. (2018). Language teacher agency. In S. Mercer & A. Kostoulas (Eds.), *Language teacher psychology* (pp. 196–210). Bristol: Multilingual Matters.

Young, J. W., Freeman, D., Hauck, M., Gomez, P. G., & Papageorgiou, S. (2014). *A design framework for the ELTeach programme assessments.* Princeton, NJ: Educational Testing Service.

7 University lecturers' perceived challenges in EMI
Implications for teacher professional development

Lê Thị Thùy Nhung

Introduction

English medium instruction (EMI) has been introduced into a number of university programmes in Vietnam over the past two decades. Despite the initial appeal of EMI, the effectiveness of EMI programmes appears to vary because many Vietnamese universities are under-resourced and are not adequately prepared for EMI implementation. According to Nguyen, Hamid, and Moni (2016) and Vu and Burns (2014), the current practice of EMI in the Vietnamese context is not fully informed by empirical evidence due to a lack of research in this area. The chapter first sketches the exponential growth of EMI in higher education worldwide and in Vietnam in particular. It reviews the empirical research on EMI and presents the results of the present qualitative study, which explored lecturers' perspectives on the use of EMI in business courses in four Vietnamese universities. It concludes with suggestions for better implementation of EMI in Vietnamese higher education institutions.

The development of EMI in higher education as a global trend

The growth of EMI in higher education in non-English-speaking countries is driven by two major forces: globalisation and internationalisation (Baldauf, 2012; Coleman, 2006; Doiz, Lasagabaster, & Sierra, 2012; Hamid & Nguyen, 2016; Hamid, Nguyen, & Baldauf, 2014; Phillipson, 2009). EMI has been introduced into universities in Europe and East Asia because of national strategies for human capital development and the internationalisation of education (Doiz et al., 2012). English has increasingly become the language of higher education across Europe (Coleman, 2004). There was a significant expansion of EMI in Europe in the past decades with more than 2,400 programmes delivered entirely in English in over 800 academic institutions in 2007 (Wächter & Maiworm, 2008).

A similar trend has been present in several Asian countries. In China, 132 universities were providing EMI courses and programmes in 2006 (Hu & Lei, 2014). English-medium teaching has become fashionable in Korean universities since the mid-2000s, with a total of 9,000 EMI courses offered by Korean universities in 2002 (Byun et al., 2011; Byun & Kim, 2011). In Japan, English-medium education is part of Japan's national agenda of internationalisation of higher education (Taguchi, 2014). In Hong Kong, six out of the eight government-funded universities offer 100% study programmes in English. Malaysia reintroduced EMI teaching at the tertiary level since 1996 after abandoning EMI for three decades (Ali, 2013). However, the rapid expansion of EMI programmes in these countries included its share of problems. The problems and issues pertaining to EMI implementation in various higher education contexts are further discussed in the next section.

Overview of EMI problems and issues

There is a large volume of research into EMI. According to Macaro (2018), many studies in Europe and North America have used surveys to identify attitudes of stakeholders towards EMI. EMI appears to generate favourable attitudes among students and lecturers. EMI is considered to prepare graduates for the international workplace and further education, as well as enhancing their English proficiency and self-confidence (Aguilar & Rodríguez, 2012; Bozdoğan & Karlıdağ, 2013; Dearden & Macaro, 2016; Earls, 2016). In some universities in East Asian countries, students' preference for EMI was mainly driven by career aspirations and the desire to study abroad (Byun et al., 2011; Chapple, 2015; Ellili-Cherif & Alkhateeb, 2015; Hu, Li, & Lei, 2014).

Mixed attitudes towards EMI among university academics have been found in various empirical studies. Young lecturers seemed to be interested in EMI teaching, while senior lecturers were generally less enthusiastic (Jensen & Thøgersen, 2011). In addition, negative attitudes towards EMI were occasionally reported. For example, in some Korean universities, lecturers showed their resistance towards EMI, claiming that EMI "deprived instructors of advantages of using a shared mother tongue, where pedagogically appropriate, with their students" (Byun et al., 2011, p. 443). Cho's (2012) survey also confirmed resistance by Korean academic staff against the enforcement of EMI policy at their university, where half of the lecturers indicated that they would choose to discontinue EMI teaching if this policy were lifted.

Researchers have also looked into the impact of EMI on students' performance and learning outcomes. EMI appears to increase students' English language proficiency, especially their specialised vocabulary knowledge (Aguilar & Rodríguez, 2012; Costa & Coleman, 2012; Yang, 2015; Yeh, 2014). However, students' reports of how well they understand content in EMI classes have been contradictory. While some students claimed they did not have problems understanding EMI lectures (Belhiah & Elhami, 2015; Joe & Lee, 2013; Ruiz-Garrido & Palmer-Silveira, 2008), others indicated that they did experience difficulty (Evans & Morrison, 2011; Hamied & Lengkanawati, 2018; Hellekjaer, 2010; Kagwesage, 2012; Nguyen, Nguyen, Nguyen, & Nguyen, 2018; Saeed, Varghese, Holst, & Ghazali, 2018). Problems with EMI lectures include complicated technical vocabulary and concepts, lecturers' unclear pronunciation and unfamiliar accents, fast delivery rate, and students' poor concentration during lectures.

Lecturers' ineffective lecturing tends to reduce students' comprehension. Some EMI lectures were lacking in clarity and elaboration (Airey & Linder, 2006; Tange, 2010). Lectures delivered in English were described as less interesting partly because there were few jokes, anecdotes, and storytelling that could deepen students' understanding of the content. Lecturers tended to give monologic lectures rather than engage students in interactive activities. These teaching behaviours hinder students' ability to understand the course content or result in students' superficial understanding of the subject matter (Kırkgöz, 2014; West, Güven, Parry, & Ergenekon, 2015).

Some lecturers admitted that the content of their lectures lacked depth and precision compared to the same lectures delivered in L1, which suggests that many lecturers are relatively inexperienced in EMI teaching (Airey, 2011). Due to difficulties with conversing in English, lecturers had to cover less material (Byun et al., 2011). In some cases, content of the lectures was reduced to 60–80% due to lecturers' slower pace of delivery and going overtime for clarification of subject matter during the class hours (Tatzl, 2011). Due to limited English proficiency, some lecturers used more formal "textbook styles" language in their English lectures and appeared to adopt an "avoiding strategy" by neither producing lecture notes nor composing written examination papers (Thøgersen & Airey, 2011). There was evidence that EMI increased lecturers' workload (Başıbek et al., 2014; Hellekjaer, 2010; Tatzl, 2011). Time was spent on looking for teaching resources, preparing for lectures, and examinations.

With respect to teaching performance, some lecturers reported having difficulty in lecturing due to linguistic constraints, resulting in their lower quality of teaching (Campagna, 2016; Guarda & Helm, 2016; Nguyen et al., 2018). Lecturers found it problematic to find appropriate linguistic resources and registers to express their ideas in English, and they even feared that they would lose the original meaning of knowledge content when translating ideas into English (Tange, 2010).

Lecturers' insufficient English proficiency not only constrains their flexibility to deliver the lectures in an interesting manner but also results in limited classroom interaction. Lecturers tended to avoid having casual exchanges with students in English during class for fear of showing their linguistic limitations and thus suffering loss of face (Tange, 2010). Generally, although senior lecturers with little experience teaching EM courses often highlight English constraints as their greatest challenge, they rarely discuss these issues openly among colleagues. The reason may be due to their having fear of damaging self-image or losing professional status if they admit their linguistic inadequacies (Tange, 2010).

Researchers also looked into how students perceived their lecturers' English proficiency. Some students were critical of their lecturers' English and blamed lecturers' limited English proficiency for causing problems with comprehension (Aguilar & Rodríguez, 2012; Byun et al., 2011; Collins, 2010; Tatzl, 2011).

Students also admitted that they lacked competence and confidence in speaking English (Aguilar & Rodríguez, 2012; Evans & Morrison, 2011; Sultana, 2014).

In brief, the bulk of research on EMI has been conducted in European contexts, and until recently there has been a paucity of research in Asian countries where there has been a noticeable increase in EMI provision in higher education (Macaro, 2018; Phillipson, 2018). Most of the studies just reviewed have examined the extent to which EMI is used at the tertiary level; however, very few studies have investigated disciplinary learning (e.g., physics, medicine, and business and management studies) through the medium of English as a foreign language.

EMI policy and development of EMI in Vietnamese higher education

In Vietnam, the official language of instruction in education is Vietnamese. However, over the past two decades, the government has encouraged the use of English to replace Vietnamese to deliver course content at the university level through several proposals, among them: *Foreign Language Education 2008–2020* (MOET, 2008); *Vietnam Educational Strategies 2009–2020* (UNESCO, 2013); and *Fundamental and Comprehensive Reform of Higher Education 2006–2020* (Vietnam Government, 2014). These documents provide various reasons for the introduction of EMI in Vietnamese higher education: to enhance graduates' employability in the international workplace and thus enhance the quality of human resources; to boost the quality of Vietnamese higher education through internationalisation; and to improve the English proficiency of Vietnamese lecturers for international research collaboration and professional exchange purposes.

The government sees EMI as one of the drivers of Vietnam's higher education. There has been an increase in EMI offerings at universities since the early 2000s. At least 70 universities have introduced EMI programmes (Hamid & Kirkpatrick, 2016; Nguyen et al., 2018). EMI has also been presented in small programmes for high-achieving students at public universities such as Advanced Programmes (*Chuong trinh tien tien*), High Quality Programmes (*Chương trinh chat luong cao*), and programmes for the gifted (*Chuong trinh cu nhan tai nang*). In addition to EMI courses and programmes, two English-medium universities have been established to offer their entire degrees in English.

The government has issued financial reward schemes to support higher education institutions that offer EMI programmes. For example, since 2008, the government has provided financial support for universities that offered Advanced Programmes. In particular, universities would receive up to 60% government funding to cover the running cost of any of their first three Advanced Programmes in operation (MOET, 2010).

The push to introduce EMI has raised concerns about the effectiveness of EMI in Vietnamese universities. Research suggests that implementation of EMI in Vietnamese universities is problematic because there is a shortage of qualified teaching staff, study materials, and resources for teaching and research (Le, 2012; Nguyen, Walkinshaw, & Pham, 2017; Vu & Burns, 2014). There is a need for further empirical research on the current practices of EMI in Vietnamese universities to add more weight to the empirical evidence.

The study

Setting

The study was carried out at two public and two private universities located in a major city in Vietnam which offer courses wholly or partly in English. One of the four universities has introduced EMI into their bachelor business degree programmes since 2002. The other three universities first introduced EMI to their degree programmes in 2004, 2009, and 2012, respectively. Three universities offered full bachelor business degree programmes in EMI mode, while the other university has introduced a few EMI courses into the business programmes in the pilot phase. One public English-medium university offered entire degrees in English.

Research questions

- What are lecturers' perception of EMI?
- What do lecturers perceive as the support for and the challenges of EMI?

Participants

A total of 22 lecturers agreed to take part in the study. The majority of the lecturers (73%) were in their late twenties and early thirties, and only three lecturers were over age 50. There were five lecturers with PhDs, while the rest held master's degrees in business and management studies. All lecturers obtained postgraduate degrees through the medium of English locally and/or abroad. Several lecturers obtained master's degrees in English-speaking countries such as the United States, Australia, and the United Kingdom. The lecturers were offered EMI teaching positions because the universities in the study preferred to recruit lecturers with international qualifications. The majority of interviewed lecturers were employed full-time at business schools. Half of them had fewer than five years of EMI teaching experience. These lecturers had mainly taught EMI courses since they started their teaching career. The rest had EMI teaching experience ranging from five to ten years.

Table 7.1 Lecturers' teaching experience (years) in EMI mode

EMI teaching experience (years)	Number	%
Under 5 years	11	50
5–10 years	10	45
Over 10 years	1	5

Data collection and analysis

The lecturers were interviewed individually for about 30–50 minutes. Although several lecturer participants claimed to speak English well, they preferred to be interviewed in Vietnamese for ease of articulation and clarity in responses. The data of the interviews were recorded and transcribed verbatim and entered into the NVivo10 software as separate text files. The data were subject to content analysis (Cohen, Manion, & Morrison, 2011), that is, analyses focused on the meaning rather than on the linguistic features of texts. The software enabled the researcher to bring together similar categories and concepts to form broader themes. Dominant themes were reported based on the frequency of recurring themes in the data. Selected quotes were translated into English by the researcher for analysis and discussion.

Findings

Perceptions of benefits of EMI

The lecturers in the study considered undertaking EMI teaching both as a job requirement and as an academic interest. Since English is a foreign language in Vietnam, there are limited opportunities for people to speak English in society at large, and so EMI teaching provided an environment where the lecturers could develop their English proficiency and at the same time enhance their professional knowledge. They had an opportunity to read English textbooks and reference materials in the original and were able to obtain updated professional materials. In their opinion, although teacher-developed materials and textbooks written in Vietnamese were easier to comprehend, they lacked a logical approach, originality, and creativity and were not subject to quality control.

> Most textbooks used for Business studies programmes in Vietnamese universities nowadays come from overseas. These books are written mostly in English. Most universities in Vietnam use the translation versions which are not accurately translated into Vietnamese. The author's original ideas might be lost in translation. If lecturers obtain knowledge from reading these materials, it's more likely that they will provide inaccurate information. I find it a lot more convenient and time saving to prepare lectures in English because I don't have to do the back translation.
>
> (Lecturer 12, University B)

The lecturers were offered better working conditions and greater financial rewards than colleagues teaching equivalent courses in Vietnamese. The two private universities offered lecturers shared office space. Their teaching staff worked in better quality facilities (in comparison with other universities), including air-conditioned classrooms, Internet access, and well resourced libraries. All the four universities charged higher tuition fees for EMI courses and programmes and thus paid lecturers an hourly rate that was about four times higher than the hourly rate for conducting Vietnamese-medium classes. In particular, full-time lecturers in one university were offered a monthly salary that was about three times higher than the amount paid to lecturers at other public universities in Vietnam.

The lecturers believed that students also benefited from EMI because it resulted in students' improved English skills, frequent update of professional knowledge, and greater employment prospects. Graduates from EMI programmes would possess knowledge of the business specialisation as well as specialised terminology in English. In addition, given the abundant resources available in English on the Internet, students who were proficient in English would be able to search for more knowledge online. More importantly, the lecturers argued that EMI students would have a competitive edge over students in regular programmes when seeking employment locally and globally:

> When it comes to applying for jobs, I think every candidate has a university degree but candidates with a high level of English proficiency will stand out in a crowd. Our graduates have been used to speaking English so they should perform in job interviews in English with confidence. This would increase their opportunities to be employed by international organisations where both English and professional knowledge are required.
>
> (Lecturer 16, University C)

Perceptions of professional challenges

Although all lecturers generally seemed to support EMI and chose to engage in EMI teaching voluntarily, they described barriers that hindered the quality of instruction in EMI courses. These included the English abilities of their own and their students, use of effective pedagogical approaches, lack of training and professional development, and institutional physical resources.

Lecturers' English abilities

With regard to lecturers' confidence in their English abilities, the lecturers were not required to show evidence of their English proficiency upon recruitment apart from their international postgraduate degrees. The lecturers who felt that they were linguistically qualified to teach EMI courses tended to be those with experience of postgraduate education abroad. Meanwhile, those without being educated overseas appeared less confident about their oral English proficiency. The senior lecturers were experienced in teaching Vietnamese medium courses and were highly knowledgeable in their subject area. However, often they were not highly proficient in English partly due to the fact that they lacked postgraduate training experience overseas and opportunities to use English for personal and professional communication. These lecturers often found it difficult to articulate their thoughts because of linguistic barriers and tended to feel more pressure delivering lectures in English than their junior colleagues. For example, an interviewed lecturer reported that one of his senior colleagues, who was knowledgeable and experienced in teaching courses in Vietnamese, had to prepare a "script" before class for his first English lectures, in which he noted major points of the lecture in English and even anticipated answers to questions that his students might ask during the lectures.

In contrast, the junior lecturers tended to be more proficient in English but were not highly knowledgeable in their professional area. Most of the lecturers started EMI teaching immediately after they completed their master's degrees, and most of them had limited teaching experience. The findings suggest the need for linguistic support for lecturers so that they could use English effectively and comfortably for communication and for teaching.

Teaching approaches

Lectures remained a dominant way of instruction in EMI class. There were few instances of student-centred activities (such as discussions, tutorials, problem solving, and group work) to enhance students' higher-order thinking. Some lecturers admitted that they found it difficult to expand the topics beyond the textbooks in order to make the lectures more interesting. They tried various strategies during lectures to assist student comprehension of subject matter such as code-switching, simplifying the subject matter by using simple language and short sentences, and making use of visual display to facilitate students' comprehension of English lectures.

> When I first delivered lectures in English, I often tried to cover everything in the textbooks because I thought the students should gain as much knowledge as they could. Then I realised the students got bored with my pouring into their heads with lots of unnecessary things. I decided to adjust my lecturing. I started to "stage" the lectures according to students' feelings. When they are still "fresh," I give them lectures. When they were tired of being loaded with the "hard to swallow" technical concepts, I organized discussions, group work, or gave them exercises to keep them awake and active in my lectures.
>
> (Lecturer 12, University B)

Since their universities had no guidelines specifying the amount of English expected to be spoken by lecturers in EMI, teaching practice seemed to vary among lecturers. Several junior lecturers claimed to speak English only during lectures and use Vietnamese for explanations of theoretical concepts and technical terms. Others had to adjust their language use according to the students' level of English proficiency and classroom situations.

Large classes prevented the lecturers from varying teaching activities, interacting individually with students, and providing detailed feedback on students' performance. While the two private universities offered small class sizes with around

25 students per class, the two public universities maintained an average of a hundred students each. Overcrowded classrooms also made it difficult for lecturers to organise assessment activities.

Lecturers with overseas postgraduate training experiences found it challenging to apply their knowledge of advanced teaching methods and best practices to the reality of university teaching in Vietnam. For example, a female lecturer, graduated from a UK university, mentioned her intention to provide tutorials for her students but failed to do so due to large class size: "I want my students to do group presentations and discussions but it's hard to do so with around 100 students in my class" (Lecturer 21, University D).

Students' English abilities

The lecturers were concerned about the wide variation in English proficiency among students. Although a majority of students met the respective universities' required entry English scores (TOEFL iBT 60 and TOEFL iBT 53, respectively), there were students from the countryside whose English competence tended to be lower than their peers from urban areas. Students' differing English abilities made it challenging for lecturers to organise learning activities and to structure lectures. Interaction between the lecturers and their students during EMI courses were described as limited. Some students rarely read books for lectures or contacted lecturers about their studies after class. One of the lecturers with experience of teaching in universities overseas expressed her disappointment at this learning behaviour.

> Regardless of my efforts to initiate topics for discussion during the courses, very few students are willing to ask questions and engage in class discussion. Many of them wait to be picked. They rarely express their opinions, unless they are being asked directly. I don't know whether they are not confident about their English or they just feel shy to speak English in front of other people.
> (Lecturers 10, University B)

Teacher professional development

Most of the lecturers in this study had not received any formal training in teaching through the medium of English. They also had very limited professional development in pedagogy. The lecturers reported that their universities offered a few informal sessions about teaching and workshops for EMI lecturers to share their teaching experience. Others claimed to attend short courses on general teaching methodologies required by their universities. Lecturers indicated that they would welcome training on EMI with regard to use of instructional language in the classroom. Some lecturers suggested a mentoring system so that novice lecturers could be guided by experienced lecturers.

> It would be ideal for us as beginning lecturers to have some mentors who have had previous experience of teaching courses in English. Also, lecturers

with education experiences in academic environments abroad could become great mentors for us. Alternatively, beginning lecturers could start their teaching career by working as tutors or co-lecturers alongside experienced lecturers and international lecturers. This will help us to learn from each other.

(Lecturer 18, University C)

The findings point to the pressing need to offer training and professional development, particularly with regard to pedagogical support for lecturers without or with limited background in teaching and education.

Resources

Basically, EMI programmes at the four universities dedicated their best physical resources to students and staff. However, there were still complaints about inadequate supplies of textbooks and reference materials. Some lecturers claimed they were encouraged to engage in research activities but were given limited access to online quality resources. One university had a policy to reward lecturers up to $US1,500 for each paper published in an international peer-reviewed journal with ISI indexing. However, the university did not support lecturers financially to access online quality research databases. The lecturers themselves had to pay to download high-quality papers for their research projects. In addition, lecturers found it difficult to obtain English textbooks and reference materials because of high cost or unavailability. They had to use unofficial or unauthorised materials available online or in the local market. The lecturers at the two public universities did not have their own office space due to a shortage of premises. As previous research indicated, inadequate resources can reduce the success of EMI programmes (Kaplan & Baldauf, 2005; Le, 2012).

Discussion

The results of interviews with lecturers produced four major findings. First, positive attitudes towards EMI were found among several lecturers. They generally supported EMI education and perceived several benefits of EMI to their professional career including improved English proficiency, enhanced disciplinary knowledge, and better financial rewards. While most universities in Vietnam have limited resources for teaching and research (Harman & Bich, 2010; Nguyen & Nguyen, 2018; Vu & Burns, 2014), the universities in the current study provided students and lecturers in EMI programmes access to comparatively better facilities and available resources.

Lecturers were motivated to engage in EMI teaching because it was well paid. This was seen as compensation for the heavy workload and the considerable time they had invested in English-medium courses. Lecturers' favourable attitudes towards EMI were evident in several studies elsewhere (Aguilar & Rodríguez, 2012; Ball & Linsay, 2012; Collins, 2010; Jensen & Thøgersen, 2011; Tatzl, 2011). However, the findings from the current study did not echo those in some other studies. For example, Korea lecturers were not in favour of English-medium teaching as they did not see much added value of EMI (Byun et al., 2011; Cho, 2012).

Second, use of effective teaching approaches remains problematic for several lecturers, which is largely a result of lack of training and professional development for EMI staff. The lecturers experienced difficulty with EMI lectures such as lack of flexibility, improvisation, and interaction with students during lectures. Several lecturers turned to code-switching to compensate for their linguistic difficulties. The findings suggest that there is a pressing need to provide pedagogical training for EMI lecturers to enhance their teaching strategies, including a more effective use of code-switching technique.

Lecturers in this study used lectures as the primary means of instruction in EMI class. Research has shown that listening to lecture monologues is a difficult task for second- and foreign-language students (Airey & Linder, 2006). In addition, lecturers' excessive use of lectures as one-way communication restricted interaction in class and thus limited opportunities for students to enhance their spoken English. It has been suggested that a more a student-centred approach in EMI classes may promote students' learning and improve their English proficiency (Lin & Lo, 2018).

Also, students' passivity contributed to lecturers' difficulty in organising teaching activities. This behaviour may be the result of insufficient English, heavy workload, or a cultural approach to learning. Traditional Vietnamese learning culture is heavily influenced by Confucian educational philosophy in which students prefer rote learning, didactic, and a transmitted approach to teaching over questioning, problem solving, and critical thinking (Ho & Hau, 2010; Mai, Terlouw, & Pilot, 2005; Nguyen, 2017; Tran, 2013). Students' passivity often was reinforced by lecturers' methods of teaching.

Third, the lecturers were concerned about the English competence of their own and their students, echoing the findings in previous studies (Le, 2012; Nguyen et al., 2017; Vu & Burns, 2014). In the study, some lecturers reported making pronunciation and grammatical mistakes during lectures. According to Lavelle (2008), such repeated errors could damage lecturers' professional image and erode their confidence. Owing to lecturers' linguistic limitations, English lectures were delivered with an absence of jokes, anecdotes, everyday examples, and storytelling. It was widely assumed by university managers in Vietnam that lecturers who earned international postgraduate degrees would enable them to become competent course instructors. This assumption appeared rather misleading because successful lecturers require not only linguistic but also academic and pedagogical competence, which few of them are likely to possess (Shohamy, 2012). The findings suggest that universities make funding and resources available for lecturers to improve their English proficiency.

Students' diverse English abilities created difficulties for the lecturers in this study. The lecturers had to spend more time searching for reference materials, preparing for lectures, and marking assignments in English. This added workload and pressure for lecturers could decrease commitment to teaching (Shohamy,

2012; Tsuneyoshi, 2005). Establishing an English threshold for EMI students and improving their English proficiency beyond that level with well designed preparatory English programmes should reduce the disparity in students' English proficiency (Byun et al., 2011).

Finally, lecturers were concerned about insufficient resources to support teaching and research. Successful implementation of EMI programmes requires adequate resources and generous funding (Kaplan & Baldauf, 2005). In this study, the lack of resources and facilities might have exerted a lot of pressure on lectures to fulfil teaching and research duties. Byun et al. (2011) suggested a more careful preparation for EMI implementation taking into account good facilities, individualised assistance, and availability of human and financial resources. Quality online resources should be made available to support lecturers with research capabilities.

Suggestions and conclusion

The chapter has presented findings from interviews with EMI lecturers at four urban universities in Vietnam. In general, the lecturers perceived the benefits of EMI for their students as well as for their own professional careers, although EMI posed numerous challenges to the business faculties in the study. They seemed to be inadequately prepared for EMI both academically and linguistically. Most of the challenges facing Vietnamese lecturers are not unique to Vietnam.

The findings of the current study suggested that some lecturers lack English proficiency and training in ways to teach EMI courses effectively. Several studies point to the need for more training of EMI lecturers in Vietnam (Le, 2012; Nguyen et al., 2017). It is recommended that lecturers be screened for proficiency in English upon recruitment (Byun et al., 2011; Kirkpatrick, 2018; Vu & Burns, 2014). Universities should stipulate an English proficiency level required for EMI lecturers. Lecturers' English proficiency could be benchmarked against international standardised tests such as TOEFL and IELTS, or/and English language qualifications such as bachelors or masters' degrees in English language teaching.

Given the context of higher education in Vietnam, it is unrealistic to employ lecturers who meet both a specified level of English language proficiency and a record of EMI teaching experience at the time of recruitment. Providing in-service training for EMI lecturers to improve their English proficiency, especially oral English skills, and their pedagogical knowledge is more practical in the current local context. Universities could provide ongoing intensive English courses designed exclusively for EMI lecturers to develop their academic English, improve their general English fluency, and boost their confidence in the presentation of discipline content in English. These language support courses should focus on the lecturers' oral presentation skills and pronunciation, and ideally should be taught by either native-speaking teachers of English or EFL experts.

Another approach to enhancing lecturers' oral English proficiency would be tandem teaching or team teaching (Cots, 2012; Klaassen & Graaff, 2001; Wilkinson, 2012), pairing discipline experts and language teaching experts in EMI classes. The language teaching experts could observe EMI lectures and provide feedback on pronunciation, vocabulary, and sentence-level expressions. The language teaching experts also could co-teach with discipline lecturers. In so doing, EMI lecturers could overcome their linguistic shortcomings and become more confident in using English in their courses. This sort of collaboration should be carefully planned and carried out to maximise its effects and minimise the ambiguities and tensions that may arise between the two experts (Cots, 2012).

Given that the majority of lecturers lack formal training in pedagogical techniques for EMI teaching, pedagogical training has been shown to help successful implementation of EMI (Ball & Linsay, 2012; Wilkinson, 2012). Pre-service training on ways to teach effectively in EMI classes is almost non-existent in Vietnam. In-service pedagogical training could include sharing teaching sessions, short courses, and workshops on pedagogical techniques for EMI classes (Ball & Linsay, 2012). Peer coaching, as noted in the literature (Klaassen & Graaff, 2001; Lavelle, 2008; Vinke et al., 1998), has been found to be helpful in assisting lecturers to enhance their teaching performance. Beginning EMI lecturers should be coached or mentored by more experienced lecturers so that the former can learn from the latter through experience sharing and practice. Also, it would be useful for universities to have communication platforms where EMI lecturers could share experiences and good practices.

As the findings from this study reveal, EMI teaching exerts a lot of stress on lecturers. As such, it is important for universities managers to recognise the pressure involved in EMI teaching and to introduce benefits such as reductions in teaching and workload, promotion, reasonable staffing of EMI programmes, adequate funding and resources, bonuses and reward schemes (Byun et al., 2011; Doiz et al., 2011; Kirkpatrick, 2018). Also, universities in Vietnam should ascertain that they have the necessary human and financial resources before they undertake EMI programmes. Given students' high tuition fees for EMI courses and programmes, it was surprising to find that some students and lecturers still lacked the resources and support needed for their daily academic activities. There should be more investment in resources and technology to ensure that facilities are adequate and accessible to both students and lecturers.

EMI has received strong support from major stakeholders in Vietnam. The current question for administrators in Vietnamese higher education is not whether or not to adopt EMI but how to implement it to maximise its benefits and minimise its problems. There is evidence that EMI can be successful if it is carefully planned, providing highly qualified teachers (in terms of both English proficiency and pedagogical knowledge), as well as students with sufficient English proficiency. Poorly implemented EMI will waste university resources and cause distress for students who had high hopes for their university studies and desirable careers following success at university.

References

Aguilar, M., & Rodríguez, R. (2012). Lecturer and student perceptions on CLIL at a Spanish university. *International Journal of Bilingual Education and Bilingualism*, *15*(2), 183–197.

Airey, J. (2011). Talking about teaching in English: Swedish university lecturers' experiences of changing teaching language. *Journal of the European Association of Languages for Specific Purposes, 22,* 35–54.

Airey, J., & Linder, C. (2006). Language and the experience of learning university physics in Sweden. *European Journal of Physics, 27*(3), 553–560.

Ali, N. (2013). A changing paradigm in language planning: English medium instruction policy at the tertiary level in Malaysia. *Current Issues in Language Planning, 14*(1), 73–92.

Baldauf, R. (2012). Language planning: Where have we been? Where might we be going? *Brazilian Review of Applied Linguistics, 12*(2), 233–248.

Ball, P., & Linsay, D. (2012). Language demands and support for English medium instruction at tertiary level: Learning from a specific context. In A. Doiz, D. Lasaga-baster, & J. Sierra (Eds.), *English medium instruction at universities: Global challenges* (pp. 44–64). Bristol: Multilingual Matters.

Başıbek, N., Dolmacı, M., Cengiz, B. C., Bür, B., Dilek, Y., & Kara, B. (2014). Lecturers' perceptions of English medium instruction at engineering departments of higher education: A study on partial Englishmedium instruction at some state universities in Turkey. *Procedia–Social and Behavioural Sciences, 116,* 1819–1825.

Belhiah, H., & Elhami, M. (2015). English as a medium of instruction in the Gulf: When students and teachers speak. *Language Policy, 14*(1), 3–23.

Bozdoğan, D., & Karlıdağ, B. (2013). A case of CLIL practice in the Turkish context: Lending an ear to students. *Asian EFL Journal, 15*(4), 89–110.

Byun, K., Chu, H., Kim, M., Park, I., Kim, S., & Jung, J. (2011). English medium teaching in Korean higher education: Policy, debates and reality. *Higher Education, 62*(4), 431–449.

Byun, K., & Kim, M. (2011). Shifting patterns of the government's policies for the internationalization of Korean higher education. *Journal of Studies in International Education, 15*(5), 467–486.

Campagna, S. (2016). English as a medium of instruction. A 'resentment study' of a micro EMI context. In S. Campagna, E. Ochse, V. Pulcini, & M. Solly (Eds.), *Languaging in and across communities: New voices, new identities. Studies in honour of giuseppina cortese* (pp. 145–168). Bern: Peter Lang.

Chapple, J. (2015). Teaching in English is not necessarily the teaching of English. *International Education Studies, 8*(3), 1.

Cho, D. (2012). English medium instruction in the university context of Korea: Tradeoff between teaching outcomes and media-initiated university ranking. *The Journal of Asia TEFL, 9*(4), 135–163.

Cohen, L., Manion, L., & Morrison, K. (2011). *Research methods in education* (7th ed.). New York: Routledge.

Coleman, J. (2004). *The language of higher education.* Paper presented at the Language and the future of Europe: Ideologies, policies and practices, University of Southampton.

Coleman, J. (2006). English medium teaching in European higher education. *Language Teaching, 39*(1), 1–14.

Collins, B. A. (2010). English medium higher education: Dilemma and problems. *Egitim Arastirmalari–Eurasian Journal of Educational Research, 39,* 97–110.

Costa, F., & Coleman, J. A. (2012). A survey of English medium instruction in Italian higher education. *International Journal of Bilingual Education and Bilingualism, 16,* 3–19.

Cots, J. (2012). Introducing English medium instruction at the university of Lleida, Spain: Intervention, beliefs and practices. In A. Doiz, D. Lasagabaster, & J. Sierra (Eds.), *English medium instruction at universities: Global challenges* (pp. 106–128). Bristol: Multilingual Matters.

Dearden, J., & Macaro, E. (2016). Higher education teachers' attitudes towards English: A three country comparison. *Studies in Second Language Learning and Teaching*, *6*(2), 3–34.

Doiz, A., Lasagabaster, D., & Sierra, J. (2011). Internationalisation, multilingualism and English medium instruction: The teachers' perspective. *World Englishes*, *30*(3), 345–359.

Doiz, A., Lasagabaster, D., & Sierra, J. (Eds.). (2012). *English medium instruction at universities: Global challenges*. Bristol: Multilingual Matters.

Earls, C. W. (2016). *Evolving agendas in European English-medium higher education: Interculturality, multilingualism and language policy*. Basingstoke: Palgrave Macmillan.

Ellili-Cherif, M., & Alkhateeb, H. (2015). College students' attitude toward the medium of instruction: Arabic versus English dilemma. *Universal Journal of Educational Research*, *3*(3), 207–213.

Evans, S., & Morrison, B. (2011). Meeting the challenges of English medium higher education: The first-year experience in Hong Kong. *English for Specific Purposes*, *30*(3), 198–208.

Guarda, M., & Helm, F. (2016). "I have discovered new teaching pathways": The link between language shift and teaching practice. *International Journal of Bilingual Education and Bilingualism*, *20*(7), 897–913.

Hamid, M. O., & Kirkpatrick, A. (2016). Foreign language policies in Asia and Australia in the Asian century. *Language Problems and Language Planning*, *40*(1), 26–46.

Hamid, M. O., & Nguyen, H. T. M. (2016). Globalization, English language policy, and teacher agency: Focus on Asia. *The International Education Journal: Comparative Perspectives*, *15*(1), 26–44.

Hamid, M. O., Nguyen, H. T. M., & Baldauf, R. B. J. (Eds.). (2014). *Language planning for medium of instruction in Asia*. Cornwall: Taylor & Francis.

Hamied, F. A., & Lengkanawati, N. S. (2018). Case study: EMI in Indonesia. In R. Barnard & Z. Hasim (Eds.), *English medium instruction programmes: Perspectives from South East Asian universities* (pp. 55–69). New York: Routledge.

Harman, G., & Bich, N. (2010). Reforming teaching and learning in Vietnam's higher education system. In G. Harman, M. Hayden, & T. N. Pham (Eds.), *Reforming higher education in Vietnam: Challenges and priorities* (pp. 65–86). Breinigsville, PA: Springer.

Hellekjaer, G. (2010). Language matters: Assessing lecture comprehension in Norwegian English medium higher education. In C. Dalton-Puffer, T. Nikula, & U. Smit (Eds.), *Language use and language learning in CLIL classroom* (pp. 233–258). Amsterdam: John Benjamins.

Ho, T. E., & Hau, K.-T. (2010). Consequences of the Confucian culture: High achievement but negative psychological attributes? *Learning and Individual Differences*, *20*(6), 571–573.

Hu, G., & Lei, J. (2014). English medium instruction in Chinese higher education: A case study. *Higher Education*, *67*, 551–567.

Hu, G., Li, L., & Lei, J. (2014). English medium instruction at a Chinese university: Rhetoric and reality. *Language Policy*, *13*(1), 21–40.

Jensen, C., & Thøgersen, J. (2011). Danish university lecturers' attitudes towards English as the medium of instruction. *Journal of the European Association of Languages for Specific Purposes, 22*, 13–34.

Joe, Y., & Lee, H.-K. (2013). Does English medium instruction benefit students in EFL contexts? A case study of medical students in Korea. *Asia-Pacific Education Researcher, 22*(2), 201–207.

Kagwesage, A. (2012). Higher education students' reflections on learning in times of academic language shift. *International Journal for the Scholarship of Teaching and Learning, 6*(2), 1–16.

Kaplan, R., & Baldauf, R. (2005). Language-in-education policy and planning. In E. Hinkel (Ed.), *Handbook of research in second language teaching and learning* (pp. 1013–1034). Mahwah, NJ: Lawrence Erlbaum.

Kırkgöz, Y. (2014). Students' perceptions of English language versus Turkish language used as the medium of instruction in higher education in Turkey. *Turkish Studies, 9*(12), 443–459.

Kirkpatrick, A. (2018). Afterword. In R. Barnard & Z. Hasim (Eds.), *English Medium Instruction programmes: Perspectives from South East Asian universities* (pp. 116–125). New York: Routledge.

Klaassen, R. G., & Graaff, D. (2001). Facing innovation: Preparing lecturers for English medium instruction in a non-native context. *European Journal of Engineering Education, 26*(3), 281–289.

Lavelle, T. (2008). English in the classroom: Meeting the challenge of English medium instruction in international business schools. In P. Mårtensson, M. Bild, & K. Nilsson (Eds.), *Teaching and learning at Business schools* (pp. 137–153). Aldershot: Gower.

Le, D. M. (2012). English as a medium of instruction at tertiary education system in Vietnam. *The Journal of Asia TEFL, 9*(2), 97–122.

Lin, A. M. Y., & Lo, Y. Y. (2018). The spread of English medium instruction programmes: Educational and research implications. In R. Barnard & Z. Hasim (Eds.), *English medium instruction programmes: Perspectives from South East Asian universities* (pp. 87–103). New York: Routledge.

Macaro, E. (2018). *English medium instruction.* Oxford: Oxford University Press.

Mai, N., Terlouw, C., & Pilot, A. (2005). Cooperative learning vs Confucian heritage culture's collectivism: Confrontation to reveal some cultural conflicts and mismatch. *Asia Europe Journal, 3*(3), 403–419.

Ministry of Education and Training (MoET). (2008). *Proposal on foreign language education in the national educational system 2008–2020*, March 26, 2012. Retrieved from www.cfl.udn.vn/uploads/uploads/Vanban/ . . . /3121_Deanngoaingu.pd . . .

Ministry of Education and Training (MoET). (2010). Advanced programmes in Vietnamese universities 2008–2015, March 26, 2012. Retrieved from dttt.vimaru.edu.vn/system/files/DeAnCTTT.pdf

Nguyen, H. M., & Nguyen, T. (2018). Professional learning for higher education academics: Systematic tensions. In T. Nguyen & T. Tran (Eds.), *Reforming the Vietnamese higher education: Global forces and local demand* (pp. 228–247). Singapore: Springer.

Nguyen, H. T. M. (2017). *Model of mentoring in language teacher education.* Cham, Switzerland: Springer.

Nguyen, H. T. M., Nguyen, T. H., Nguyen, V. H., & Nguyen, T. T. T. (2018). Local challenges to global needs in English language education in Vietnam: The perspective of language policy and planning. In C. C. S. Kheng (Ed.), *Un(intended) language planning in a globalising world: Multiple levels of players at work* (pp. 213–232). Berlin: Gruyter.

Nguyen, H. T., Hamid, M. O., & Moni, K. (2016). English-medium instruction and self-governance in higher education: The journey of a Vietnamese university through the institutional autonomy regime. *Higher Education, 72*(5), 669–683.

Nguyen, H. T., Walkinshaw, I., & Pham, H. H. (2017). EMI programs in a Vietnamese university: Language, pedagogy and policy issues. In B. Fenton-Smith, P. Humphreys, & I. Walkinshaw (Eds.), *English medium instruction in higher education in Asia-Pacific: From policy to pedagogy* (pp. 37–52). Cham, Switzerland: Springer International.

Phillipson, R. (2009). English in higher education: Panacea or pandemic? *Angles on the English Speaking World, 9,* 29–57.

Phillipson, R. (2018). Foreword. In R. Barnard & Z. Hasim (Eds.), *English medium instruction programmes: Perspectives from South East Asian universities* (pp. xi–xv). New York: Routledge.

Ruiz-Garrido, M., & Palmer-Silveira, J. (2008). Content learning in business communication: A teaching experience within the new European framework. In I. Fortanet-Gómez & C. Räisänen (Eds.), *ESP in European higher education: Integrating language and content* (pp. 147–164). Amsterdam: John Benjamins.

Saeed, M., Varghese, M., Holst, M., & Ghazali, K. (2018). EMI in Malaysia: Student voices. In R. Barnard & Z. Hasim (Eds.), *English medium instruction programmes: Perspectives from South East Asian universities* (pp. 70–86). New York: Routledge.

Shohamy, E. (2012). A critical perspective on the use of English as a medium of instruction at universities. In A. Doiz, D. Lasagabaster, & J. M. Sierra (Eds.), *English medium instruction at universities: Global challenges* (pp. 196–210). Bristol: Multilingual Matters.

Sultana, S. (2014). English as a medium of instruction in Bangladesh's higher education: Empowering or disadvantaging students. *Asian EFL Journal, 16*(1), 11–52.

Taguchi, N. (2014). Pragmatic socialization in an English medium university in Japan. *IRAL: International Review of Applied Linguistics in Language Teaching, 52*(2), 157–181.

Tange, H. (2010). Caught in the tower of Babel: University lecturers' experiences with internationalisation. *Language and Intercultural Communication, 10*(2), 137–149.

Tatzl, D. (2011). English medium masters' programmes at an Austrian university of applied sciences: Attitudes, experiences and challenges. *Journal of English for Academic Purposes, 10*(4), 252–270.

Thøgersen, J., & Airey, J. (2011). Lecturing undergraduate science in Danish and in English: A comparison of speaking rate and rhetorical style. *English for Specific Purposes, 30*(3), 209–221.

Tran, T. T. (2013). Is the learning approach of students from the Confucian heritage culture problematic? *Educational Research for Policy and Practice, 12*(1), 57–65.

Tsuneyoshi, R. (2005). Internationalization strategies in Japan: The dilemmas and possibilities of study abroad programs using English. *Journal of Research in International Education, 4*(1), 65–86.

UNESCO. (2013). *Vietnam's education strategies: 2009–2020,* October 15, 2013. Retrieved from http://planipolis.iiep.unesco.org/upload/Viet%20Nam/Viet_Nam_Education_%20strategy_2009-2020_viet.pdf

Vietnam Government. (2014). *Fundamental and comprehensive reform of higher education 2006–2020.* December 5. Retrieved from www.chinhphu.vn/portal/page/portal/

chinhphu/hethongvanban?class_id=509&_page=4&mode=detail&document_id=14954

Vinke, A. A., Snippe, J., & Jochems, W. (1998). English medium content courses in non-English higher education: A study of lecturer experiences and teaching behaviours. *Teaching in Higher Education, 3*(3), 383–394.

Vu, T. T. N., & Burns, A. (2014). English as a medium of instruction: Challenges for Vietnamese tertiary lecturers. *The Journal of Asia TEFL, 11*(3), 1–31.

Wächter, B., & Maiworm, F. (2008). *English-taught programmes in European higher education: The picture in 2007.* Bonn: Lemmens.

West, R., Güven, A., Parry, J., & Ergenekon, T. (2015). *The state of English in higher education in Turkey: A baseline study.* Ankara: British Council.

Wilkinson, R. (2012). English medium instruction at a Dutch university: Challenges and pitfalls. In A. Doiz, D. Lasagabaster, & J. Sierra (Eds.), *English medium instruction at universities: Global challenges* (pp. 3–24). Bristol: Multilingual Matters.

Yang, W. (2015). Content and language integrated learning next in Asia: Evidence of learners' achievement in CLIL education from a Taiwan tertiary degree programme. *International Journal of Bilingual Education and Bilingualism, 18*(4), 361–382.

Yeh, C.-C. (2014). Taiwanese students' experiences and attitudes towards English-medium courses in tertiary education. *RELC Journal, 45*(3), 305–319.

8 Teachers' implementation of computer-assisted language learning in the context of educational change in Vietnam

Nguyen Thi Hong Nhat

Introduction

Computer-assisted language learning (CALL) is one of many global and important innovations in the field of language learning and teaching (van den Branden, 2009). Like many countries in Asia, Vietnam has introduced CALL innovations to enhance foreign language education, especially English in response to the country's integration into the increasingly globalised world. One of many recent innovations is a large-scale national training course undertaken in 2014 by the Ministry of Education and Training (MOET). The aim of the course was to equip English-as-a-foreign-language (EFL) teachers across the country to use computer-mediated technologies in their own classes, as well as to become trainers for other teachers. Accordingly, MOET authorised VietCALL in 2014 to deliver a nationwide professional development (PD) course in CALL for in-service EFL teachers at all levels (MOET, 2014). This PD programme aims at equipping EFL teachers with the knowledge and skills to design, operate, and manage a Moodle-based course (a free open-source learning management system), as well as to employ a wide range of Web 2.0 tools in language teaching and learning.

In this chapter, as a part of a bigger project on evaluating this educational innovation, I examined the impact of the MOET course on teaching practice with the technology of Vietnamese tertiary EFL teachers at their own institutions. Adopting a case study approach, this study collected data through interviews and observations with five EFL teachers nine months after the MOET course. This study is of importance as little research has looked at the actual implementation and outcomes of CALL courses (Luu, 2015; McNeil, 2013; Wong & Benson, 2006). It is especially necessary in the context of Vietnam as it helps to provide research-based information for MOET to implement future CALL courses (VietCALL, 2014).

This chapter begins with an overview of the literature on the interaction between CALL education and training and the classroom and the obstacles to CALL integration. Then it explains the methodology adopted in the study. Finally, it discusses the key findings of the research and their implications that can be carefully taken to plan and implement future educational innovations in Vietnam and in other similar contexts.

Literature review

The interaction between coursework and the classroom

While there are several studies of teachers' views on PD courses, little is known about the impact of those courses on teachers' teaching practices in different contexts. The existing literature suggests that CALL courses can change teachers' attitudes and increase their confidence and competence in technology but that they are not sufficient to provide any significant improvement in teachers' practice (Egbert et al., 2002; Kessler, 2006). There is a gap between what teachers are taught in CALL courses and what they are able to do in the classroom because they encounter certain contextual difficulties in the process of transferring the knowledge they acquire in these courses to their language teaching practice (Chao, 2015; Dooly, 2009; Egbert et al., 2002; Son, 2014). For example, Son's (2014) study found that some of the teachers in his study did not use CALL in their teaching practice even after they had taken a formal CALL course in Australia. The study highlighted that lack of time and access to computer facilities were two of the most common reasons for the teachers' limited use of CALL at their institutions. Also, the literature suggests that a CALL course is not sufficient for significant improvement in teacher practice (Kessler, 2006; Kilickaya & Seferoglu, 2013).

While many studies evaluate the impact of CALL courses on teachers' attitudes and technology literacy, not much research has been done on their impact on teachers' ability to use CALL (Arnold & Ducate, 2015). Two of very few studies investigating the impact of CALL courses on teachers' actual use and development of CALL materials are by Kilickaya and Seferoglu (2013) and Tai (2015). For example, Kilickaya and Seferoglu (2013) conducted an examination of CALL-based materials used and developed by 25 in-service English-as-a-foreign-language teachers in Turkey after one year of a CALL course. This study showed a change in teachers' practice when they used a variety of CALL-based materials and tools. Regarding the methodology used in these studies, research has relied mainly on self-reported data from questionnaires and interviews with teachers and has not triangulated data through classroom observation. Overall, the existing literature calls for more studies to investigate the impact of CALL training on teachers' actual use of technology through observation data (Arnold & Ducate, 2015; Kessler, 2006). So far no studies have looked at teachers' teaching practice with technologies after the MOET course. Thus, more research is needed to provide empirically based information for MOET to implement future teacher professional development in Vietnam (VietCALL, 2014).

Obstacles to CALL integration

Attempts have been made to identify and classify multiple challenges that hinder CALL integration in different contexts. These factors can be of all kinds: "social, cultural, economical, systemic, structural and even spatial" (Levy & Caws, 2016,

p. 96). They can include lack of resources, time pressure, lack of teacher training, lack of guidelines, lack of support, inadequate facilities, restricted curriculum and inflexible computer settings (e.g., Dinh, 2015; Kessler, 2007). In addition to these, the rate of technological change raises another barrier to technology integration (Chambers & Bax, 2006).

It can be seen that obstacles to CALL vary across contexts and that many of these problems have been true historically and applied to both developed and developing teaching contexts. Egbert (2010) pointed out a variety of challenges that teachers in various parts of the world are experiencing. These challenges include a lack of education and training in pre-service and in-service education, limited general access to technology, limited connections, no or obsolete software, limited hardware, set curriculum, limited time, big classes, limited training, limited funding, limited administrative support, lack of culturally relevant electronic resources, and lack of student strategies for electronic media use. In confirmation of what has been found generally, in Vietnam the same problems have been found (e.g., Dinh, 2015; Le, 2015; Peeraer & Van-Petegem, 2011, 2012; Pham, 2015).

Taken together, it can be seen that there are a number of obstacles to CALL integration. While many of them occur in many contexts, some are more context specific. The existing literature mainly drew on self-reported data from surveys and interviews with teachers. The review points to the importance of using observation data to investigating actual CALL practices.

Methodology

As part of a larger research project, the current study set out to investigate tertiary EFL teachers' teaching practices with technologies in the context of when the Vietnamese government introduced the MOET course to improve their skills and knowledge in order to use technologies in teaching.

More specifically, this study aims to answer the following two research questions:

1 What knowledge and skills did the teachers learn from the MOET course and apply to their actual teaching?
2 What contextual factors influenced the teachers' use of technologies in their teaching of listening skills at their own institutions?

In order to achieve the aim of the current study, which is to understand Vietnamese EFL teachers' practices with technologies in the context of educational change, the researcher employed a qualitative research design. More specifically, a case study approach was adopted to investigate the research questions of this study.

A case study approach has been valued as a useful method of providing "a thick description of a complex issue within a cultural context" (Dörnyei, 2007, p. 155). This approach allows researchers to investigate teaching practice in a context from which individual case study teachers are instances of the system.

Moreover, as van Lier (2005) asserted, "Case study research has become a key method for researching changes in complex phenomena over time" (p. 195). Case studies can provide insight into teachers' experience over extended periods and point to consequences of education reform on the working life of teachers.

This paper reports the results of the study, which employed data from two main sources of evidence: (1) interviews (see Appendix A for the interview questions) and (2) observation (see Appendix B for the observation protocol). Table 8.1 summarises the data collection methods, the timing of data collection, and the data collected for this study.

The five case study teachers

The five case study teachers Dat and Ngoc (university A), Diem and Hoa (university B), and Minh (university C) were Vietnamese teachers of English for English-major students at the tertiary level in Vietnam. They were chosen based on their teaching and academic backgrounds, voluntary participation, and availability. Table 8.2 provides a detailed overview of the five case study teachers.

The five teachers perceived different levels of CALL materials development experience. The scale of material development experience is developed based on Hertz's (1987, p. 183) scale as follows:

Level 1: I have used available online materials to develop a task (e.g., a YouTube video).
Level 2: I have developed content for CALL materials but I don't have any programming expertise (e.g., PowerPoint slide).
Level 3: I have developed my own materials using a CALL authoring system (e.g., a Hot Potatoes exercise).
Level 4: I have developed a CALL software program (e.g., a vocabulary app for mobile phone).

Among the five teachers, Dat and Diem had experience as users of existing materials (Level 1), and Ngoc, Minh, and Hoa had experience as users of authoring software (Level 3).

Table 8.1 Data collection methods

Time	Instruments	Data for analysis
July and August 2015 – 9 months after the MOET course	1 Teacher demographic survey 2 Teacher interviews 3 Classroom observation 4 Classroom documents 5 Teachers' reflection reports	• 5 survey responses • 5 interviews (about 30 minutes each) • Field notes on 5 lessons • Classroom documents of 5 lessons (textbooks, handouts, syllabus) • 5 teachers' reflection reports

Table 8.2 Overview of case study teachers

	DAT	NGOC	MINH	DIEM	HOA
Age	38	32	30	32	33
Gender	Male	Female	Female	Female	Female
Previous degree	PhD in linguistics MA in TESOL BA in TESOL	MA in TESOL BA in EFL	MA in TESOL BA in EFL	MA in TESOL BA in EFL	MA in TESOL BA in EFL
Teaching experience	Lecturer of EFL at a provincial university in Vietnam (13 years)	Lecturer of EFL at a provincial university in Vietnam (7 years)	Lecturer of EFL at a university in the capital of Vietnam (6 years)	Lecturer of EFL at a provincial university in Vietnam (7 years)	Lecturer of EFL at a provincial university in Vietnam (8 years)
Experience outside Vietnam	PhD programme in Australia	MA programme in England	MA programme in New Zealand	MA programme in Vietnam	MA programme in Vietnam
Confidence and competence with technology (1 = low; 5 = high)	3	4	4	3	3
Level of CALL materials development experience*	1	3	3	1	3
Became a trainer	No	No	Yes	No	No
Implemented Moodle	No	No	No	No	No

Note: All the teachers' names are pseudonyms.

Key findings

The data analysis provided information about each teacher's learning from the MOET course, their practice of teaching listening skills, and their use of technology. However, the scope of this paper does not allow enough space to present the findings related to each of the five case study teachers. The chapter now continues with an analysis of two case study teachers Dat and Minh. Finally, it presents the summary of the findings around the research questions that were answered by the data analysis.

Dat

Dat was the only male teacher among the five. He was also the oldest and had the most teaching experience, and he was one of the two teachers having the lowest level of CALL materials development experience. Dat worked for a provincial university, and at the time of attending the MOET course, he had recently returned to work from his overseas PhD study.

Learning from the MOET course

Dat reported that he did not gain much knowledge and skills from the MOET course. He stated that he had known about many tools introduced in the course such as Google Drive and Hot Potatoes. One tool that was new to him was Moodle. Dat supplied three reasons for not using this tool. First, access to technology was limited, and the Internet was very weak. As noted earlier, as Dat's university is a provincial one, it lags behind universities in big cities regarding investment in facilities. Second, Dat found Moodle "quite complicated to follow in such a short period of time of training" and "self-learning this tool is time-consuming." He was "so busy with conventional classroom duties" when having to teach every day from morning to afternoon that he found it "so difficult to arrange time to find out more about it." Third, he commented that "Moodle is not what I need." He reported that he thought Moodle was a learning management system rather than software for learning and teaching. In his opinion, "[T]his tool can help teachers to track students' learning progress but is not very engaging to students." Dat expressed a wish to learn some software that directly supported the learning and teaching of different language subjects such as listening, writing, speaking, and reading. As mentioned in (Table 2.1), in the Vietnam language, subjects are usually organised according to skills.

Use of technologies

With regard to his use of technologies, Dat reported that he did not use much CALL technology but "effectively used" and had "no difficulties" with the teaching aids he employed. Regarding hardware, Dat "use[d] simple technologies" such as projectors, speakers, and laptops. Dat employed strategies to compensate for the deficiencies of the facilities in his university. The Listening 2 class met twice per week for two hours in a language lab. However, as Dat reported "the Internet connection [was] limited and the sound system and most of the headphones [were] broken." The observation data showed that there were no computers for the students to listen individually and to focus on the segments that they as individuals might find problematic. Dat decided to bring his own laptop and store listening files on it. The observation data showed that the students together listened to the listening text through a speaker connected to the teacher's laptop. Regarding software, he only used Windows Media Player to play audio files in his laptop and did not use Audacity, the software he was taught in the MOET course. Dat explained that Audacity is typically used to design listening tests; however, he was not assigned the role of test design for this course.

Minh

Minh was the youngest teacher among the five case study teachers. Unlike the other four teachers, Minh worked for a university in the capital of Vietnam. This university is a high-ranked university in Vietnam, and it attracts many students with good study results at high school. Minh had used CALL technologies before the MOET course, and she was one of the three teachers rating the experience of CALL materials development at three.

Learning from the MOET course

After the MOET course, Minh became a trainer for other CALL courses at her university. Minh, the only one among the five teachers to do so, had this opportunity because her university ran other courses. MOET did not provide institutions with guidelines on how to make use of the knowledge and skills taught in the MOET course. Thus, it was up to each university to decide whether the teachers would become trainers.

In addition to becoming a trainer, Minh reported that she had learnt many new things from the MOET course and put them into practice, including how to use Story Jumper, Google Drive, and Audacity. However, like the other four teachers, Minh had not yet used Moodle for any language courses she taught. Minh pointed out two main reasons that hindered her use of this tool. The first one was related to facilities. She reported that although she taught at a university in the capital of Vietnam, Hanoi, which has received significant investment in technology infrastructure, access to the Internet and computer labs was still limited to some areas of the campus. Second, Minh asserted that her university "[did] not yet have any policies to implement Moodle courses systematically." In her opinion, the university should help teachers design, manage, and maintain online courses, which saves the time teachers need to develop content for those courses.

Use of technologies

Minh commented that her university also had computer laboratories, but she did not use them due to three reasons. She explained that if she wanted to use them in any lessons, she had to book them with the equipment department in advance and that the rooms were often fully booked. Also, she reported that she did not like the layout of the labs as students sat in enclosed tables, making it very hard for interaction between teachers and students. Finally, she said that, as the rooms were far away from the normal classrooms, it took time for both the teacher and students to move between classrooms. Thus, Minh decided to use traditional classrooms that were not equipped with speakers, desktop computers, and projectors. Although Minh experienced difficulty with the inadequate facilities, she showed determination and managed to prepare the necessary equipment to implement listening tasks successfully. This was illustrated in the classroom observation. On the day of observed teaching, Minh borrowed an audiocassette and a projector from the equipment department. She also brought her own laptop to play the video files. During the lesson, the speakers of the cassette player did not work properly, and the sound was not loud enough. Reflecting on this situation, she said that to guarantee lessons go well next time, "the only alternative was to use [her] own speakers" (Minh-TR 1; original in English).

A summary of the data analysis

Learning from the MOET course (RQ1)

The results from the case study indicated that nine months after the teachers returned from the MOET course, they did not implement much CALL in their teaching. Among the five teachers, only Minh became a trainer for other CALL courses as her university such courses and invited her to become a trainer. Minh and Dat reported learning and using a few specific tools from the MOET course. However, none of the five teachers used Moodle, even though the key objective of the MOET course was to train teachers in the design of Moodle-based courses.

Contextual factors influencing CALL use (RQ2)

The analysis of case study data identified many interrelated factors that limited the teachers' adoption of Moodle as well as the implementation of CALL in general. They included the lack of a link between CALL training and teaching practices, inadequate guidelines for CALL implementation, and limited access to facilities and Internet connections. These factors are discussed in detail in the next section.

Discussion

The results indicated that there was not a close link between the MOET course and the teachers' practices at their home institutions, which limited the teachers' transfer of knowledge gained from the course into their classroom. This concurs with results in earlier studies (e.g., Chao, 2015; Dinh, 2009; Egbert et al., 2002), which showed that a mismatch between course materials and teaching contexts is a reason that limits teachers' application of what they learned.

A possible explanation for the limited use of Moodle by the teachers in this study might be related to the top-down management of the educational system in Vietnam. As in many other Asian countries where the education system is centralised (Do & Do, 2014; Phan & Hamid, 2017), in Vietnam, most PD courses are delivered based on standardised content packages provided by MOET. Due to the pre-packaged and standardised nature of courses' content, they may not able to acknowledge teachers' needs in their contexts. Similarly, the Vietnamese government introduced the MOET course as a national top-down decision. The course was independently developed and run by VietCALL on behalf of MOET. There was a lack of communication and discussion among different stakeholders, including VietCALL, universities, departments, and teachers about the choice of technologies, including Moodle, to be introduced in the course. Therefore, it can be seen that Moodle was not immediately related to the teachers' needs in their everyday teaching at the local contexts. Also, according to the regulation on textbook prescription, they had to teach with a textbook in their language courses. However, MOET introduced Moodle for the teachers to develop their own courses that would be used separately from their classrooms and textbooks. As Moodle was not something that was compatible with teachers' current practices, the teachers found the tool irrelevant to their teaching needs.

Guidelines for CALL implementation

The current study also identified that a lack of guidelines for CALL implementation at both the MOET level and institutional level was another issue limiting the use of CALL by the teacher participants. In Vietnam, written guidelines are commonly issued and used by MOET to provide and to guide universities on academic affairs (Do & Do, 2014). With regard to this, MOET provided several guidelines on the integration of technologies into language teaching in Vietnam. However, this study indicated that although the existing policies showed a high expectation from MOET that universities enhance the use of technologies, they did not provide specific guidelines on the way the MOET initiative was integrated with each university system and policy framework. This study found that there was a lack of specific guidelines disseminated from MOET to universities and from universities to teachers regarding how to support teachers' use, in their home institutions, of the knowledge and skills acquired from the MOET course. This finding confirms the fact that in the context of Vietnam, there was a lack of specific guidelines from MOET to universities to implement education policies in general (e.g., Mai, 2014; Phan & Hamid, 2017) and on how to integrate technologies in language teaching in particular (Dang, 2013; Dinh, 2015, Peeraer & Van-Petegem, 2011). This resonates with the experience of language teachers reported in previous research on technology use in education in the Asian region and other contexts (e.g., Lee, Hung, & Cheah, 2008; Yildiz & Tatar, 2010).

Technologies and time availability

Further obstacles to the implementation of CALL at the institution level in Vietnam, which are also very common in other contexts (e.g., Son, 2014; Sumi, 2011), are teachers' lack of time for CALL materials development and limited access to facilities and Internet connections. Due to a heavy workload, the teachers in this study had little time for CALL materials development. As one of the teachers said, they "*[had] to teach from the morning to the late afternoon every day* (emphasis added)." Thus, they found it very hard to arrange time for CALL implementation, which generally requires more time and effort from teachers for preparation and planning.

The issue of facility constraints also arises as a major concern. The study found that teachers lacked sufficient tools to implement CALL. Their institutions had limited facilities, unstable Internet connections, and inappropriate room layouts, which discouraged teachers from using CALL. For example, Minh taught in traditional classrooms that were not equipped with desktops, speakers, and projectors. The situation was no better in Dat's university. Although he taught in a multimedia room, it was like a traditional classroom because the system was broken and the Internet connection was very weak. A possible explanation for this might be that while MOET allocated certain funding from the Project 2020 to invest in facilities, due to the lack of resources, their investment was limited to some institutions (Dang, 2013). In reality, while some universities in big cities are equipped with modern devices and Internet access, other universities have very limited access to equipment and Internet.

These results support previous studies, especially by Le (2015) and Dinh (2015), into obstacles to CALL, which indicate that unstable Internet connections and inadequate facilities and lack of time have been prevalent historically in Vietnam. The difficulties the Vietnamese teachers faced have been identified previously in many different contexts, in both developed countries (Chambers & Bax, 2006; Levy, 1997) and in limited technology contexts as noted in Egbert (2010).

Implications of the study

This section of the chapter discusses the key implications of these findings that can be used to plan and implement future educational innovations in Vietnam and in other similar contexts.

Designing education and training in CALL: understanding teachers and their contexts

One of the very important findings of this study is that the disconnect between what happened in the MOET course and what happened in the teachers' practices at their home institutions afterwards. As the National Foreign Languages

Project 2020 (NFLP 2020) is planned to continue delivering CALL training for language teachers in the coming years (MOET, 2016), this finding holds important implications for the design of future courses in Vietnam. For CALL education and training initiatives to be successful, they need to be designed such that they are tailored to the needs of specific groups of teachers working in their contexts. Specific knowledge of teachers as a group and as individuals, of the curriculum, and of institutional contexts is important to prepare a relevant and practical training. This study points to the importance of understanding teachers and their contexts to develop effective contextualised training programs for teachers. In this way, the study strongly supports the ideas of Graves (2009), Healey (2012) and Son and Windeatt (2017a). With this knowledge, designers of CALL courses will be able to ensure a correspondence between what the courses do and what teachers want, which can facilitate the possibility that the knowledge and skills acquired from courses will be integrated in the classroom.

In order to design CALL education and training that is relevant, meaningful, and practical for teachers, a needs analysis should be conducted to gather the needs of teachers in their local contexts. As teachers play a pivotal role in CALL implementation (Hubbard, 2008), their voices should be listened to so that their needs can be catered for. Needs analysis should take into account what teachers know and can do before they start the training, and it should understand what pedagogical and institutional constraints they will face on exit. Such an analysis would guide CALL trainers and educational leaders to select appropriate content for training that is directly related to their teaching practices.

Planning and supporting CALL implementation

Another important implication is the need for MOET to have comprehensive plans to diffuse CALL in the long term. In the context of a low-resource country like Vietnam, it is important to prioritise clear actions within their plans. Lessons from the past show that teacher training is crucial for CALL implementation (Davies, 1997); thus MOET planning of in-service training and pre-service training is very important. So far, it can be seen that while MOET had a stated goal to train local teachers to become trainers at their institutions, simply sending teachers to training courses is not enough. Training and development programs delivered by MOET have still been fragmented and one-off. Moreover, there has been very little support for CALL implementation at the local level. It is therefore argued that in order to increase the long-term impact as well as to save the costs of training courses, MOET should plan for and support CALL implementation better. Given the fact that the Vietnamese government is considering continuing NFLP 2020 to 2025, MOET needs to draft specific plans regarding the type of future training and how to support teachers after training in order to diffuse CALL in local contexts. Plans could be either short term (a one-year plan) or longer term (e.g., three-year or five-year plans).

From the institutional level, universities should seriously consider the way to address primary barriers to teachers' implementation of CALL (e.g., textbook and syllabus prescription, lack of guidelines, time constraints, and inadequate facilities). The study found that none of the case study teachers in three universities used Moodle, as this tool was not available or supported in the teachers' institutions. Teachers will not use and will not be able to use CALL if they "*lack so many things*" as noted by one teacher participant. Thus, institutions should provide support for teachers if they want their teachers to use CALL. Each university should conduct a critical examination of their current situation to think of the most effective way to address these barriers in the local context.

Perhaps instead of these barriers being treated equally, they should be put in order of priority according to the conditions and the needs of the context. Maybe in one situation, time is the biggest problem to be addressed. If teachers "have to teach from the morning to the late afternoon every day," it will be very hard for them to arrange time for CALL materials development. It is necessary to deeply consider different alternatives to address time constraints. One option could be to allocate time for teachers not only to learn but to also try out new technologies and reflect on classroom experiences. For example, teachers could have a non-teaching day for training once per month. Having time for training and experimenting with new technologies would mean teachers have opportunities for decontextualised practice that enables them to develop an understanding of how new tools can be integrated into their current practice for effective learning.

Conclusion

This chapter presents EFL practices of teaching with technology at the tertiary level in Vietnam in a context where the Vietnamese government introduced a national innovation with the MOET course as central to enhancing CALL in that country. It can be seen that the government is creating opportunities for teachers to become more autonomous and to make changes in their teaching in terms of technology but still within a fairly structured framework. This study reveals that Vietnam is heading in the right direction at the national level but that more work needs to be done to guide universities and teachers at the university level.

As the teacher plays the crucial role in the implementation of innovations (Fullan, 2007; van den Branden, 2009), as is strongly confirmed in this study, they need not only training but also support from the system so that they might be more autonomous in their own practices. The results of this study agree with that of Fullan (2007): making change "is not just an individual problem; it is a system problem" (p. 153). In other words, it is not just the question of individual teachers making changes. As much as individual teachers need to make changes, the system needs to make changes for teachers to grow and become more autonomous. Given the fact that MOET plans to run other CALL courses to 2025, there is a need for complementary actions, strategies and training to make teachers more confident and secure in implementing CALL. This goal may be achieved through a process of open and collaborative communication among and between stakeholders at different levels within the system. All stakeholders need to be involved for the successful integration of CALL. In this way, the quality of language teaching with technology in Vietnam can flourish.

References

Arnold, N., & Ducate, L. (2015). Contextualized views of practices and competencies in CALL teacher education research. *Language Learning & Technology, 19*(1), 1–9. Retrieved from http://llt.msu.edu/issues/february2015/commentary.pdf

Chambers, A., & Bax, S. (2006). Making CALL work: Towards normalisation. *System, 34*(4), 465–479.

Chao, C-c. (2015). Rethinking transfer: Learning from call teacher education as consequential transition. *Language Learning & Technology, 19*(1), 102–118.

Dang, X. T. (2013). *ICT in foreign language teaching in an innovative university in Vietnam: Current practices and factors affecting ICT use.* Doctoral thesis, La Trobe University, Bundoora, Australia. Retrieved from http://hdl.handle.net/1959.9/499506

Davies, G. (1997). *Lessons from the past, lessons for the future: 20 years of CALL.* Retrieved from www.camsoftpartners.co.uk/coegdd1.htm#conc1

Dinh, H. T. B. (2009, February). *Factors influencing EFL novice teachers' adoption of technologies in classroom practice.* Proceeding of the 5th CAMTESOL conference. Retrieved from www.scribd.com/document/100267661/CamTESOL-Selected-Papers-Vol-5-2009

Dinh, H. T. B. (2015). *Factors influencing English as a Foreign Language (EFL) teachers' use of Information and Communication Technology (ICT) in classroom practice: A mixed methods study at Hanoi University, Vietnam.* Doctoral thesis, RMIT University, Melbourne, Australia. Retrieved from https://researchbank.rmit.edu.au/view/rmit:161364

Do, H. M., & Do, T. N. Q. (2014). Higher and tertiary education in Vietnam. In L. T. Tran, S. Marginson, H. Do, Q. Do, T. Le, N. Nguyen, T. Vu, T. Pham, & H. Nguyen (Eds.), *Higher education in Vietnam: Flexibility, mobility and practicality in the global knowledge economy* (pp. 29–53). Basingstoke: Palgrave Macmillan.

Dooly, M. (2009). New competencies in a new era? Examining the impact of a teacher training project. *ReCALL, 21*(3), 352–369.

Dörnyei, Z. (2007). *Research methods in applied linguistics: Quantitative, qualitative, and mixed methodologies.* Oxford: Oxford University Press.

Egbert, J. (Ed.). (2010). *CALL in limited technology contexts.* San Marcos: CALICO, Texas State University.

Egbert, J., Paulus, T. M., & Nakamichi, Y. (2002). The impact of call instruction on classroom computer use: A foundation for rethinking technology in teacher education. *Language Learning and Technology, 6*(3), 108–126.

Fullan, M. (2007). *The new meaning of educational change* (4th ed). New York: Teachers College Press.Graves, K. (2009). The curriculum of second language teacher education. In A. Burns & J. C. Richards (Eds.), *The Cambridge guide to pedagogy and practice in second language teaching* (pp. 37–49). New York: Cambridge University Press.

Healey, D. (2012). Planning a distance education course for language teachers: What administrators need to consider. In L. England (Ed.), *Online language teacher education: TESOL perspectives* (pp. 172–184). New York: Routledge.

Hertz, R. M. (1987). *Computers in the language classroom.* Menlo Park, CA: Addison-Wesley.

Hubbard, P. (2008). CALL and the future of language teacher education. *CALICO Journal, 25*(2), 175–188.

Kessler, G. (2006). Assessing CALL teacher training: What are we doing and what could we do better? In P. Hubbard & M. Levy (Eds.), *Teacher education in CALL* (pp. 22–42). Amsterdam: John Benjamins.

Kessler, G. (2007). Formal and informal CALL preparation and teacher attitude toward technology. *Computer Assisted Language Learning, 20*(2), 173–188. doi:10.1080/09588220701331394.

Kilickaya, F., & Seferoglu, G. (2013). The impact of call instruction on English language teachers' use of technology in language teaching. *Second and Multiple Language Acquisition, 1*(1), 20–38.

Le, X. M. (2015). *Lecturers' adoption and integration of information and communication technology in English teacher education at two universities in the Mekong Delta, Vietnam*. Doctoral thesis, University of Sydney.

Lee, Y. J., Hung, D., & Cheah, H. M. (2008). IT and educational policy in the Asia-pacific region. In J. Voogt & G. Knezek (Eds.), *International handbook of information technology in primary and secondary education*, Vol. 20 (pp. 1119–1132). New York: Springer.Levy, M. (1997). *Computer-assisted language learning: Context and conceptualization*. New York: Clarendon.

Levy, M., & Caws, C. (2016). CALL design and research: Taking a micro and macro view. In C. Caws & M.-J. Hamel (Eds.), *Language-learner computer interactions: Theory, methodology and CALL applications*. Amsterdam, The Netherlands: Benjamins.

Luu, T. P. L. (2015). *The effects of computer-assisted listening instruction on Vietnamese teachers and students of English*. Doctoral thesis, University of Auckland, Auckland, Australia. Retrieved from https://researchspace.auckland.ac.nz/handle/2292/25379

Mai, N. K. (2014). Towards a holistic approach to developing the language proficiency of Vietnamese primary teachers of English. *Electronic Journal of Foreign Language Teaching, 11*(2), 341–357.

McNeil, L. (2013). Exploring the relationship between situated activity and CALL learning in teacher education. *ReCALL, 25*(2), 215–232.

MOET. (2014). *Thông tư số 01/2014/TT-BGDĐT ban hành Khung năng lực ngoại ngữ 6 bậc dùng cho Việt Nam* [Circular N0 01/2014/TT-BGDĐT on the language proficiency framework in Vietnam]. MOET. Hanoi, MOET.

MOET. (2016). *Hội nghị trực tuyến về triển khai giai đoạn 2016–2020, định hướng đến năm 2025 của Đề án Ngoại Ngữ Quốc Gia 2020* [Online conference on the implementation of Vietnam's National Foreign Languages 2020 Project in the period 2016–2020, orienting to 2025].

Peeraer, J., & Van-Petegem, P. (2011). ICT in teacher education in an emerging developing country: Vietnam's baseline situation at the start of "The Year of ICT". *Computers & Education, 56*(4), 974–982.

Peeraer, J., & Van-Petegem, P. (2012). Information and communication technology in teacher education in Vietnam: From policy to practice. *Educational Research for Policy and Practice, 11*(2), 89–103.Pham, T. N. (2015). *Interpersonal interaction: A study of an online English language learning environment at a Vietnamese university*. Doctoral thesis, Victoria University, Melbourne, Australia. Retrieved from http://vuir.vu.edu.au/id/eprint/29786

Phan, T. T. H., & Hamid, M. O. (2017). Learner autonomy in foreign language policies in Vietnamese universities: An exploration of teacher agency from a socio-cultural perspective. *Current Issues in Language Planning, 18*(1), 39–56.

Son, J.-B. (2014). Moving beyond basics: From CALL coursework to classroom practice and professional development. In J.-B. Son (Ed.), *Computer-assisted language learning: Learners, teachers, and tools* (pp. 122–149). Newcastle upon Tyne: Cambridge Scholars Publishing.

Son, J.-B., & Windeatt, S. (2017a). Teacher training in computer-assisted language learning: Voices of teacher educators. In J.-B. Son & S. Windeatt (Eds.), *Language teacher education and technology: Approaches and practices* (pp. 1–17). London: Bloomsbury Academic.

Sumi, S. (2011). Voices from EFL teachers: A qualitative investigation of teachers' use of CALL. In M. Levy, F. Blin, C. B. Siskin, & O. Takeuchi (Eds.), *World-CALL: International perspectives on computer-assisted language learning* (Vol. 5, pp. 293–312). New York: Routledge.

Tai, S.-J. D. (2015). From TPACK-in-action workshops to classrooms: CALL competency developed and integrated. *Language Learning & Technology, 19*(1), 139–164.

van den Branden, K. (2009). Diffusion and implementation of innovations. In M. H. Long & C. J. Doughty (Eds.), *The handbook of language teaching* (pp. 659–672). Oxford: Blackwell. doi:10.1002/9781444315783.ch35.

van Lier, L. (2005). Case study. In E. Hinkel (Ed.), *Handbook of research in second language teaching and learning* (pp. 195–208). Mahwah, NJ: Lawrence Erlbaum Associates.VietCALL. (2014). *Báo cáo chiến lược ứng dụng công nghệ thông tin trong dạy và học ngoại ngữ* [Action plan for the enhancement of CALL]. Hanoi: NFLP 2020.

Wong, L., & Benson, P. (2006). In-service CALL education: What happens after the course is over?. In P. Hubbard & M. Levy (Eds.), *Teacher education in CALL* (pp. 250–264). Amsterdam, The Netherlands: Benjamins.

Yildiz, S., & Tatar, S. (2010). Overcoming limited instructional planning and vision in Turkish schools. In J. Egbert (Ed.), *CALL in limited technology contexts*. San Marcos, TX: CALICO.

Appendix A
Questions for semi-structured interviews

Part 1: CALL practice

1 Do you use any skills and knowledge that you acquired from MOET's training courses in CALL in your EFL teaching? If yes, please give some details. If no, please explain why.
2 What barriers to CALL do you face in your current environment? Please specify.
3 In what ways could your School/Department better support you in your CALL work?

Part 2: Listening and CALL

4 Do you teach listening and do you have any difficulties in teaching this skill? If yes, please explain in details.
5 Can you describe a typical listening lesson that you normally conduct with your students? Please explain in details.
6 Have you used any skills and knowledge that you acquired from MOET's course in CALL in your teaching of Listening? If yes, please give some details. If no, please explain why.

Part 3: Textbooks

7 What do you like and dislike of the currently used textbooks for listening at your institution? Please give more details.
8 How do you think technologies can help to fill in the gaps in the textbook?
9 According to policies, you can adapt and supplement textbooks by using technologies; have you done that? If yes, please give more details. If No, please give the reasons.
10 (6,456 words)

Appendix B
Class observation protocol

1 General information

Institution: ID

Teacher: ID

Date and time:

Number of learners:

Materials:

Learners' language level:

Lesson name:

Learners' competence with technologies:

Availability of technologies:

Objectives of the lesson:

. . . .

. . . .

. . . .

2 Classroom configuration

3 Procedures

Time	Teachers' activities and language	Students' activities and language

9   An evaluation of the intercultural orientation of secondary English textbooks in Vietnam

How well are students prepared to communicate in global contexts?

Nguyen Thi Thuy Minh and
Cao Thi Hong Phuong

Background

With the global spread of English as a means of international communication, there is an increasing demand for people in non-English-speaking countries to learn and master the language. In the particular context of Vietnam, recognising the benefits of the English language for the country and its citizens in the world arena, the government has recently launched an English language education initiative, known as National Foreign Languages Project 2020 (NFLP 2020), in order to enhance the quality of English language teaching and learning in the national education system. An objective of the project is to enable school learners to become effective English language users who can function successfully in multilingual and multicultural environments (Le & Do, 2012). This is expressed in the most recent National English Language Draft Syllabus, which states that English language education should aim at "providing learners with an important means of international communication, which will enable them . . . to explore different cultures, hence contributing to building mutual understanding among nations and developing their own capacity as global citizens" (Ministry of Education and Training (MOET), 2018, p. 3).

Nonetheless, despite the strong emphasis placed on global cultural awareness and intercultural citizenship (Byram, 2011) in the English language education policy of Vietnam, it is observed that monocultural and monolingual norms still largely underpin actual teaching and assessment practices. In the *Framework of Foreign Language Proficiency for Vietnam* (MOET, 2014), for example, "native speaker (NS) standards" are often referenced as the benchmark for evaluating English users in Vietnam while other varieties are not considered (Ho & Nguyen, Chapter 10, this volume). Similarly, multiculturalism is barely portrayed in instructional materials, while British English models and norms of communication are over-emphasized (Dang & Seals, 2018). These practices, however, cannot adequately prepare learners to communicate in the context of globalisation and multiculturalism where English users are not only from Anglophone countries but can come from all different linguistic and cultural backgrounds. As plausibly pointed out by Byram, Gribkova, and Starkey (2002, p. 11), in such a context, "it is not possible to anticipate all the knowledge one might need in interacting with people of other cultures." Therefore, it would be more beneficial for learners if, in addition to knowledge about one particular "NS" variety of English, they are also equipped with a broader repertoire of intercultural knowledge, skills, and attitudes to help them interact and "develop . . . human relationship[s]" with people of more diverse languages and cultures (Byram et al., 2002, p. 7).

Aim and rationales of the study

As part of the NFLP 2020, a series of new English textbooks have been developed for use in schools nationwide in order to renovate teaching practices and cultivate students' abilities to communicate effectively in intercultural situations (Hoang, 2016). The goal of our chapter is hence to examine the extent to which these books enable teachers to achieve the aim of developing competent intercultural speakers in order to recommend implications for English language teaching (ELT) in the context of Vietnam. Intercultural speakers, as defined by Byram et al. (2002, pp. 9–10), are mediators between cultures who understand intercultural human relationships and who are able to engage with multiple norms and perspectives, seeing such interaction as an enriching experience. Our analysis will be centred on the Project's upper-secondary school English textbooks, which have not yet been investigated in previous research (Dang & Seals, 2018, evaluated primary-level textbooks).

Our focus on textbook evaluation stems from the fact that although textbooks are the "visible heart of any ELT programme" (Sheldon, 1988, p. 237), research has repeatedly shown that they do not adequately prepare learners to communicate in a multicultural, highly diversified, and globalised world (Hu & McKay, 2014; Kiss, 2018; Nguyen, 2011). Although globalisation has radically expanded the communicative needs of English learners, textbooks still tend to privilege NS cultural norms and values over other cultural practices, thus failing to raise learners' awareness of multiple perspectives inherent in intercultural communication and prepare them to cope with this diversity (Dang & Seals, 2018; Shin, Eslami, & Chen, 2011; Syrbe & Rose, 2016). Textbooks have also been found to present a monolithic, static view of culture (Syrbe & Rose, 2016), which may lead to "overly simplistic and stereotypical understandings of . . . cultures and people," thus hindering rather than aiding communication across cultures (Baker, 2015, p. 134). These findings are not surprising, given the mismatch between textbooks and theories of language learning and teaching often reported in the literature (see Tomlinson, 2016, for a collection of studies on this issue). This indicates that textbooks need to be carefully evaluated before being adopted for a language programme. Textbook evaluation can help teachers select the most appropriate books for their teaching purposes and students' learning objectives. In the case of prescribed textbooks, such as the NFLP 2020 textbooks, textbook evaluation will also help inform teachers of the strengths and weaknesses of the books and thus assist them in the process of textbook adaptation.

An intercultural approach to teaching English as a lingua franca

As stated earlier, successful communication in the globalised context requires more than knowledge of the target language culture. It requires that learners acquire intercultural (communicative) competence (ICC), or the ability to ensure mutual understanding among people of different language and cultural backgrounds and to communicate effectively and appropriately with one another as "complex human beings with multiple identities and [our] own individuality" (Byram et al., 2002, p. 10). The notion of ICC has emerged over the past years to respond to the criticism that the conventional model of communicative competence (CC) has become inadequate in accounting for language learning and use in intercultural situations, and therefore there is a need for an alternative pedagogic model (Alptekin, 2002; Byram, Holmes, & Savvides, 2013; Byram & Wagner, 2018; McKay, 2002).

The CC model emphasises that learners need to develop not only knowledge of the grammar of the target language but also the ability to use this knowledge to communicate meanings appropriately for purpose, audience and social contexts in the target language setting (Canale & Swain, 1980). In other words, learning to use a second language is equated to learning to express oneself in the way that is appropriate for the cultural values and ideologies of the people who speak the language. However, as Alptekin (2002) has pointed out, the CC model with its standardized NS norms is based on the monolithic perception of language and culture, which is simply flawed, as there is no single correct and appropriate way to use English. The CC model also tends to neglect the lingua franca status of the English language and the fact that NS norms may not be at all relevant in intercultural communication involving multilingual English users of different languages and cultures, for whom the ability to understand one another is more essential for successful communication than conformity to the cultural norms of the target language community. As such, it has become clear that the monolingual English-speaking model is inadequate to meet the communicative needs of learners in the globalised context, who learn English not to become similar to English NSs but to use the language effectively for specific communication purposes in local and international settings, while preserving their own cultural identities (Canagarajah, 2006).

In a similar vein, Byram et al. (2002, p. 9) have indicated that the assumption that the aim of language learning is to "imitate a native speaker both in linguistic competence, in knowledge of what is 'appropriate' language, and in knowledge about a country and its 'culture'" represents simplistic understandings of social identity based solely on national origins. This simplification disregards the multiplicity and fluidity of identity. As further explained by Byram et al. (2002), although we acquire our cultural values, beliefs, and behaviours through growing up in our cultural community, we do not have only one identity. On the contrary, we are all different individuals with distinctive perspectives and qualities, which constantly develop and expand as we enter a new social group. However, by assuming that learning a language means becoming like a person from the culture speaking that language, the CC model necessarily "reduces the individual from a complex human being to someone who is representative of a country or 'culture,'" seeing them through a single identity (Byram et al., 2002, p. 9). This may lead to generalisations and stereotypical assumptions, which can undermine mutual understanding and impede our communication with other people.

Unlike the CC model, the ICC model does not assume such a static and stereotyped view of language, identity, and culture. On the contrary, it emphasises the importance of developing an awareness that people have different social identities and the corresponding ability to engage with such complexity and multiple perspectives in intercultural interaction (Byram et al., 2002). To this end, the ICC model proposes that instead of being imposed with the unrealistic idea that they should acquire the NS competence, learners need to develop intercultural awareness that is more useful for successful communication across diverse linguacultural boundaries. According to Byram (1997), this awareness includes the understanding that appropriateness of norms is culturally relative and an openness to other cultures (*savoir être*); knowledge about other cultures and how one's own culture is likely perceived by other cultural communities (*savoirs*); the ability to see things from a different cultural perspective and evaluate how differences might give rise to misunderstanding (*savoir comprehendre*); the ability to acquire new knowledge about other cultures and to apply this knowledge to real-life communication (*savoir apprendre/faire*); and critical awareness of self and other (*savoir s'engager*).

In order to support learners in developing these *savoirs*, the ICC emphasises the need to bring together materials from different origins to create a "sphere of interculturality" (Kramsch, 1993), in which learners are encouraged to compare and critically reflect on cultural materials with different perspectives in order to develop self-awareness and awareness of others (Byram et al., 2002). An example of how this can be done in the classroom includes getting students to compare texts about how a specific issue is dealt with in two different societies to help them learn to consider the same issue from different perspectives, thereby avoiding presumptions and enhancing awareness of ideological pluralisms (Müller-Hartmann & Schocker-von, 2007). Another example is analysis of texts for implicit meanings and ideologies to encourage learners to engage with texts critically and develop the ability to identify and challenge cultural biases (Byram et al., 2002). As strongly stressed by Byram et al. (2002), the ICC approach to materials is always inclusive and critical.

Teachers' use of instructional materials

Textbooks are an important source of language input and cultural knowledge in most foreign-language teaching contexts and can exert a major influence on learners' language and cultural ideologies. However, they do not necessarily present a neutral view of social reality but more often present selective forms of knowledge suited to authors' and publishers' interpretations of this reality (Ilieva, 2018). Although teachers need to develop a critical stance towards textbook use so that they can exploit the textbook in a way that does not limit but enriches students' learning experience and empowers them as critical text consumers and producers, research has indicated that this is not always the case (e.g., Forman, 2014; Grossman & Thompson, 2008). Tomlinson (2012), for example, notes that while experienced teachers are not constrained by prescribed textbooks and often adapt teaching materials to suit the needs of their students, novice teachers tend to view textbooks as an absolute authority and rely heavily on textbooks for guidance. Similarly, Grossman and Thompson (2008) have shown that beginning teachers' classroom practices are largely shaped by teaching materials; however, as their knowledge of students and the curriculum grows, they become better aware of the need to adapt the materials.

An important explanation for the new teachers' tendency to uncritically "latch onto" textbooks is the lack of adequate training during pre-service education, which seems to limit their experience with materials analysis and adaptation for real classroom teaching (Grossman & Thompson, 2008). As such, it is important that teachers have opportunities to critically reflect on curriculum materials not only during pre-service training but also as part of their continuing professional development (Grossman & Thompson, 2008). When teachers develop practical knowledge and strategies to use textbook resources for context-appropriate teaching, they can successfully decentre the NS-based resources prescribed in textbooks and provide learners with opportunities to learn beyond the scope of these resources (Yu, 2018).

Since teachers' beliefs and values can determine how they engage with teaching materials, thereby having an effect on students' learning (Grossman & Thompson, 2008; Nguyen, 2013), it is also important that teachers become aware of their own values and perspectives and challenge their own stereotypes (Byram et al., 2002). With specific respect to the context of English as a lingua franca (Seidlhofer, 2005), that would mean developing the awareness that textbooks presenting only voices and values of the target language community are biased and unhelpful in fostering intercultural sensitivity and respect for cultural pluralism. Consequently, teachers need to ensure the use of inclusive materials that reflect multiple perspectives and voices and that engage their learners in discussions of the materials from critical perspectives in order to enable them to develop as intercultural citizens who understand the subtleties and complexities involved in intercultural interaction (Ndura, 2004). As discussed by Byram et al. (2002), the aim of teaching ICC after all is not to transmit cultural information because culture is not static and teachable as a set of separate facts. Rather, it is about raising learners' awareness of the dynamic processes of intercultural interaction and how one's beliefs and perceptions about oneself and others may influence the outcome of these processes.

The present study

Research questions

In light of these discussions, our chapter aims to evaluate the extent to which the NFLP 2020's secondary textbooks support students in developing intercultural awareness for communication with people from different first language backgrounds in the context of globalisation and multiculturalism. Specifically, based on Byram et al.'s (2002) discussion of materials to promote the intercultural learning just discussed, we focus on two issues: (1) the use of inclusive materials from an intercultural and critical perspectives and (2) the depiction of culture itself in the books.

Concerning the first issue, we ask to what extent materials from different origins are included in the books and what students are expected to do with these materials. That is, are students given opportunities to relate the materials to their real-life experiences and analyse the materials for deep-level cultural learning, or are they positioned as passive recipients of a one-way transmission of information without opportunities to compare and analyse the materials critically to develop awareness of self and others?

Regarding the second issue, we ask whether the books present a static or dynamic view of cultures (whether culture is depicted as invariable and unchanging or as fluid and complex) and to what extent multiple cultural values and ideologies are represented.

The books

The textbook series analysed in our chapter included three books *English 10*, *English 11*, and *English 12*, and their accompanying audio material, which were intended for Vietnamese grade 10 (aged 16), grade 11 (aged 17), and grade 12 (aged 18) students. As stated in the books' prefaces, the books adopted a theme-based curriculum approved by the Ministry of Education and Training. This curriculum placed a strong emphasis on developing students' communicative competence, intercultural awareness, sense of global citizenship, and knowledge and appreciation of the Vietnamese language and culture. Each book contained ten teaching units to be taught over a period of 105 instructional hours, with three hours per week. The books' various sections were focused on developing students' linguistic competence, communication skills, and cross-cultural knowledge, including knowledge about the Vietnamese culture and cultures of Anglophone and other ASEAN countries.

Analysis

Following the analytical procedures of Weninger and Kiss (2013) and Kiss (2018) for examining cultural contents in ELT materials, the units of analysis for our textbook analysis were both texts and pedagogical tasks accompanying them. Our coding categories, adapted from previous textbook studies (e.g., Hu & McKay, 2014; Syrbe & Rose, 2016), included directly observable items such as types of cultural contexts described (local, Anglophone/Western, other Asian, or cross-cultural), task requirements (comprehension-based versus analytical and reflective), and depiction of culture (as fixed Anglophone cultures versus as fluid global cultures), and cultural values (Anglophone/Western versus local). With regard to the coding of cultural contexts, note that our analysis did not make a distinction between Anglophone and other Western contexts because speakers' national identities were not always provided, making it impossible to assign them to one culture or another. For practicality's sake, hence, we considered both speakers' groups together.

The data analysis procedures were as follows. First, we tested the coding categories on two units (Unit 1 and Unit 2) in *English 10* book and modified the categories iteratively until they fitted the data completely and no further modifications were needed. The second author then used the finalised scheme to independently code the remainder of the data. Her coding was finally cross-checked by the first author, and discrepancies in coding results were discussed until consensus was reached.

Findings and discussion

Inclusiveness of cultures and promotion of intercultural awareness

As discussed earlier, in order to promote intercultural awareness among students, it is important that materials from different origins and with different perspectives be used together and that students be invited to reflect upon these materials through different lenses (Byram et al., 2002; Kramsch, 1993). Consequently, our first research question focuses on whether the books are inclusive of a variety of cultures and enable students to critically engage with the cultural material to support their intercultural learning.

Our analysis shows that although a wide range of cultural contexts were present in the books, these contents were not equally represented. Cultural contents related to Anglophone/Western contexts and local contexts received the most attention, respectively contributing to 36% and 27% of all three books' contents. On the other hand, features related to other Asian (e.g., China, Japan, and ASEAN nations) and cross-cultural contexts were seriously under-represented (11% and 9% of the books' contents, respectively).

The prevalence of Anglo-American/Western cultural contents is not unexpected and corroborates previous ELT textbook evaluation research (e.g., Hu & McKay, 2014; Shin et al., 2011; Syrbe & Rose, 2016). However, the strong emphasis on the local context is a very much welcomed feature of this textbook series. As stated, learners in multilingual contexts often study English for a designated purpose, such as for higher education, work, or travel, rather than to replace their first language and culture. In cross-cultural situations, English language may also be used as a vehicle for mutlilingual speakers to express who they are culturally. Thus, the provision of topics related to students' own country and culture can equip them not only with knowledge of their own cultural contexts but also with linguistic means required for communicating about their country, people, and culture. As several scholars have plausibly argued, intercultural awareness involves not only acquiring knowledge about another culture but importantly an understanding of one's own culture in relation to another, as in learning about another culture, one requires knowledge of one's own culture (Kramsch, 1993; McKay, 2002). Textbooks with localised input are therefore helpful in promoting this perspective.

Nonetheless, the paucity of the Asian contexts may invite criticism. As pointed out by Vietnamese scholars such as Ton and Pham (2010), in the past 20 years the need to learn English in Vietnam has been motivated by the influx of foreign investment from several Asian countries such as Singapore, Hongkong, and Malaysia. As such, it can be anticipated that for Vietnamese learners of English, knowledge of regional countries is of no less importance than learning about Anglophone cultures. In order to prepare students to use English in this intercultural context, it is therefore important that Asian countries and cultures be represented more equally in instructional materials. A larger proportion of the cultural contents should also be related to cross-cultural contexts in which materials of different origins and with different perspectives are juxtaposed and examined so that students' intercultural awareness can be enhanced. Such learning experiences are essential to enable learners to act as mediators between cultures who are capable of negotiating mutliple perspectives, yet without losing their identities (Byram, 2003).

With regard to how cultural contents were treated and whether students were offered opportunities to engage with the material in a meaningful way, our analysis of text-based tasks indicates both strengths and limitations. The strengths lie in the plethora of tasks provided in each unit to enable students to relate the material to their own daily life and to the wider local society (80% of all tasks accompanying cultural material). A typical example is the text-based tasks found in *English 11* Unit 3, "Generation gap." This unit appeals to Vietnamese students because it affords them multiple opportunities to associate their real-world experiences and cultural knowledge of local family structure and dynamics. At the beginning of the unit, students listen to two foreign speakers, Sam and Ann, exchanging their opinions about the generation gap and family relationhsips. After answering some factual questions about the text, students have a chance to share their experience living in a neuclear or an extended family and what they like and dislike about each type of family. In the subsequent *Reading* section, there is a text about conflict between parents and teenage children, which is again followed by comprehension-based activities and pair-work discussion, e.g., "Do you get into conflict with your parents? Share your experience with your partner." Students subsequently have a chance to discuss how conflict in their family might arise out of the generation gap and how it could be resolved, using ideas and language input provided in the *Speaking* and *Listening* sections. In the *Writing* section, students write a letter about their family rules to an imagined

English friend who is going to stay with their family on a cultural homestay programme. Then in *Communication and Culture*, they read a text about the rise of multigenerational houseolds in the United States and the UK, answer factual questions, and subsequently discuss current family trends in Vietnam. At the end of the unit, students conduct an interview with other teenagers about their intergenerational conflict experience and report the results to the class. It is noted that the remainder of units across the three books were designed in the same manner. That is, apart from tasks aiming to check students' understanding of factual information (20% of the tasks), there were always explicit efforts to involve students' personal relevant experience in relation to the material in order to enable them to use English to describe their local experiences in intra-/international communication (see Xu, 2013 for a similar discussion on this point).

On the other hand, the limitations of the books mainly concern the absence of tasks that enable students to critically engage with more profound cultural values and ideologies implicitly embedded in the material. In all three books, cultural contents were primarily presented as factual information about countries, places, people, practices, and cultural artefacts, which was subsequently used as a basis for students to express their own culture (see the previous discussion). However, there was no attempt to encourage students to move beyond the texts' surface for deeper cultural meanings. Unit 1 in *English 10* represents such a missed opportunity. In *Getting Started*, students are presented a conversation between a teenager and his uncle about the different ways in which household duties are divided in their families. In the teenager's family, both parents work, and hence the chores are split equally among all family members, whereas in his uncle's family, the wife handles all the chores because the husband is responsible for the household finances. Students are subsequently asked to indicate their understanding of the conversation by deciding the truthfulness of a number of statements about the conversation. In follow-up activities, students are guided to identify meanings of new lexical items occurring in the conversation and finally discuss with their friends how household duties are shared among members of their families. It is clear that the focus of these activities is on language development, not cultural learning. Hence, although the discussion might effectively enable students to associate their relevant experiences in a meaningful way, more could yet be done to promote critical cultural awareness. For example, students could be guided to compare the two types of households depicted in the conversation and discuss the changing beliefs and values about gender roles that underlie household labour division in many modern Vietnamese families. Such a discussion not only enables students to examine and challenge their own assumptions and stereotypes but also helps them see cultural values not as static but as contestable and negotiable.

A similar example can be found in Unit 7 of the same book. In *Getting Started*, students listen to two Western speakers discussing Vietnamese traditional and modern weddings and answer comprehension questions about the conversation. In fact, this text could effectively be used for students to discuss how Vietnamese cultural practices and values might be seen from an outsider's perspective, thereby critically reflecting upon their culture in relation to others. Students could also be invited to challenge some generalisations made by the speakers (e.g., parents pay for their adult children's weddings and guests give money as presents) and suggest another perspective. Unfortunately, however, throughout the books, there was a lack of conscious effort to engage students in such learning experiences (see Shin et al., 2011 for similar discussions).

Depictions of culture and cultural values

According to Liddicoat (2001), although culture is always dynamic, it is, unfortunately, more often than not seen through a static lens in language education. This static view treats culture as unvarying and cultural knowledge as discrete facts that can be transmitted in the way we acquire factual information. Emerging models of culture, however, view culture as a set of variable practices that can be enacted differently by individual members of the culture and continually created and recreated as they participate in interaction with other members. In this sense, cultural knowledge is not about learning facts about another culture but knowing how to engage with it (Liddicoat, 2001). This view of culture is considered more capable of representing cultural variability and dynamics in postmodern globalisation and thus has increasingly been advocated in ELT pedagogy (Xu, 2013). On the other hand, the fact-based approach to culture has been criticised for its simplification and incapability to account for cultural diversity and fluidity in intercultural interaction (Fang, 2011).

Notwithstanding this criticism, the fact-based approach still finds its way into many ELT textbooks (Shin et al., 2011; Syrbe & Rose, 2016). This also holds true for the books examined in our study. We found that cultures were largely portrayed in these books as monolithic entities that are invariable and impermeable. Although there were some multicultural depictions (e.g., Singapore is a multicultural society, or Vietnam has over 50 ethnic groups, etc.), it is observed that stereotypical, inflexible presentations of countries and people (e.g., Vietnamese people strongly believe in life after death, or Americans hold high values about hard work and self-reliance) were more typical (12 out of 16 instances in which countries and cultures are mentioned). Such depictions actively contribute to the myth of cultural homogeneity (Matsuda & Matsuda, 2011) and hence are deemed untenable in today's globalised world, where global and local norms come into frequent contact and are constantly negotiated. As noted by Canagarajah (2006), the strong "transcultural flows" between nations have entailed an increasing hybridity of languages, communities, and cultures. As such, cultures can change, be shaped, negotiated, and recreated "in each instance of communication" (Syrbe & Rose, 2016, p. 10). Unfortunately, this dynamic, fluid, and negotiated aspect of culture was not sufficiently emphasised in the books to help raise students' awareness of the complexities, yet adaptability and malleability of "doing culture" in globalised communication.

Another noteworthy finding regarding the depiction of culture in the examined books is the biased representation of cultural values and ideologies in favour of Anglo-American countries. As with previous studies (e.g., Babaii & Sheikhi,

2018; Hu & McKay, 2014), we found in the contents of these books various examples in which qualities and values often identified with the West were openly valorised. In a listening text in Unit 3 in *English 11*, for example, two Vietnamese students discuss how they admire a common friend for being independent, self-reliant, and confident – i.e., values that are mostly associated with individualism-oriented societies but are less emphasised in a collectivism-oriented society such as Vietnam. On the other hand, values often associated with collectivism-oriented cultures such as interdependence, involvement, and modesty are barely portrayed. The fact that externally imposed values are depicted as being embraced rather than approached from a critical perspective by Vietnamese young people represents a clear case of "inculcation" that has been in current ELT scholarship (Fairclough, 2001). As such, instead of empowering students to engage with the material from an intercultural perspective, the books tend to position them as passive recipients of the "hidden curriculum."

In another example, cross-cultural materials with different perspectives are used not to engage students in critical cultural awareness but to celebrate American values. In a text discussing parenting practices across cultures (Unit 3 in *English 11*), American parents are depicted as liberal and respectful of their children's autonomy (e.g., teaching children to live independently, showing respect for them, letting them voice their opinions, etc.) – in other words, a parenting style that is generally deemed progressive and endorsed in the modern Western philosophy of education. These practices are placed in direct juxtaposition with Vietnamese parenting styles, which are depicted in a less positive light such as being protective and authoritarian (e.g., providing for children but seldom asking for children's opinions), thus subtly "othering" the Vietnamese parenting values as inferior and less desirable. A similar example was found in a text describing what success means to the Vietnamese as opposed to the Americans (Unit 7 in *English 10*). While the American culture is positively portrayed as valuing self-made and self-driven individuals ("success is the result of hard work and self-reliance"), the Vietnamese culture is portrayed, apparently in a much less favourable light, as placing more value on superficial things such as wealth and status when defining success. Strikingly, however, in none of the tasks accompanying these texts are students invited to challenge the generalisations and offer an alternative perspective on the issues discussed.

It should also be noted that many of the exo-normative values popularized in the books can be difficult for local students to associate because they may not exist at all in the local cultural schemas. For example, in one unit students are asked to discuss whether they should take a gap year after secondary school to explore their future options, despite the fact that this concept may be totally foreign to students' lived experiences. Also, although the discussion involves local students, the book presents an image of a Western teenager traveling the world and holding a signboard in his hand that says "A world of opportunities. Take a gap year" (Unit 3 in *English 11*). Such presentations tend to promote an out-group's perspective, while disregarding students' own cultural experiences and hence are likely to alienate them and make them feel marginalised.

In sum, as indicated by many scholars, textbooks are "carrier of cultures and ideologies" (Xu, 2013, p. 5). In the case of the books examined in our study, these cultures and ideologies appeared to be dominantly Western-based. Obviously, if textbooks are to promote respect for diversity and empower students to function effectively in the context of globalisation and multiculturalism without losing the sense of who they are culturally, it is imperative that no single cultural or ideological stance be afforded a dominant position (Xu, 2013). Instead, students should be made aware of pluralistic ideologies and allowed to draw on their multilingual resources to negotiate these diversities and express their subjectivity.

Implications and conclusion

An important objective of the Vietnamese government's NFLP 2020 is to develop intercultural language users who can successfully participate in global contexts. Our study therefore aimed to evaluate to what extent this objective has been achieved in the Project's upper secondary school ELT textbooks. We have found that, despite an attempt to globalise their cultural contents, the books do not fully enable teachers to develop intercultural awareness among their students.

First, although intercultural communication in the context of English as a lingua franca involves a wide spectrum of speakers from vastly diverse backgrounds, the books tend to focus merely on preparing students to use English for communication with Anglophone/Western English users. This is seen in the inclusion of a greater proportion of texts about Anglo-American/Western cultures than texts about other international contexts (e.g., other Asian countries). As such, it is questionable that the books present lingua-cultural materials that are entirely representative of what Vietnamese students require for future intercultural communication.

Second, although materials from different origins are used, and there is a wealth of tasks to enable students to relate these materials to their lived experiences and practice language skills, the materials are rarely approached from an intercultural and critical perspective to facilitate intercultural learning. As discussed earlier, intercultural learning requires not knowledge transmission but opportunities for critical engagement with the materials to raise students' awareness of underlying values and meanings and to enable them to challenge generalisations and consider phenomena from multiple perspectives. However, such opportunities are lacking in the books.

The development of intercultural awareness also requires that students be exposed to a multifaceted view of culture and be empowered to identify with multiple voices and perspectives. However, we have found that the books tend to display a strong favour for monolingual Anglophone/Western cultures and a static view of culture and hence do not seem to effectively support students in expanding their cultural awareness, thereby fostering respect for cultural diversity.

Despite this criticism, however, it is worth noting that the strengths of the books lie in the inclusion of localised material to enrich learners' knowledge of their own culture. Local cultural materials are scarcely included in locally produced textbooks (e.g., see Hu & McKay, 2014; Tajeddin & Teimournezhad, 2015). Therefore, this inclusion is a much welcomed feature of the books in our study. A word of caution is also in order here regarding the interpretation of our findings. That is, since our analysis concerns primarily opportunities for intercultural learning, our study does not by any means diminish the quality of the books in other aspects, e.g., language skills development. Also, since the books are only one component of the curriculum, and we do not know how they are implemented in the actual classroom to impact students' intercultural learning, our study by no means suggests the lack of success of the NFLP 2020 overall.

Still, in the light of these findings, some important implications can be suggested with regard to building teachers' capacity in exploiting textbooks for teaching ICC in the context of ELT in Vietnam. To begin with, because teachers are mediators between curriculum and students' learning and a curriculum produces effects on students mainly by virtue of having an effect on teachers (Grossman & Thompson, 2008), it is first and foremost important that teachers have the requisite content knowledge base for successfully achieving curriculum goals. In other words, in order for teachers to make the best use of textbooks to cultivate students' intercultural awareness, teachers themselves need to have an adequate understanding of culture, the role of teaching culture in ELT, as well as what developing intercultural awareness means in practice for them and their students.

Although little is known about how secondary school English teachers in Vietnam view and address culture in the classroom, studies in the university context have indicated that Vietnamese teachers may have fairly limited understandings in this aspect. For example, Ho (2011) found that teachers generally held a static view of culture and believed in the subordinate role of culture in language teaching, which may have led to their neglect of teaching ICC. Similarly, Nguyen (2013) found that regardless of their teaching experience, many university teachers did not seem to be aware of their integrated role as teachers of both language and culture and therefore tended to prioritize teaching language over teaching cultural knowledge. On the rare occasions they addressed culture, their teaching tended to focus more on transmitting cultural information than on developing learners' critical awareness of deeper-level cultural elements such as values and beliefs. Their teaching was also heavily dependent on the contents prescribed in textbooks, which tended to present culture in a biased way. This was largely due to their own limited cultural knowledge and lack of proper training in teaching intercultural communication.

Clearly, such studies as these have suggested that in order to support teachers in utilising the textbook for intercultural teaching, it is essential to first of all raise teachers' awareness of the importance of integrating intercultural teaching into ELT and to enhance their ICC as well as capacity in teaching ICC. Presumably, this can be done by incorporating more cultural information and suggestions about how to teach it in teachers' books. Currently, such information is absent in the teacher's manuals accompanying the books under inquiry in our study. Further, teachers' professional development workshops could also focus more on the role of ICC in language teaching. For example, teachers can be guided to work with Byram's (1997) model of ICC to develop a better idea of what ICC involves and how to teach it most effectively. This kind of workshop may also direct teachers to self-access resources dealing with ICC development for teachers' subsequent independent professional learning.

Next, teachers also need to be supported in how to work with textbooks in order to leverage these resources to benefit students' learning while overcoming the resources' potential limitations. Given that, as cultural artefacts, textbooks are ideological, teachers need to adopt a critical stance and reflective approach towards textbook use so that they can assist their students to become aware of and able to challenge ideologies imposed by textbooks. As pointed out by Byram et al. (2002, p. 21), "Textbooks can be presented in a way that suggests that the materials are authoritative and definitive or in an intercultural and critical perspective." Therefore, in order to use textbooks effectively to facilitate students' intercultural skills, teachers should be guided in how to evaluate and customise teaching materials to reflect current thinking in ELT and intercultural language teaching as well as to suit their teaching contexts. For example, in the specific context of ELT in Vietnam, because of the restricted number of classroom hours allocated to English teaching in the school curriculum (105 hours), not all *savoirs* in Byram's model can be addressed. Therefore, to make the best use of the limited time and make room for intercultural learning in textbooks, teachers need to develop effective selection strategies to help them determine what is important to teach and what is not, basing their decisions on the specific needs and levels of their classrooms. Obviously, in order to assist teachers in this aspect, greater autonomy should be given to them in terms of textbook modification and adaptation.

References

Alptekin, C. (2002). Towards intercultural communicative competence in ELT. *ELT Journal, 56*(1), 57–64.

Babaii, E., & Sheikhi, M. (2018). Traces of neoliberalism in English teaching materials: A critical discourse analysis. *Critical Discourse Studies, 15*(3), 247–264.

Baker, W. (2015). Research into practice: Cultural and intercultural awareness. *Language Teaching, 48*(1), 130–141.

Byram, M. (1997). *Teaching and assessing intercultural communicative competence.* Clevedon: Multilingual Matters.

Byram, M. (2003). Cultural studies and foreign language teaching. In B. Susan (Ed.), *Studying British cultures: An introduction* (pp. 57–69). London: Routledge.

Byram, M. (2011). Intercultural citizenship from an international perspective. *Journal of the NUS Teaching Academy, 1*(1), 10–20.

Byram, M., Gribkova, B., & Starkey, H. (2002). Developing the intercultural dimension in language teaching. *A practical introduction for teachers.* Strasbourg: Council of Europe.

Byram, M., Holmes, P., & Savvides, N. (2013). Intercultural communicative competence in foreign language education: Questions of theory, practice and research. *The Language Learning Journal, 41*(3), 251–253.

Byram, M., & Wagner, M. (2018). Making a difference: Language teaching for inter-cultural and international dialogue. *Foreign Language Annals, 51*(1), 140–151.

Canagarajah, S. (2006). Changing communicative needs, revised assessment objectives: Testing English as an international language. *Language Assessment Quarterly, 3*(3), 229–242.

Canale, M., & Swain, M. (1980). Theoretical bases of communicative approaches to second language teaching and testing. *Applied Linguistics, 1*(1), 1–47.

Dang, T. C. T., & Seals, C. (2018). An evaluation of primary English textbooks in Vietnam: A sociolinguistic perspective. *TESOL Journal, 9*(1), 93–113.

Fairclough, N. (2001). *Language and power* (2nd ed.). London: Routledge.

Fang, G. (2011). Linguistic capital: Continuity and change in educational language polices for South Asians in Hong Kong primary schools. *Current Issues in Language Planning, 12*(2), 251–263.

Forman, R. (2014). How local teachers respond to the culture and language of a global English as a foreign language textbook. *Language, Culture, and Curriculum, 27*(1), 72–88.

Grossman, P., & Thompson, C. (2008). Learning from curriculum materials: Scaffolds for new teachers? *Teaching and Teacher Education, 24*(8), 2014–2026.

Ho, S. T. K. (2011). *An investigation of intercultural teaching and learning in tertiary EFL classrooms in Vietnam.* Unpublished PhD thesis. Wellington, New Zealand, Victoria University of Wellington.

Ho, T. M. H., & Nguyen, T. H. (2020). English as a lingua franca for Vietnam: Current issues and future directions. In V. C. Le, H. T. M. Nguyen, T. T. M. Nguyen, & R. Bernard (eds.). *Building teacher capacity in English Language Teaching in Vietnam* (pp. 166–183). London: Routledge.

Hoang, V. V. (2016). Renovation in curriculum design and textbook development: An effective solution to improving the quality of English teaching in Vietnamese schools in the context of integration and globalization. *VNU Journal of Science: Education Research, 32*(4), 9–20.

Hu, G., & McKay, S. L. (2014). Multilingualism as portrayed in a Chinese English textbook. In J. Conteh & G. Meier (Eds.), *The multilingual turn in languages education: Opportunities and challenges* (pp. 64–88). Clevedon: Multilingual Matters.

Ilieva, R. (2018). Textbooks. In J. I. Liontas, T. International Association, & M. DelliCarpini (Eds.), *The TESOL encyclopedia of English language teaching* (pp. 1–13). Hoboken: John Wiley & Sons.

Kiss, T. (2018). Developing intercultural communicative competence: An example of the new college English textbook series. *Indonesian JELT, 12*(1), 79–98.

Kramsch, C. J. (1993). *Context and culture in language teaching.* Oxford: Oxford University Press.

Le, V. C., & Do, T. M. C. (2012). Teacher preparation for primary school English education: Case of Vietnam. In B.Spolsky & Y. Moon (Eds.), *Primary school English language education in Asia* (pp. 106–128). New York: Taylor &Francis.

Liddicoat, A. (2001). Static and dynamic views of culture and intercultural language acquisition. *New Zealand Language Teacher, 27*, 47–58.

Matsuda, A., & Matsuda, P. (2011). Globalizing writing studies: The case of U.S. technical communication textbooks. *Written Communication, 28*(2), 172–192.

McKay, S. L. (2002). *Teaching English as an international language: Rethinking goals and perspectives.* New York: Oxford University Press.

MOET. (2014). *Implementing the 6-level framework of foreign language proficiency for Vietnam* [Ban Hanh Khung Nang Luc Ngoai Ngu 6 bac Danh cho Viet Nam]. Hanoi: Ministry of Education of Vietnam.

MOET. (2018). *National English language draft syllabus* [Du Thao Chuong Trinh Tieng Anh Thi Diem]. Hanoi: Ministry of Education of Vietnam.

Müller-Hartmann, A., & Schocker-von, D. M. (2007). *Introduction to English language teaching.* Stuttgart: Klett.

Ndura, E. (2004). ESL and cultural bias: An analysis of elementary through high school textbooks in the Western United States of America. *Language, Culture and Curriculum, 17,* 143–153.

Nguyen, T. L. (2013). *Integrating culture into Vietnamese university EFL teaching: A critical ethnographic study.* Unpublished PhD thesis. Auckland, New Zealand, Auckland University of Technology.

Nguyen, T. T. M. (2011). Learning to communicate in a globalised world: To what extent do school textbooks facilitate the development of intercultural pragmatic competence? *RELC Journal, 42*(1), 17–30.

Seidlhofer, B. (2005). English as a lingua franca. *ELT Journal, 59*(4), 339–341.

Sheldon, L. E. (1988). Evaluating ELT textbooks and materials. *ELT Journal, 42*(4).

Shin, J., Eslami, Z. R., & Chen, W.-C. (2011). Presentation of local and international culture in current international English-language teaching textbooks. *Language, Culture and Curriculum, 24*(3), 253–268.

Syrbe, M., & Rose, H. (2016). An evaluation of the global orientation of English textbooks in Germany. *Innovation in Language Learning and Teaching,* 1–12.

Tajeddin, Z., & Teimournezhad, S. (2015). Exploring the hidden agenda in the representation of culture in international and localised ELT textbooks. *The Language Learning Journal, 43*(2), 180–193.

Tomlinson, B. (2012). Materials development for language teaching and learning. *Language Teaching, 45*(2), 143–179.

Tomlinson, B. (Ed.). (2016). *SLA research and materials development for language learning.* New York: Routledge.

Ton, N. N. H., & Pham, H. H. (2010). Vietnamese teachers' and students' perceptions of global English. *Language Education in Asia, 1*(1), 48–61.

Weninger, C., & Kiss, T. (2013). Culture in English as a foreign language textbooks: A semiotic approach. *TESOL Quarterly, 47*(4), 694–716.

Xu, Z. (2013). Globalization, culture and ELT materials: A focus on China. *Multilingual Education, 3*(1), 6.

Yu, M. H. (2018). Exploring the orientation and use of textbook lingua-cultural resources to teach and learn English for lingua franca communication. *The Asia-Pacific Education Researcher, 27,* 257–266.

10 English as a lingua franca for Vietnam

Current issues and future directions

My Hau Thi Ho and Hanh Thi Nguyen

Introduction

As the Vietnamese government is making efforts to increase the country's foreign language capacities, a native speaker (NS) model seems to be assumed to be the target of language education. This view is expressed in the description of various language skills in the *Framework of Foreign Language Proficiency for Vietnam* (Ministry of Education and Training of Vietnam, 2014), which frequently references *người bản ngữ* [native L1 speakers] and *giọng chuẩn* [standard pronunciation] as the benchmark for evaluating English users in Vietnam (pp. 9–12, 26, 27). Also, in the specifications for the implementation of Project 2020 (Ministry of Education and Training of Vietnam, 2008), the importance of *giáo viên bản ngữ* [native L1 teachers] is repeatedly stated (pp. 35–39) and universities in Vietnam are encouraged to recruit NS teachers (pp. 34–35). At the National Conference on teaching English at High Schools, broadcast live on Vietnamese television on October 19, 2011, the director of a regional Department of Education and Training in Vietnam criticized English teachers in Vietnam for *nói tiếng Anh theo giọng Việt* [speaking English with a Vietnamese accent]" and considered this a hindrance to learning. This rejection of norm deviance, even in accent, reflects a rigid belief in the NS target.

Globally, concerns about linguistic imperialism (Canagarajah, 1999; Pennycook, 1994; Phillipson, 1992) have led to reactions against the entitlement to ownership of the English language by its NSs (e.g., Alptekin, 2002; Braine, 2010; Cook, 1999; Mahboob, 2010) in favour of the teaching of English as a lingua franca (ELF) or English as an international language (EIL) (e.g., Jenkins, 2006; McKay, 2002; Modiano, 2001; Pakir, 2009; Seidlhofer, 2004). However, until recently, discussions on this issue have involved mainly researchers from or working in the Inner Circle countries (Kachru, 1985), that is, countries such as the UK, United States, Canada, Australia, and New Zealand, in which English has explicit or default official status and most people speak it as a first language. A problem with this imbalance is that the application of "political correctness" and "democracy" by Western ELT can risk "imposing a powerful hegemony of its own" (Waters, 2007, p. 355). Holliday (2007) argued that "English-speaking Western researchers . . . must not presume to speak for, or to represent colleagues or students who locate themselves on the periphery, but simply to learn what they tell us about our own discourse" (p. 365).

Given this direction, Vietnamese users of English should decide for themselves what English varieties are best suited for their needs and goals. The problem is that there is little empirical research on how educators and learners in Vietnam perceive ELF and its use in English education. This study thus seeks to examine Vietnamese teachers' and learners' views regarding ELF and the possibility of teaching and learning ELF in Vietnam.

English as a lingua franca

Definitions

Modiano (2001) conceptualised ELF as "a mode of communication which allows people to interact with others without aligning themselves to ideological positioning indicative of specific mother-tongue speech community" (p. 170).

House (1999) noted that ELF is used in "interactions between members of two or more different linguacultures in English, for none of whom English is the mother tongue" (p. 74). In ELF interactions, speakers often engage in mutual accommodation to facilitate intelligibility (e.g., Firth, 2009; Kaur, 2011; Kirkpatrick, Subhan, & Walkinshaw, 2016); and in many cases, it is the NSs of English who need to accommodate their language use to comply with the norms agreed on by ELF speakers (Jenkins, 2006). Importantly, ELF is not a monolithic variety of English (Jenkins, 2006; Jenkins & Leung, 2019); anyone in international interactions can employ widely used linguistic forms that are intelligible across different groups of speakers of English (Cogo, 2012; Dewey, 2013). When it comes to teaching and learning, however, there is often uncertainty among teachers and students about the relationship between the English they actually use and the English they should teach and learn.

Issues in teaching and learning ELF

Teaching and learning ELF can be problematic because of the difficulty in identifying the specific characteristics of a lingua franca, since the achievement of mutual intelligibility depends on the context of the interactions (Jenkins, 2009). No consistency in form goes beyond the participants, that is, each combination of interactants can negotiate their own variety of lingua franca use in terms of proficiency level, use of code-mixing, degree of pidginisation, and so on.

Proponents of ELF have basically responded to this issue in two ways. One is to uncover core features common to all varieties of ELF based on analysis of a large corpora of ELF communication. Jenkins (2005), for example, referred to Seidlhofer's (2004) Vienna–Oxford International Corpus of English (VOICE) project to recommend common core pronunciation features and lexicogrammatical features for ELF, in contrast with NS pronunciation and lexicogrammar. The premise of these ELF features is that, in practice, even without "good" pronunciation and grammar, people can still communicate effectively. The general purpose of the core feature inventories is to demonstrate the possibilities of codification based on current English usage among non-native speakers (NNSs), whose influence is ignored if the NS model is seen as the only model for practice and teaching. At the same time, these inventories, being developed in the context of Europe, are not intended to be prescriptive for teaching and curriculum development everywhere.

A second solution is to view ELF as embodying the processes and strategies of adaptation by NNSs to attain mutual intelligibility in verbal or written discourse in conversations and Internet communications. These processes and strategies have been identified in studies on ELF interactions (e.g., Cogo & Jenkins, 2010; Firth, 2009; Kaur, 2011; Kirkpatrick, Subhan, and Walkinshaw, 2016; Mauranen & Ranta, 2009). This approach conceptualises language as being constructed in interaction and reflecting the speakers' identities rather than being fixed rules, forms, functions, and pronunciation (Dewey, 2013). With respect to language teaching and learning, a focus on how ELF speakers adapt, invent, and improvise linguistic resources for communicative purposes can be useful guides in assisting learners in classrooms to develop effective pragmatic strategies for more successful intercultural communication and greater cultural awareness.

It has been recommended that the choice of which language standard to use in language teaching and learning "must be made locally, even individually" (Petzold, 2002, p. 424) and must be based on "the uses the learners will make of the language" (Berns, 2006, p. 725). The question is then, "Which choice is preferred in a given context by teachers, students, policymakers, and members of society?" We will next examine what has been found regarding perceptions of ideal English models in Vietnam.

Teachers' and learners' perception of English varieties in Vietnam

Empirical studies on Vietnamese teachers' and learners' language attitudes show that learners typically subscribe to the NS model.

Nguyễn (2013), in a small-scale survey of 17 Vietnamese students studying in the Philippines, revealed that the Vietnamese students preferred NS models of English, i.e., American and British Englishes, and considered other varieties incorrect and unoriginal. This unquestioned preference for the NS model as the target of learning was also found in studies on the teaching and learning of English pronunciation by Vietnamese learners (e.g., Cunningham, 2013). Another survey by Walkinshaw and Duong (2012) revealed that Vietnamese college-level students valued teachers who have experience in teaching, good qualifications, friendly personality, enthusiasm, interesting classes, understanding of students' culture, and, importantly, excellent English abilities. Although overall the students did not prioritise NSs, NS model idealisation was implicitly expressed in their preference for English pronunciation.

Subscription to the NS model while being aware of the reality of actual English use leads to a paradox that Vietnamese teachers and learners face.

Tôn and Phạm (2010), in a survey and interviews with college-level students and teachers in Central Vietnam, found that while the NS variety is preferred in teaching and learning in order to meet curricular and testing demands, the participants also reported speaking English mostly to NNSs in real life. This paradox, which has also been identified in other countries (e.g., Braine, 2010; Holliday, Aboshiha, & Swan, 2015; Mahboob, 2010), points to the tension and contradiction between the current practice of teaching the NS model of English (UK and U.S. varieties) and increased practical need to teach NNS varieties.

Tôn and Phạm (2010) observed that teachers and students alike were ambiguous and confused about the best model for future teaching and learning, since both NS and NNS models had advantages and drawbacks. They suggested that, although there were no simple answers to the paradox, teachers should focus on teaching NS English because (1) students need to be intelligible in global communication, (2) materials for other varieties were not available, and (3) teaching all English varieties is not feasible. They also recommended that students "should be encouraged to explore other varieties through out-of class learning opportunities" (p. 59). In a later study also on college students in Central Vietnam,

Ngô (2013) added that teachers' and learners' preference for an NS model is deeply rooted in the standard language ideology and the reproduction of pedagogies and language values emanated from the West. These ideologies and values are mutually reinforced by teachers and students, and therefore a remedy is to raise teachers' awareness of ELF by incorporating content about ELF in pre- and in-service teacher training programmes.

Research questions

This chapter aims to extend current understandings about learners' and teachers' perceptions about ELF in Vietnam by focusing on how Vietnamese users of English perceive ELF. Rather than making theory-driven suggestions for the future, we aim to find out what Vietnamese users of English consider to be suitable English varieties for Vietnam. Specifically, we attempt to address these questions:

1 What are the teachers' and learners' perceptions of ELF?
2 Which variety/varieties of English do the participants consider the most appropriate to be taught in Vietnam?

Methodology

Participants

Unlike previous studies (e.g., Ngô, 2013; Tôn & Phạm, 2010), we elicited the viewpoints not only of university teachers and regular students but also of working part-time students and employed English major graduates. By covering all four groups, we aim to provide a clearer picture about the reality of actual

English use. Also, to extend current research (Ngô, 2013; Tôn & Ph m, 2010), we recruited participants (evenly distributed) from both a mid-sized urban centre, Huế, and a mega urban centre, Hồ Chí Minh City.

Forty-two participants, representative of all groups, were interviewed in eight face-to-face focus groups (six groups of five and two groups of six). Teachers were grouped together, and current and former students were grouped together. Before the focus group interviews, a face-to-face survey was administered to 240 participants (including the interviewees) with equal representation from each of the four groups. The survey revealed their overall profiles and helped identify trends in their viewpoints, which informed the interview questions. The teachers had an average of 10.7 years of teaching experience (from 6 months to 30 years). Sixty-five percent of the teachers reported using English while abroad, and 61.7% reported using English outside the classroom. The English majors were at intermediate level, with 15% reporting that they used English while abroad, 46.7% reported using English outside class and none reported using English in their jobs. The part-time students were non-traditional students who were working while attending private English classes. They had intermediate-level English, with 13.3% reporting that they used English while abroad, 55% reporting using English outside of class, and 43.3% reporting using English in their jobs. The English major graduates were recent graduates, with 56.7% reporting that they used English while abroad, 55% reported using English outside of class, and 95% reported using English in their jobs. Thus, the part-time students and graduates were the groups with the most experience using English in real life, even more than the teachers.

Instruments

Framed by the research questions and based on the trends revealed by the survey, interview questions were developed. The first author provided participants these questions a few minutes before the start of the focus group interviews. This gave them just enough time to think about the questions without preparing "correct" answers. The researcher used an interview plan as a guide but remained flexible as a moderator and facilitator, which involved initiating the discussion, asking for clarification and using probes when necessary, and moving the discussions on to the next topic when no new content was expressed. The interviews were conducted in the participants' and the researcher's native language, Vietnamese. Extracts presented in this chapter have been translated into English.

Data collection

Participants' consent was obtained and data were collected in accordance with the ethics approval by LaTrobe University (2008). The group interviews were audio recorded and were between 1.5 and 2.5 hours long. The interviews' transcripts totalled 113, 837 words.

Analytical procedure

Following Grounded Theory, axial coding (Strauss & Corbin, 1998) was applied on the group interviews transcripts in order to generate data-driven themes. Responses were entered under headings, and subheadings that were generated by the participants' responses and similar responses were grouped into thematic categories until coding exhausted all categories. The group interviews were interpreted as co-constructed interactions, that is, participants' responses were indexically formulated vis-a-vis the other interviewees and the researcher as a moderator. Thus, when focusing on specific interview responses, we analysed both *what* they said and *how* they said it in order to uncover meanings (Holstein & Gubrium, 2004). This deeper discourse analysis is a step further compared to previous studies on users' perceptions of and attitudes towards English varieties in Vietnam (e.g., Tôn & Phạm, 2010; Ngô, 2013).

Findings

Perceptions of English as a lingua franca

Although most participants were aware of the mismatch between the English norm taught in school and the English varieties in actual use (see also Tôn & Phạm, 2010), they were not familiar with the concept of English as a lingua franca. Only after the interviewer outlined the main characteristics of ELF were they able to express their viewpoints about it. The participants' attitudes towards ELF were mixed and can be categorised as (1) ambivalent, (2) positive, and (3) negative.

Ambivalence towards ELF

The participants' ambivalence towards ELF is seen in comments from about half of the participants in the group interviews, in which they displayed hesitation regarding whether they should observe NS standards or welcome new tendencies. Specifically, some participants expressed excitement and explicitly voiced support for ELF in one part of an interview only to state strong preference for NS English in another part of the interview.

Some participants' ambivalence towards ELF can also be seen in the implicit meanings in their expressed acceptance of ELF, such as in Extract 1.

Extract 1

1   G5: Some people, even native speakers from the UK, when they come
2   here, I noticed that they themselves, they don't really use, they are
3   not so rigid about their culture because they have travelled and
4   worked in a lot of countries, so I see that they have, like, they have,
5   sort of adapted quite well to the cultures of other countries, so I
6   think we shouldn't force ourselves to follow any specific cultural
7   standards.

G5 recognised the possibilities for linguistic and cultural flexibility among NSs. Ironically, in doing so, she was subscribing to a NS model of flexibility. G5 started with a description of what NSs do (lines 1–5) then used "so" (line 5) to indicate the upshot that "we" (Vietnamese) followed suit (lines 5–7).

Positive attitudes towards English as a lingua franca

There were 76 comments indicating clear support for ELF, with the reasons being its flexibility, recognition of local and regional variety, and denial of the absolute superiority of NS English norms and rules. The positive features of ELF mentioned were mutual comprehensibility despite variations, authentic reflection of real-life communication and thus better preparation for students, and the ease to learn ELF compared to NS English, resulting in students being more motivated, more confident, and more encouraged.

It is noteworthy that these viewpoints came mainly from the Huế participants, especially the part-time learners and graduates, who had work experience communicating with NNSs of English. The majority of the Huế part-time learners group even contended that ELF would sooner or later become a tendency that English learners in Vietnam would have to follow. A possible explanation is that more experience in actual English use by the graduates and part-time students may have led to their higher acceptance of variation and diversity. Second, higher tolerance for regional variation in Vietnamese among the Huế participants (Huế is not a major dialect in Vietnam) might have resulted in higher tolerance of variation in English (see, for example, Obeid, 2015, on how learners' attitudes towards language varieties in their L1 can be transferred into the L2).

The participants' acceptance of ELF were expressed at both the abstract general level and the concrete personal level, as seen in Extract 2.

Extract 2

1 *L2*: English is just a tool to connect cultures together.
2   So when we communicate, we have to keep something that belongs
3   to us and we have to be more sensitive to the cultural aspects of our
4   interlocutors, that is we have to be flexible.

L2 displayed linguistic and cultural flexibility (see Baker, 2009; Kaur, 2011; Sweeney & Hua, 2010). She started first with a definition of what English is (line 1), then appealed to the general value of self-identity (lines 2–3), and the value of accommodation to the recipients (lines 3–4).

Extract 3 exemplifies how the participants sometimes related their positive view on ELF with their personal feelings and experiences.

Extract 3

1 *L7*: Also there's a psychological aspect, I think it's important,
2   like when we talk to Indian people and when we talk in Australia.

3   To tell the truth, when we use English in Australia we have to be
4   mindful and talk in certain ways, whereas with Indian people, we
5   talk in a more liberated way, and sometimes we are even praised
6   (for our English).
7   *Several people*: Ah, that's right, because they are like us, we aren't
8   afraid . . . (laugh) we aren't afraid of being judged.
9   *L7*: Then what kind of English are we using that makes us feel so
10   liberated, it's true, you see.
11 *Several people*: Yes, yes, and it seems friendly, yes.

L7 highlighted "psychological aspect" as a reason to support ELF (line 1) and mentioned the positive feeling of being "liberated" and being "praised" (lines 4–5, 10). Similarly, the other participants mentioned being "afraid of being judged," the impression of NNS English being "friendly," and produced laughter with several agreement tokens (lines 7–8, 11), thus orienting to the emotional and personal aspects of using ELF as described by L7. It appears that their acceptance of ELF was argued for on the basis of emotions and personal experience.

Negative attitudes towards English as a lingua franca

A majority of the interview responses, however, were not in favour of ELF. Perceptions of NNS varieties were commonly quite negative. Their rationales for rejecting ELF were preference for NS norms, the artificial nature of ELF, and problems with adopting ELF.

Many participants in all of the groups (31 out of 42) explicitly opted for NS English as a classroom model, with the most frequent reason being that NS accent was preferable. Some commented that people "looked down" on local varieties and that the dominance of NS English should be embraced because it is both inevitable and beneficial in conferring "world ownership" of English. The idea that ELF would encourage more democracy in language use was deemed by the participants to be "impractical." The notion introduced by the interviewer that ELF might offer more equality and resistance to imperialism seemed not to hold sway among the participants, perhaps for two reasons. First, most participants were unaware of the phenomenon of linguistic imperialism. This is an abstract concept that requires some critical examination and reflection, and some participants may not have had the chance to consider it in-depth. Second, as one participant put it, ELF was unrealistic because ultimately most people learn English to serve their practical purposes (i.e., for employment or further education). This was a valid observation and was very relevant to Vietnam. Inequality in employment and higher education due to a difference in English proficiency levels is clear in Vietnam: the salaries of people with better English skills may be ten times higher than their counterparts working in a state-run organisation (Phạm, 2006). Furthermore, those who want to further their studies abroad need to take standardised tests based on British or American English such as the International English Language Testing System (IELTS) test or the Test of

English as a Foreign Language (TOEFL). Behind many of the participants' comments was the recognition that, in the linguistic market, "standard" English has more cultural capital than ELF (see Holborow, 2015).

Those participants who considered NS English natural and ELF artificial based their argument on the fact that NS English is connected with a nation, whereas ELF is a language of no nation. They argued that if language could not be separated from culture, there could not be a culture-free language such as ELF. These concerns and doubts have indeed been expressed by some educators elsewhere (Alptekin, 2002; Llurda, 2004; Modiano, 2001; Tarone, 2005). However, the issue of culture in ELF can be seen in a more empowered and dynamic way.

Smit (2010) advocated for "transcultural identities" (p. 73) in which learners appropriate the target language for their own identity expressions, and Baker (2011) pointed out that "by co-constructing a third space, ELF interactants negotiate their specific 'ELF culture'" (pp. 199–200). That is, with ELF, learners do not have to imitate NSs, they can use English freely in their own way as long as mutual understanding is achieved, and they can share their own cultures rather than conforming to an NS culture. Regarding self-expression, "World Englishes" literatures (Y. Kachru & Smith, 2008) and "contact" literatures (B. Kachru, 1986) are well documented in Outer Circle countries. If ELF is embraced in Expanding Circle countries, similar literatures may develop there. Finally, even the premise that language and culture must be tied together has been disputed (Risager, 2006). The participants' perception of the cultural problem with ELF seems to reflect a lack of self-determinism and commitment to ELF.

By far the most frequently mentioned argument against ELF had to do with the problems it might cause. Overall, however, the participants' responses were often uninformed and revealed a lack of critical reflection. The most important problem with ELF mentioned by the participants was decreased mutual intelligibility among NNSs of English if a large number of variations are accepted (see also Deterding & Kirkpatrick, 2006, regarding the ASEAN context). However, this may be an oversimplified view of communication. When in context and with negotiation of meaning, most issues in understanding can be resolved (e.g., McKay & Bockhorst-Heng, 2008). Another issue with ELF according to many participants is that ELF features are errors (see also Peckham, Kalocsai, Kovács, & Sherman, 2008, as cited in Jenkins, 2009). Some participants even questioned whether learners had to learn "wrong" English. However, Fiedler (2010) pointed out that to perceive deviations from NS norms as errors is to hold a deficit view towards NNS English. A more self-assertive view would be to see learners as "multicompetent speakers" rather than as "failed native speakers" (Cook, 1999, p. 204). The participants' view thus reflects a lack of self-assertion regarding their own English use.

Many participants believed that a consequence of accepting ELF would make English polluted with uncontrollable developments. Some feared that this would lead to a lack of reference for accuracy in their own language use. Teachers admitted that they themselves made errors, so they had to expect even more errors by their students. With a "narrow" NS standard in place, the result would at least be "controllable variations," a much better situation than if "variations of variations" were allowed. The reality of this practical concern has been acknowledged elsewhere (Petzold, 2002). However, this would be a problem only if users continue to subscribe to existing norms. When "errors" are widespread and accepted in a community, they inevitably become new norms, as has been seen in the history of any language as well as in EIL (McKay & Bockhorst-Heng, 2008). The participants' comments, again, reflect an uninformed view regarding the nature of language change and a lack of self-empowerment.

The participants also identified the learning burden resulting from including a large number of variations (29 responses from six out of eight groups). They believed that teaching, learning, and assessment would be jeopardised due to a lack of a codified system. They pointed out that even if ELF features were codified systematically, learners would then have to learn all the different variations/standards, thus adding a learning burden. Therefore, NS standard would be "less complicated" for learning and teaching. The difficulty of reaching common norms in ELF has been pointed out by Mollin (2006) in the context of Europe and Kirkpatrick (2010) in South East Asia. Also, as mentioned, codification has its own thorny problems. Mainly, codification may be constructed at the expense of fluidity, hybridity, and contingency, which is a defining feature of ELF (Ferguson, 2009; Jenkins, Cogo, & Dewey, 2011). Further, the codification of ELF may turn it into a reduced variety of English and, more problematically, a new device for exclusion (Elder & Davies, 2006). However, it is possible that ELF be treated not as a "replacement for traditional EFL" but as a "pedagogical alternative" (Jenkins, 2007, p. xii; see also Phan, 2016). By becoming familiar with variations in context, learners may be able to achieve intelligibility through negotiation, accommodation, and appropriation (Canagarajah, 2007; Kirpatrick, 2016; Leyland, 2011).

Choice of English varieties for Vietnam

Although the participants acknowledged NS English to be difficult, they indicated that they would love to learn it: 31 out of 42 participants advocated NS English as a model for teaching and learning. While this overwhelming preference for NS English is not surprising, what we are more interested in is the participants' suggestions for incorporating ELF in teaching and learning.

The most frequent suggestion across the eight interviews (58 out of 104 interview responses) was that NS English should continue to be a model for teaching and learning. The idea of having ELF as a model was rejected in six out of the eight focus groups. Of note, this rejection was stronger in the HCMC groups, who were also less amenable to the integration of some ELF elements whilst retaining the principal model of NS English. In contrast, some of the participants from Huế, especially the working learners, were willing to experiment. This finding may provide a sliver of hope: as learners engage more with the reality of English outside of class, they may become more open to accepting and learning ELF features.

When the participants did give suggestions for changes in the present state of language teaching and learning, the most prevalent suggestion (46 responses by 22 participants in seven focus groups) was to emphasise learners' communication skills and not require learners to be near-native in speaking, which could build up learners' confidence (see also Honna, 2012, on developing intercultural accommodation skills). Here again, tolerance for variation in pronunciation and even grammar was the most frequent suggestion among the Huế part-time learners. In fact, part-time learners in both HCMC and Huế were more flexible and open with English norms, perhaps because they have had more experience with communicating with NNSs in real life (Extract 4).

Extract 4

1   *H3*: We can accept different ways of speaking, this way is OK, that way
2   is also OK, in general, not to be too strict about pronunciation.
3   Similarly, with writing, different options should be accepted. You
4   can write this way, or that way. For example, presently we accept,
5   let's say, "colour" can be written in the longer or shorter spelling,
6   both are correct. So in the future it's just like that, if you write -s
7   after "look" for third person singular, that's OK, but if you don't,
8   that's OK, too.

H3, a part-time learner, advocated flexibility (line 1) by pointing to the relative norms in NS models (line 3–6) as the basis to accept specific NNS norms (lines 6–8).

The second most frequent suggestion relating to changes in English teaching/learning was about localising language and materials (42 comments by 15 participants in five focus groups). The participants agreed that the language as well as the context of the teaching materials should be familiar to learners and should reflect language use in practice (see also McKay & Bockhorst-Heng, 2008; Tupas, 2010). We noted that the topic of localisation was expressed mainly by Huế participants and more by teachers than by learners. Among the learners, more graduates than current students mentioned this suggestion, perhaps reflecting the impact of real-life communication at the workplace on the recognition of the relevance of local content in teaching materials.

The consensus for language localisation sometimes emerged gradually through discussion rather than being stated up front as a firm position, as seen in Extract 5.

Extract 5

1   *L7*: So it's just in research as Ho7 said before.
2   There needs to be a model, for example, "How are you?" . . .
3   like . . .
4   *Ng7*: That's right, we have to give some situations so that people can
5   understand.
6   *Int*: "Where are you going?" . . . such model

7 *L7*: Yes, yes, you see, so there should be 1 to 2 models that
8   South East Asian ELF speakers often use.
9 *Ho7*: If only South East Asian or Asian nations, for example, use such
10   English for communication among those countries, then they will
11   naturally get used to that, they get used to using that, they'll keep
12   using "Where are you going?" instead of "How are you?" then in
13   about a few . . .
14 *Nh7*: Then people in other places will get used to it and eventually
15   understand it.
16 *Ng7*: Other places will understand.
17 *L7*: If we design our materials in that way, then in about 10 years,
18   our learners will behave like that [Nh7 shows agreement] to a
19   certain extent. If now we develop our materials following such
20   English models . . .
21 *Ho7*: I think it depends on what extent the society will accept and use it.
22 *L7*: "How are you? – Fine, thank you," then down below asking
23   about whether the wife has given birth yet . . . for example. . . . In
24   about 10 years, learners will talk like that.
25 *Ng7*: That's right. I also think so.
26 *L7*: Now we have to start to do it, otherwise we still . . .
27 *Ng7*: Because previously our Asian or Vietnamese people didn't know
28   English. In the past, there was only French in Vietnam. Now that
29   more people who know English will use English in the Asian way,
30   then it will have a different position from the past, won't it?
31 *L7*: Yes . . .

L7 suggested the need for a concrete model for teaching ELF (lines 1–3). Another participant, Ng7, consolidated the idea by adding that specific situations needed to be given to introduce ELF features in context (line 3). When the interviewer forwarded an example of an ELF feature, an expression often used in greetings in Vietnam and Southeast Asia (lines 4–5), L7 agreed enthusiastically (lines 7–8). The other participants projected the success of such an ELF model (lines 9–16), and L7 went further to specify concrete actions teachers could take and the impact of an ELF model in ten years (lines 17–20). One participant (Ho7) expressed a slight hesitation, referring to the contingency of society's acceptance (line 21), but L7 argued for the future of ELF by providing an example of a hypothetical conversation in which the greetings followed an NS model only to become out of place and disjunctive when local content about intimate family affairs were talked about (lines 22–24). L7's position was aligned with that of another participant, Ng7 (line 25), which may have prompted L7 not only to suggest immediate actions but also to point out a potential negative outcome if the current situation were maintained (line 26). Ng7's further support for a future with ELF in Vietnam was based on a contrast with the past and collectivity with other Southeast Asian countries (lines 27–30), to which L7 also agreed (line 31). Thus, through collaborative turns, the participants moved from expressing the need for uptaking the interviewer's concrete example of ELF and developing a clearer sense of an ELF model for teaching, as well as rationales to support the need for such a model.

This idea of forming a regional variety of English echoes Yano (2001), who suggested that English might orient itself around regional varieties because the use of English intra-regionally will be more frequent than inter-regionally. However, being aware of practical challenges in reality, some participants proposed raising awareness for prospective teachers by introducing a component of World Englishes/ELF to the present curriculum of teacher training.

Another proposal from some participants (5 comments) was to increase learners' exposure to real-life English use in the workplace, which, by extension, can increase their exposure to different varieties of English. A graduate suggested that the curriculum include opportunities for learners to interact with English-speaking people outside of class in their local communities. This suggestion reflects this student's perception of the gap between textbook English and real-life English. It is also not a far-fetched suggestion, as experiential learning in ESP has been shown to be highly fruitful (e.g., Bremner, 2012; Lockwood, 2007).

Related to these teaching suggestions, many participants criticised the disconnect between the Ministry's adoption of the Common European Framework of Reference for Languages (CEFR), hence a British English standard, and educators' practical concerns regarding local linguistic and pedagogical factors, as well as students' actual abilities. Furthermore, several participants voiced critical evaluations of parents' and the general public's *sính ngoại* [xenophile] attitude, expressed in their blind preference for NS teachers.

Discussion and future directions

The findings reveal that university students, teachers, and recent graduates had mixed views towards ELF, with a majority having either a negative or an ambivalent attitude and with part-time learners and recent graduates having a higher tendency to accept ELF. The participants' reasons for their positions ranged from personal experience to ideological beliefs and practical concerns. We believe that these findings can contribute to the building of teachers' capacity in several important ways.

First, teachers' capacity can be expanded by increasing self-assertion and self-determination. The participants' positive points about the values and necessity of ELF can empower teachers to introduce English varieties in the curriculum and free themselves as well as their students from a subscription to "standard" English. That NS English is a commodity in the linguistic marketplace in Vietnam and internationally is an undeniable reality. However, rather than accepting and perpetuating this status quo, educators have the responsibility to inform learners about the relevance and importance of local varieties and international varieties of English. This is because another undeniable reality is that, for many learners, having NS proficiency is both unattainable and unnecessary (see also Jenkins & Leung, 2019). The finding that many participants with a negative view towards

ELF were not aware of the notion of linguistic imperialism and were uninformed about how ELF communication actually works suggests that a first step towards preparing learners for the real world is to introduce critical thinking about the historical and cultural contexts of language varieties (see also Matsuda & Friedrich, 2011). Indeed, Widdowson (2013) suggested that the ELF perspective, which associates learning and use more closely than the NS model does, can help learners utilise their own linguistic resources and unique communicative strategies for effective interaction. Learners' ability to adapt their linguistic resources in communication should not be underestimated (Sung, 2013). Our data hinted that when participants felt that they could express themselves freely, or when they collaborated in discussions, they were more open to accepting norms other than the NS model. This suggests that when users of English as a second language felt empowered, their acceptance of NNS norms could become a closer possibility.

Teachers wishing to introduce ELF to their students can review the participants' specific concerns about ELF that are reported above in order to inform their intervention efforts to increase students' acceptance of ELF. Anticipating students' reservations and referring to historical and contemporary evidence in Vietnam and other countries can help debunk misconceptions about ELF. Further, given the finding that those with more real-world experience using English were more open to ELF, another step to increase teachers' capacity would be to expose themselves as well as their students to authentic materials in different English varieties and to seek and create opportunities to engage in real-life interactions outside of the classroom, both face-to-face and online. Through these direct experiences, learners may be able to recognise, accept, and embrace different NNS varieties (see also Mansfield & Poppi, 2012; Nero, 2012; Ngô, 2013; Tôn & Phạm, 2010).

The participants' discussion of ELF's future in Vietnam also provided important suggestions for policymaking to build teachers' capacity. Their dissatisfaction with externally based language standards suggests that future policies need to be connected with the reality of language teaching and learning in Vietnam, where NNS varieties are more relevant than NS standards. In keeping with local reality, language policies should not normalise and perpetuate linguistic imperialism. Explicit statements of acceptance of NNS varieties and clear guidelines about how they may be integrated into teaching curricula will help pave the way for a future in which learners are ready for real-world communication and feel confident and proud of their own language varieties.

References

Alptekin, C. (2002). Towards intercultural communicative competence in ELT. *ELT Journal, 56*(1), 57–64.

Baker, W. (2009). The cultures of English as a lingua franca. *TESOL Quarterly, 43*(4), 567–592.

Baker, W. (2011). Culture and identity through ELF in Asia: Fact or fiction? In A. Archibald, A. Cogo, & J. Jenkins (Eds.), *Latest trends in ELF research* (pp. 35–52). Newcastle upon Tyne: Cambridge Scholars Publishing.

Berns, M. (2006). World Englishes and communicative competence. In B. Kachru, Y. Kachru, & C. L. Nelson (Eds.), *The handbook of world Englishes* (pp. 718–730). Singapore: Blackwell Publishing.

Braine, G. (2010). *Non-native-speaker English teachers: Research, pedagogy, and professional growth*. New York: Routledge.

Bremner, S. (2012). Socialization and the acquisition of professional discourse: A case study in the PR industry. *Written Communication, 29*(1), 7–32.

Canagarajah, A. S. (1999). On EFL teachers, awareness, and agency. *ELT Journal, 53*(3), 207–214.

Canagarajah, S. (2007). Lingua franca English, multilingual communities, and language acquisition. *The Modern Language Journal, 91*(Focus Issue), 923–939.

Cogo, A. (2012). English as a lingua franca: Concepts, use, and implications. *ELT Journal, 66*(1), 97–105.

Cogo, A., & Jenkins, J. (2010). English as a lingua franca in Europe: A mismatch between policy and practice. *European Journal of Language Policy, 2*(2), 271–294.

Cook, V. (1999). Going beyond the native speaker in language teaching. *TESOL Quarterly, 33*(2), 185–209.

Cunningham, U. (2013). Teachability and learnability of English pronunciation features for Vietnamese-speaking learners. In E. Waniek-Klimczak & L. R. Shockey (Eds.), *Teaching and researching English accents in native and non-native speakers* (pp. 3–14). Berlin: Springer-Verlag.

Deterding, D., & Kirkpatrick, A. (2006). Emerging South East Asian Englishes and intelligibility. *World Englishes, 25*(3–4), 391–409.

Dewey, M. (2013). The distinctiveness of English as a lingua franca. *ELT Journal, 67*(3), 346–349.

Elder, C., & Davies, A. (2006). Assessing English as a lingua franca. *Annual Review of Applied Linguistics, 26*, 282–301.

Ferguson, G. (2009). Issues in researching English as a lingua franca: A conceptual enquiry. *International Journal of Applied Linguistics, 19*(2), 117–135.

Fiedler, S. (2010). The English-as-a-lingua-franca approach – Linguistic fair play? *Language Problems & Language Planning, 34*(3), 201–221.

Firth, A. (2009). The "lingua franca" factor. *Intercultural Pragmatics, 6*(2), 147–170.

Holborow, M. (2015). *Language and neoliberalism*. London and New York: Routledge.

Holliday, A. (2007). Response to "ELT and 'the spirit of the times'". *ELT Journal, 61*(4), 360–365.

Holliday, A., Aboshiha, P., & Swan, A. (2015). *(En)countering native-speakerism: Global perspectives*. New York: Palgrave Macmillan.

Holstein, J., & Gubrium, J. (2004). The active interview. In D. Silverman (Ed.), *Qualitative research: Theory, method, and practice* (2nd ed., pp. 140–161). London: Sage Publications.

Honna, N. (2012). The pedagogical implications of English as a multicultural lingua franca. *Journal of English as a Lingua Franca, 1*(1), 191–197.

House, J. (1999). Misunderstanding in intercultural communication: Interactions in English as a lingua franca and the myth of mutual intelligibility. In C. Gnutzmann (Ed.), *Teaching and learning English as a global language* (pp. 73–89). Tübingen: Stauffenburg.

Jenkins, J. (2005). Teaching pronunciation for English as a Lingua Franca: A sociopolitical perspective. In C. Gnutzmann & F. Intemann (Eds.), *The globalisation of*

English and the English language classroom (pp. 145–158). Göttingen and Tübingen: Gunter Narr.

Jenkins, J. (2006). Current perspectives on teaching world Englishes and English as a lingua franca. *TESOL Quarterly, 40*(1), 157–181.

Jenkins, J. (2007). *English as a lingua franca: Attitude and identity.* Oxford: Oxford University Press.

Jenkins, J. (2009). English as a lingua franca: Interpretations and attitudes. *World Englishes, 28*(2), 200–207.

Jenkins, J., Cogo, A., & Dewey, M. (2011). Review of developments in research into English as a lingua franca. *Language Teaching, 44*(3), 281–315.

Jenkins, J., & Leung, C. (2019). From mythical 'standard' to standard reality: The need for alternatives to standardized English language tests. *Language Teaching, 52*(1), 86–110.

Kachru, B. (1985). Standards, codification, and sociolinguistic realism: The English language in the outer circle. In R. Quirk & H. Widdowson (Eds.), *English in the world: Teaching and learning the language and the literature.* Cambridge: Cambridge University Press.

Kachru, B. (1986). *The alchemy of English: The spread, functions, and models of non-native Englishes.* Oxford: Pergamon.

Kachru, Y., & Smith, L. E. (2008). *Cultures, contexts, and world Englishes.* New York and London: Routledge.

Kaur, J. (2011). Intercultural communication in English as a lingua franca: Some sources of misunderstanding. *Intercultural Pragmatics, 8*(1), 93–116.

Kirkpatrick, A. (Ed.). (2010). *The Routledge handbook of world Englishes.* New York: Routledge.

Kirkpatrick, A., Subhan, S., & Walkinshaw, I. (2016). English as a lingua franca in East and Southeast Asia: Implications for diplomatic and intercultural communication. In P. Friedrich (Ed.), *English for diplomatic purposes* (pp. 75–93). Bristol: Multilingual Matters.

Leyland, C. (2011). For mutual intelligibility, must English as a Lingua Franca be standardised? *ARECLS, 8*, 25–45.

Llurda, E. (2004). Non-native-speaker teachers and English as an international language. *International Journal of Applied Linguistics, 14*(3), 314–323.

Lockwood, J. (2007). An interdisciplinary approach to teaching adults English in the workplace. In J. Cummins & C. Davison (Eds.), *International handbook of English language teaching* (pp. 403–412). New York: Springer.

Mahboob, A. (Ed.). (2010). *The NNEST lens: Non-native English speakers in TESOL.* Newcastle upon Tyne: Cambridge Scholars Publishing.

Mansfield, G., & Poppi, F. (2012). The English as a foreign language/lingua franca debate: Sensitising teachers of English as a foreign language towards teaching English as a lingua franca. *Profile Issues in Teachers' Professional Development, 14*(1), 159–172.

Matsuda, A., & Friedrich, P. (2011). English as an international language: A curriculum blueprint. *World Englishes, 30*(3), 332–344.

Mauranen, A., & Ranta, E. (Eds.). (2009). *English as a lingua franca: Studies and findings.* Newcastle upon Tyne: Cambridge Scholars Publishing.

McKay, S. L. (2002). *Teaching English as an international language: An introduction to the role of English as an international language and its implications for language teaching.* Oxford: Oxford University Press.

McKay, S. L., & Bockhorst-Heng, W. D. (2008). *International English in its socio-linguistic contexts: Towards a socially sensitive EIL pedagogy.* New York: Blackwell.

Ministry of Education and Training of Vietnam. (2008). *Đề án dạy và học ngoại ngữ trong hệ thống giáo dục quốc dân giai đoạn 2008–2020* [Project to teach and learn foreign languages in the national education system in 2008–2020]. Ministry of Education and Training of Vietnam.

Ministry of Education and Training of Vietnam. (2014). *Ban hành khung năng lực ngoại ngữ 6 bậc dành cho Việt Nam* [Implementing the 6-level proficiency framework for Vietnam]. Ministry of Education and Training of Vietnam.

Modiano, M. (2001). Ideology and the ELT practitioner. *International Journal of Applied Linguistics, 11*(2), 159–173.

Mollin, S. (2006). English as a lingua franca: A new variety in the new expanding circle? *Nordic Journal of English Studies, 5*(2), 41–57.

Nero, S. (2012). Languages without borders: TESOL in a transient world. *TESL Canada Journal, 29*(2), 143.

Ngô, L. H. P. (2013). *An investigation into Vietnamese teachers' and students' perception of English as a Lingua Franca.* Unpublished MA Thesis, University of Southampton.

Nguyễn, D. C. (2013). Cultural diversity in English language teaching: Learners' voices. *English Language Teaching, 6*(4), 1–7.

Obeid, S. A. (2015). The transfer of L1 attitudes towards L2 varieties: A preliminary investigation. *TESOL Working Paper Series, 13*, 31–52.

Pakir, A. (2009). English as a lingua franca: Analyzing research frameworks in international English, world Englishes, and ELF. *World Englishes, 28*(2), 224–235.

Pennycook, A. (1994). *The Cultural politics of English as an international language.* London: Longman.

Peckham, D., Kalocsai, K., Kovács, E., & Sherman, T. (2008). English and multilingualism, or English only in a multilingual Europe? In *Languages in a Network of Excellence in Europe*, unpublished project report, Work Package 7.

Petzold, R. (2002). Toward a pedagogical model for ELT. *World Englishes, 21*(3), 422–426.

Phạm, H. H. (2006). The global spread of English: Ethical and pedagogic implications for ESL/EFL teachers. *Journal of Asia TEFL, 3*(1), 21–32.

Phan, L. H. (2016). English and identity: A reflection and implications for future research. *Journal of Asian Pacific Communication, 26*(2), 348–355.

Phillipson, R. (1992). *Linguistic imperialism.* Oxford: Oxford University Press.

Risager, K. (2006). *Language and culture: Global flows and local complexity.* Clevedon: Multilingual Matters.

Seidlhofer, B. (2004). Research perspectives on teaching English as a Lingua Franca. *Annual Review of Applied Linguistics, 24*(1), 209–239.

Smit, U. (2010). *English as a lingua franca in higher education* (Vol. 2). Berlin: De Gruyter Mouton.

Strauss, A., & Corbin, J. (1998). *Basics of qualitative research: Techniques and procedures for developing grounded theory* (2nd ed.). Thousand Oaks, CA: Sage Publications.

Sung, C. C. M. (2013). English as a lingua franca and English language teaching: A way forward. *ELT Journal, 67*(3), 350–353.

Sweeney, E., & Hua, Z. (2010). Accommodating toward your audience. Do native speakers of English know how to accommodate their communication strategies toward non-native speakers of English? *Journal of Business Communication, 47*(4), 477–504.

Tarone, E. (2005). Schools of fish: English for access to international academic and professional communities. *The Journal of Asia TEFL, 2*(1), 1–20.

Tôn, N. N. H., & Phạm, H. H. (2010). Vietnamese teachers' and students' perceptions of global English. *Language Education in Asia, 1*(1), 48–61.

Tupas, T. R. F. (2010). Which norms in everyday practice: And why? In A. Kirkpatrick (Ed.), *The Routledge handbook of world Englishes* (pp. 567–579). New York: Routledge.

Walkinshaw, I., & Duong, T. H. O. (2012). Native- and non-native speaking English teachers in Vietnam: Weighing the benefits. *TESL-EJ, 16*(3), 1–17.

Waters, A. (2007). ELT and "the spirit of the times". *ELT Journal, 61*(4), 353–359.

Widdowson, H. G. (2013). ELF and EFL: What's the difference? Comments on Michael Swan. *Journal of English as a Lingua Franca, 2*(1), 187–193.

Yano, Y. (2001). World Englishes in 2000 and beyond. *World Englishes, 20*(2), 119–131.

11 Building teacher capacity for ELT in Vietnam

Ways forward

Le Van Canh and Roger Barnard

A language education policy in practice is part of what Cochran-Smith (2003) terms the "unforgivable complexity of teaching," a reality that is discussed and acknowledged throughout this volume. The crucial theme that emerges in most of the chapters in this volume is the tension between what is intended by policymakers and what is implemented by teachers in their classrooms (Ball, 2006; Grassick & Wedell, 2018; Li, 2010). The tension is attributed to multiple causes, such as innovations in curricula and assessment, but perhaps the most important are learner- and teacher-related factors (Liddicoat & Baldauf, 2008). It has been commonly recognised (Hu, 2002; Li, 1998; Li & Baldauf, 2010; Nunan, 2003) that unsuccessful implementation of language education policies is due to the failure to consider the specific challenges that teachers confront in their teaching practices.

Curricular innovations

Common European Framework of Reference for Languages (CEFR)

Perhaps the most important of these challenges are significant shifts in the perception of the language to be taught and assessed. In the case of Vietnam, the Ministry of Education and Training (MOET) has decided to use the Common European Framework of References for Languages (CEFR) as an instrument of its policy to mandate proficiency levels for different groups of learners and teachers. It is hoped that this will give a new impetus to the desired outcomes in teaching and learning English as an international language.

The problem of the decision to use the CEFR lies in the assumption of its context-independent nature. As Krumm (2007, p. 667) puts it:

> [I]n a world of social, cultural, and individual heterogeneity, one instrument and approach can neither address all situations and contexts nor meet all needs. Although the CEFR is not intended to be applied uniformly to everybody, in some cases it is applied in just such a fashion.

In Chapter 1, Le explains that the introduction of CEFR in Vietnam has been abrupt and hasty without adequately considering its contextual constraints. The framework has been adopted as an assessment blueprint, and a locally developed language proficiency test has been introduced called Vietnamese Standardised Test of English Proficiency (VSTEP), but without changing the criteria for the different levels of proficiency. The lack of credibility in VSTEP has led many universities to abandon VSTEP in favour of internationally recognised proficiency tests such as IELTS (International English Language Testing System) and TOEFL (Test of English as a Foreign Language). In short, the introduction of the CEFR into the national benchmarking of English proficiency, which is forcefully supported by political and educational authorities, has created enormous demands on both learners and teachers. Trim's (1996, p. 282) observation that "there will always be people who are trying to use it as an instrument of power" is correct in the case of Vietnam.

English as a lingua franca (ELF)

Although communicative competence has been defined as the goal of English language learning and teaching in Vietnam, communication needs to be reconceptualised. The ability of communicating in English in diverse contexts is now considered more important than linguistic accuracy, invariably measured according to the standards of native-speaking users of the language. In many, if not most parts of the world, communication in English most frequently occurs among speakers of English using the language as a lingua franca (ELF). This raises new questions about the generalisability of the CEFR to all languages and varieties (Leung, 2013; McNamara, 2012; Pilkinton-Pihko, 2013; Seidlhofer, 2003). For instance, Pilkinton-Pihko (2013) illustrates the prominence of specific native speaker (NS) language ideologies in the CEFR, which, she concludes, limit the ability of applying the framework to ELF contexts. As a result, Hynninen (2014) calls for the need to consider the CEFR from an ELF perspective and to consider the limitations of the framework when dealing with ELF communication. In the era of globalisation, communication involving non-native speakers is perceived as a realistic situation that Vietnamese learners will be facing and need to be prepared for. This clearly has implications for policymakers, curriculum developers, and educational institutions alike

The issue was discussed by Ho and Nguyen in Chapter 10 of this volume. Their focus group discussions revealed that university students, teachers, and recent graduates had mixed views towards ELF. However, the authors felt that, when they collaborated in discussions, their participants were open to accepting norms other than the NS model because they were dissatisfied with externally based proficiency standards. The authors suggested that future policies need to be connected with the reality of language teaching and learning in Vietnam, where NNS varieties are more relevant than NS standards.

Intercultural communicative competence (ICC)

The move away from "native speakerism" has also had another impact on the English language curriculum in Vietnam: one of the important objectives of the

NFLP 2020 is to develop Vietnamese speakers' ability to communicate in English in multilingual and multicultural contexts. In other words, intercultural communicative competence (ICC) should be one of the important goals of English language education in Vietnam. According to Byram and Fleming (1998, p. 11):

> Instead of the assumption that learners should model themselves on the "native speaker," it is becoming apparent to teachers and their learners that successful cross-cultural communication depends on the acquisition of abilities to understand different modes of thinking and living, as they are embodied in the language to be learnt, and to reconcile or mediate between different modes present in any specific interaction. This is not the "communicative competence" on which people using the same language in the same, or closely related, cultures rely; it is an "intercultural communicative competence" which has some common ground with communicative competence, but which also has many unique characteristics.

This issue was considered in Chapter 9 by Nguyen and Cao in their evaluation of the extent to which ICC has been promoted in upper secondary school textbooks. They found that, although there are moves in the books to globalise their cultural contents, they do not fully enable teachers to develop intercultural awareness among their students. The authors recommended that efforts should be made to sensitise teachers to the importance of ICC and (as Byram and Fleming said) its "unique characteristics" and that they should be guided to systematically evaluate and effectively customise the coverage in the textbooks.

Given the fact that a great majority of learners need to learn ELF for intercultural communication, teacher education institutions in Vietnam should be prompted to engage both pre-service and in-service EFL teachers in appropriate reflection-based activities that will empower them in promoting their learners' cultural identities and in alleviating negative attitudes towards non-native varieties of English (Sifakis, 2009). This is really a great challenge in Vietnamese context where teaching is perceived as covering the prescribed textbook and where effective EFL teaching is assessed in terms of examination pass rates, while both teachers' and students' proficiency is assessed against the native speakers' norms.

English as the medium of instruction (EMI)

Another curricular innovation promoted by NFLP 2020 has been the recent introduction of university programmes taught through the medium of English. In this respect, Vietnam is following the trend across Asian universities, following the lead from Europe.

> Such has been the spread and speed of this development that Ernesto Macaro (2018) has likened it to an unstoppable train running off the rails. Using a different metaphor, Robert Philippson described it as a pandemic.
>
> (Barnard, 2018, p. 1)

The reason for these alarming images is that EMI policies are almost invariably imposed by government and/or university authorities without investigating or even fully considering the readiness of staff and students to deal with the complexity of teaching or learning in a second language.

In Chapter 7, Nhung reported a qualitative study in which she interviewed Vietnamese lecturers to elicit their perspectives on the implementation EMI in four universities. Her findings suggested that although her participants saw that EMI could benefit their students as well as their own professional careers, some of them lacked adequate English proficiency, and the majority had had no formal training in appropriate pedagogical techniques. Adequate resources and facilities were usually unavailable. Consequently, the lecturers felt under considerable stress. In this respect, the findings concur with those reported elsewhere in the Asian region (e.g., Ryan, 2018). Nhung concludes that poorly implemented EMI programmes waste resources and lead to distress among students, as well as teachers. The issue in Vietnam is not whether to adopt EMI but to devise ways to minimise its problems and maximise its benefits. Shohamy (2013) argues that the move to EMI requires not only "a big shift in the approach to language teaching" (p. 197) but also the acceptance of a superior status and prestige of English to the national language. This is unlikely to happen in Vietnam, at least in the near future. The Vietnamese deputy prime minister, Vu Duc Dam, has recently responded to the proposal of elevating English to the second language in Vietnam that no foreign language is given the status of second or third language in Vietnam (*Dan Tri*, December 12, 2018). Therefore, "the adoption of bilingual supportive scaffolding practices" (Doiz, Lasagabaster & Sierra (2013, p. 213) or "translanguaging" (Garcia & Wei, 2014, p. 80), according to which language takes on the role of medium- and content-accommodating "bilingual language practices" (Garcia & Wei, 2014, p. 80) of all participants is worth considering.

Computer-assisted language learning (CALL)

Another national innovation promoted by the Ministry of Education and Training has been the enhancement and increase of CALL programmes in Vietnamese universities. It has been maintained that "globalization is effected by two inseparable mediation tools, technology and English; and to respond to the rapid changes brought about by globalization, all countries have been trying to ensure that they are adequately equipped with these two skills" (Tsui and Tollefson, 2007, p. 1).

In Chapter 8, Nhat reported the impact of a CALL training course on five university lecturers' teaching of listening skills and the contextual factors that influenced their use of CALL technology. Her findings revealed that, several months after the training course, the participants made very little use of CALL technology and in particular of the Moodle platform that was heavily promoted in the course. The interview data identified many interrelated factors that limited the teachers' adoption of Moodle as well as the implementation of CALL in general. They included the lack of a link between CALL training and teaching practices, inadequate guidelines for CALL implementation, and limited access to facilities and Internet connections. The author concluded that, given that MOET plans to run more CALL training courses over the next several years, steps need to be taken to enhance lecturer's technical skills and confidence to use CALL technology effectively and autonomously. She suggested that this might be achieved through open communication and collaborative effort on the part of all stakeholders.

Teacher competence

Maintaining and developing teachers' expertise and good practices are essential for successful education and an international concern (Avalos, 2011). The implications of all the chapters in the book reviewed so far lead inevitably to the central importance of the teaching and learning context to the success or otherwise of curricular innovations. The authors of each of these chapters have made specific recommendations to raise the competence of the teachers concerned. More generally, teacher competence, demonstrated in their effective teaching, is key to the achievement of the goals of ELT in Vietnam and indeed in any context (Wedell, 2008). That teachers play a decisive role in the implementation of the language-in-education policy is uncontroversial. So is the role played by pre-service and in-service teacher education in developing teacher capacity (Freeman & Johnson, 1998). Four of the other chapters in this book have used the findings of case studies to critique key aspects of teachers' professional development envisaged by the NFLP 2020: pre-service education; in-service programmes; and the lack of attention paid to emotional factors.

Pre-service English language teacher education (PELTE)

In Chapter 2, Vu and Dudzik pointed out that PELTE programmes are foundational in building teacher capacity. They applied a multi-method approach to data collection to critique the effectiveness of the PELTE curriculum at leading English teacher education institutions. Data derived from documents, survey, interviews, and focus groups were analysed using Vietnam's English Teacher Competencies Framework (ETCF). The authors found that the student-teachers were given a solid foundation in certain of the framework's domains, such as knowledge of SLA theories, literary content, and technology. Professional values and processes such as reflection, research, cooperation and collaboration, creativity and critical thinking were also moderately represented. However, more than 42% of the competencies defined in the ETCF were weakly represented in the syllabi, including most of Domain 5 – learning in and from practice and being informed by context. These findings led the authors to make a number of suggestions for improving the ETCF. These included prioritising the competences to meet the needs of teachers in their real-life teaching, establishing effective apprenticeship of observation, and providing student-teachers with authentic pedagogic tasks, classroom case studies, and real teaching experiences. The authors concluded that the curriculum demonstrated a move towards a more comprehensive preparation of pre-service teachers' capacity. However, as there were limited connections between their education and real-life practices, much of the curriculum seemed to fall short of the students' expectations, and they questioned their own professional readiness. These findings are not surprising. There is widespread agreement in the second language teacher education literature that while pre-service teacher training is necessary, it fails to prepare teachers adequately for their real-life practices (e.g., Farrell, 2012; Mann, 2005) because the language class "is an arena of subjective and intersubjective realities which are worked out, changed, and maintained. . . . [These activities] continually specify and mould the activities of teaching and learning" (Breen, 2001, p. 28). Burns and Knox (2011, p. 19) view the language classroom as a complex and dynamic system where "unforeseen (and unidentified) factors can have an unpredictable impact, [and] the participants . . . are in a state of flux." Therefore, pre-service training needs to be bridged with in-service training (Farrell, 2012).

Mandatory in-service training (INSET)

In Chapter 4, the capacity-building potential of INSET was discussed by Le in terms of the effectiveness of the government-funded programmes provided by the NFLP 2020 Management Board and run by university staff. He held focus groups of a hundred randomly selected primary and secondary teachers working in 11 provinces, all of whom had completed either a 50-hour methodology course or a 120-hour language improvement course mandated by MOET. He also observed lessons taught by 53 of the teachers in all the 11 provinces. His focus group data indicated that the teachers were dissatisfied with the content and organisation of the courses: they felt that the courses did not meet their needs, and attendance at the courses became a burden as they had to complete daily work-related and family responsibilities; they also felt humiliated because they were viewed by others as underqualified. The observational data revealed that they were unable to put into practice the methods and techniques recommended in the INSET courses, many of which were irrelevant to their actual contexts; they tended to revert to their conventional (and ineffective) practices. In conclusion, Le argues that, in the present circumstances, mandatory INSET courses should remain the dominant approach to professional development for practising English teachers in Vietnam because of teachers' limited opportunities for a dialogical engagement with globally emerging discourses. However, he suggests that they should be supported with locally appropriate policies that could motivate every teacher to become a lifelong learner and should take into account the teachers' knowledge, beliefs, and emotions so that a local path to a stronger professional identity can be constructed for individual teachers. As INSET is necessary to the updating of teachers' knowledge and teaching skills, at least in Vietnamese contexts, radical changes in the INSET approach are needed. We would recommend a constructivist curriculum that is designed on the basis of teachers' perceived needs. More importantly, follow-up monitoring and support strategies should be incorporated in future courses to fill the gap between INSET input and teachers' contextually situated needs. These strategies would be intended to encourage teachers to try out the new teaching ideas provided in the INSET course and to provide feedback on their classroom teaching as well as the kinds of adjustments they feel are needed. Without these strategies, INSET can hardly result in the desired level of "follow-up," i.e., impact on teachers' conceptual changes and their classroom practices (Waters, 2006). Follow-up support is particularly fundamental to Vietnamese teachers, who, influenced by the Buddhist view of knowledge, tend to privilege knowledge that is acquired through everyday experience more than the abstract or theoretical knowledge that is formally provided.

In a similar vein, Nguyen, Phan, and Le, in Chapter 5, call for radical changes in teachers' professional development by moving beyond the concept of learning in one-off workshops, lectures, or seminars towards collaborative and needs-based learning. Viewed from Vygotsky's (1978) developmental theories, "mediated activity" is essential to the development of higher psychological functions. Accordingly, collaboration is essential to the professional development of teachers. However, while collaboration can be a beneficial process in teachers' learning, it is important to note that teachers' engagement in collaborative learning is multidimensional and resource bounded. Duncombe and Armour (2004) clarify the difference between productive collaborative opportunities and unproductive everyday discussions in the forms of experience swapping, sympathy, and support. Thus, for collaboration to be effective to the professional development of teachers, it must be structured. In Vietnam, because a great majority of EFL teachers work in resource-poor environments, they are rarely facilitated to view teaching from angles other than their tacit knowledge shaped by their collective beliefs (Le, 2011). Hardly do they have the opportunities to reflect together on their work practices or to review the underlying theoretical knowledge of teaching and learning (Day, 1999; Farrell, 2015, 2019). Neither do they have regular access to asymmetrical collaboration in a scaffolded setting that contains different levels of support or facilitation within a group (Le, 2019). This raises the need to research and develop local scaffolded settings when a facilitator with a higher level of expertise is accessible and can facilitate professional discussion or support finding a solution.

Teacher language proficiency

Language proficiency is believed to constitute a core dimension of second language teachers' professional competence. Every English language teacher is required to achieve a certain level of proficiency in the language to teach it so that we can serve as models for our students and provide them with valuable language input that can help them learn. However, there is still no agreed-upon level of proficiency that an English language teacher needs to teach effectively, and there may never be because the requirement varies from context to context. As mentioned by Le (Chapter 1) and Grassick (Chapter 3), benchmarks referenced to the CEFR have been established for teachers in Vietnam. The aim is for 100% of teachers to meet the required threshold level: CEFR B2 for primary teachers and CEFR C1 for lower secondary school teachers. These benchmarks are unrealistically high, and a majority of in-service teachers are unsurprisingly unable to achieve them despite great national and personal investment. The problem is that it is not clear whether teachers' improved English proficiency leads to their improved classroom practices. As Richards (2017, p. 28) has noted:

> The relationship between the language proficiency of language teachers' and their ability to teach in the language is complex, and often problematic both for teachers who recognise limitations in their language abilities as well as for providers of training and professional development programmes for teachers.

Richards goes on to argue that while "language knowledge and ability is [sic] central to the professional identity of language teachers . . . language proficiency and teaching ability are not the same thing" (p. 28). To address this complexity, Freeman and Katz (Chapter 6), drawing on their experience in Vietnamese and other EFL contexts, redefine the relationship between language proficiency and classroom pedagogy through their English-for-teaching – a type of English for specific purpose – initiative. Despite the ideological view on teachers' language proficiency, it is neither realistic nor necessary to expect teachers working in bi/multilingual environments to acquire a high overall proficiency. It seems that English-for-teaching is much more achievable for teachers to learn and allows them to manage their classrooms in English and still provide their students with valuable language input. However, more research is needed to address the potential challenges of the crossover between English-for-teaching and overall English proficiency.

Emotional factors

The issue of building and developing teacher capacity in response to the requirements of new language-in-education policies in diverse contexts has been complicated by new insights in the process of teacher learning. Viewed from a social cognitive perspective in psychology (Golombek & Doran, 2014; Kubanyiova, 2012), teacher learning is an emotionally driven process. For example, Golombek and Doran (2014, p. 105) maintain, "Emotion, cognition, and activity continuously interact and influence each other, on both conscious and unconscious levels, as teachers plan, enact, and reflect on their teaching." Thus, not only are emotions vital to teacher learning, but they are also influential to teachers' changes in teaching practices.

The role of emotion in teacher learning (Woff & De Costa, 2017) is further supported by Grassick (Chapter 3), who conducted a series of semi-structured individual interviews with six experienced primary teachers working in urban or rural schools. They had all followed a three-month language and methodology course intended to equip them with the enhanced linguistic knowledge and appropriate pedagogical skills to deal with the new communicative primary English curriculum. The interview data revealed that the courses gave rise to feelings of uncertainty about what was expected of them and doubts about their professional competence. The support they received was insufficient and irrelevant to their classroom realities, and this, compounded by the very limited opportunities to practise and use the language outside the classroom, led them to "muddle along as best they could." There was an absence of collegial collaboration, giving rise to feelings of isolation and anxiety. Grassick concludes that her small-scale study attempted to bring attention to the emotionality of educational change so that those involved in policy planning and implementation might appreciate that educational change is "socially complex" (Fullan, 2015). The study emphasised the need to look beyond a technical-managerial process of language policy change to a greater understanding of the role that teachers' feelings and emotional experiences play. Research on the mutually constitutive effects of agency, identity, emotion, and conceptual change for language teachers is needed to gain deeper insights into the social origins of affect and its dynamic relationship to cognitive development, as well as to the reconstruction of agency and identity. From sociocultural perspectives, emotions deserve theoretical status equal to that of cognition (Verity, 2000).

Further research and professional development

Educational policies, like all others, should be informed by research carefully conducted before they are formulated and implemented. However, for the innovations discussed this book, it is too late to "look before you leap" by undertaking exploratory research to consider the feasibility of what is proposed. Nhung said in the conclusion to her chapter, "The issue in Vietnam is not whether to adopt English Medium Instruction but to devise ways to minimise its problems and maximise its benefits." The same applies to the curricular innovations reported in the other chapters. One way to do this is for MOET to set up an archive of abstracts of all relevant research carried out in Vietnam relating to such innovations and make a continuously updated register of these details available to potential and actual researchers. Some of these might well be commissioned by MOET to undertake specific projects; university departments and staff might also follow up on the implications of studies conducted in areas of interest.

In the light of what has been said in the previous three sections, it is clear that any research needs to be conducted holistically – taking an ecological perspective of as much as possible of the complex interplay of factors. There is some value in collecting quantitative data from (quasi-)experiments and surveys as support for other data. However, a need in educational research should be, as we said in the introduction to this final chapter, to identify, address, and – hopefully – solve the *specific* challenges that teachers confront in their teaching practice. Therefore, the bias should be towards interpretive research that explores phenomena occurring in their natural settings: for example, observation of lessons taught by teachers in their normal classes, and the beliefs, knowledge, skills, and experience of those intended to be involved in any particular curriculum innovation. This implies that such research should be conducted within the case study paradigm: only by the in-depth investigation of a small number of people, places, and events can one seek to understand the complex reality of teaching. Of course, case studies cannot be replicable or their findings generalised, but the accumulation of such studies enables a portfolio to be built upon which to base policies that would be context sensitive.

There are many approaches to collecting qualitative data: conventional means such as interviews and observations; approaches such as focus groups, stimulated recall sessions, and think-aloud protocols; narratives derived from diaries, reflective journals, and narrative frames; collaborative methods such as peer observation, shared tasks, and joint lesson planning. These are carefully explained in research methods textbooks (e.g., Cohen, Manion & Morrison, 2018), and several have been illustrated in collections of methodological case studies (e.g., Barnard & Burns (2012). It is also important that such data should be subjected to the systematic process of grounded analysis (Charmaz, 2014), whereby data from various sources are collated, triangulated, and constantly interrogated to identify convergences and divergences among them, so that common patterns and themes emerge. By this means, the data are allowed to "speak for themselves" so that researchers can devise a situated explanation for their findings. Doing so would prevent the data being squeezed into or ignored by decontextualised categories provided by predetermined theoretical frameworks.

Much has been said in this book about the professional development of teachers, and at this late stage, we would like to draw attention to the common view that teachers should be provided with relevant contextualised ideas, materials, and methods in structured programmes. There is obviously a need for this, but a truly authentic approach to capacity building should start from the teachers themselves. Perhaps the most important skill that can be developed among teachers is systematic reflective practice (Farrell, 2007, 2013, 2015, 2019), and some of the many ways that reflection for action, in action, and on action can be carried out are exemplified in Barnard & Ryan (2017). The point is that experience itself teaches you nothing; it is only by reflecting while or after doing something that sense can be made of what has happened and that decisions can be made to improve practice in the future. Reflective practice – "the capacity to reflect on action so as to engage in a process of continuous learning" (Schon, 1983) – shifts the focus from teachers *being* developed to teachers *doing* it for themselves – a bottom-up approach that the teacher initiates and leads to self-regulated teacher learning and autonomous professional practice. However, reflection has to be mediated by expert teacher educators to be effective (Le, 2017). According to Freeman (2016: 221), "improvement in teaching comes when teachers can turn actions that are automatic and routine into ones that are considered. . . . This shift from automatic to considered actions supports a more professionalized view of teaching." For this shift to happen, teachers need to be assisted to develop their vision of who they want to become through their mindfulness of the impact of their pedagogy upon student learning as well as of the contextually situated strategies to transform their practices towards greater levels of professional expertise. To be more specific, that shift has to be mediated with appropriate cultural and psychological tools that can engage teachers in the ongoing learning to teach with the hand, the heart and the head.

References

Avalos, B. (2011). Teacher professional development in teaching and teacher education over ten years. *Teaching and Teacher Education, 27*, 10–20.

Ball, S. (2006). *Education policy and social class: The selected works of Stephen J. Ball.* London: Routledge.

Barnard, R., & Burns, A. (Eds.). (2012). *Researching language teacher cognition and practice: International case studies.* Bristol: Multilingual Matters.

Barnard, R., & Hasim. Z. (Eds.). (2018). *English medium instruction programmes: Perspectives from South East Asian universities.* London: Routledge.

Barnard, R., & Ryan, J. (Eds.). (2017). *Reflective practice: Voices from the field.* London: Routledge.

Breen, M. P. (2001). The social context for language learning: A neglected situation? In C. N. Candlin & N. Mercer (Eds.), *English language teaching in its social context: A reader* (pp. 122–144). London: Routledge.

Burns, A., & Knox, J. S. (2011). Classrooms as complex adaptive systems: A relational model. *TESL-EJ, 15*(1), 1–25.

Byram, M., & Fleming, M. (1998). Introduction. In M. Byram & M. Fleming (Eds.), *Language learning in intercultural perspective: Approaches through drama and ethnography* (pp. 1–10). Cambridge: Cambridge University Press.

Charmaz, K. (2014). *Constructing grounded theory* (2nd ed.). Thousand Oaks, CA: Sage Publications.

Cochran-Smith, M. (2003). The unforgivable complexity of teaching: Avoiding simplicity in an age of accountability. *Journal of Teacher Education, 54*(1), 3–5.

Cohen, L., Manion, L., & Morrison, K. (2018). *Research methods in education* (8th ed.). London: Routledge.

Dan Tri. (December 12, 2018). *Phó Thủ tướng: Không có tiếng nước ngoài nào là ngôn ngữ chính thức thứ 2, 3 tại VN* [No foreign language is the second or third official language in Vietnam]. Retrieved from https://dantri.com.vn/giao-duc-khuyen-hoc/pho-thu-tuong-khong-co-tieng-nuoc-ngoai-nao-la-ngon-ngu-chinh-thuc-thu-23-tai-viet-nam-20181212070832819.htm

Day, C. (1999). Professional development and reflective practice: Purposes, processes and partnerships. *Pedagogy, Culture & Society, 7*(2), 221–233.

Doiz, A., Lasagabaster, D., & Sierra, J. M. (2013). Future challenges for English-medium instruction at the tertiary level. In A. Doiz, D. Lasagabaster, & J. M. Sierra (Eds.), *English-medium instruction at universities: Global challenges* (pp. 213–221). Clevedon: Multilingual Matters.

Duncombe, R., & Armour, K. M. (2004). Collaborative professional learning: From theory to practice. *Journal of In-Service Education, 30*(1), 141–166.

Farrell, T. S. C. (2007). *Reflective teaching: From research to practice.* London: Continuum.

Farrell, T. S. C. (2012). Novice-service language teacher development: Bridging the gap between preservice and in-service education and development. *TESOL Quarterly, 46*(3), 435–449.

Farrell, T. S. C. (2013). *Reflective writing for language teachers.* Sheffield: Equinox.

Farrell, T. S. C. (2015). *Promoting teacher reflection in second language education: A framework for TESOL professionals.* New York: Routledge.

Farrell. T. S. C. (2019). "My training has failed me": Inconvenient truths about second language teacher education (SLTE). *TESL-EJ, 22*(4), 1–16.

Freeman, D. (2016). *Educating second language teachers.* New York: Oxford University Press.

Freeman, D., & Johnson, K. E. (1998). Reconceptualising the knowledge-base of language teacher education. *TESOL Quarterly, 32*(3), 397–417.

Fullan, M. (2015). *The new meaning of educational change* (5th ed.). New York: Teacher College Press.

Garcia, O., & Wei, L. (2014). *Translanguaging.* New York: Palgrave Macmillan.

Golombek, P., & Doran, M. (2014). Unifying cognition, emotion, and activity in language teacher professional development. *Teaching and Teacher Education, 39*, 102–111.

Grassick, L., & Wedell, M. (2018). Temporal dissonance, contextual confusion and risk: Learning from experiences of teachers living with curriculum change. In M. Wedell & L. Grassick (Eds.), *International perspectives on teachers living with curriculum change* (pp. 247–271). London: Palgrave Macmillan.

Hu, G. (2002). Potential cultural resistance to pedagogical imports: The case of communicative language teaching in China. *Language, Culture and Curriculum, 15*(2), 93–105.

Hynninen, N. (2014). The Common European framework of reference from the perspective of English as a lingua franca: What we can learn from a focus on language regulation. *Journal of English as a Lingua Franca (JELF), 3*(2), 293–316.

Krumm, H.-J. (2007). Profiles instead of levels: The CEFR and its (ab)uses in the context of migration. *The Modern Language Journal, 91*(4), 667–669.

Kubanyiova, M. (2012). *Teacher development in action: Understanding language teachers' conceptual change.* New York: Palgrave Macmillan.

Le, V. C. (2011). *Form-focused instruction: A case study of Vietnamese teachers' beliefs and practices.* Unpublished doctoral thesis. Hamilton, New Zealand, University of Waikato.

Le, V. C. (2017). Reflection on action: Lesson transcript. In R. Barnard & J. Ryan (Eds.), *Reflective practice: Voices from the field* (pp. 128–139). London: Routledge.

Le, V. C. (2019). Unpacking the complexity of learning to teach English to young learners: A narrative inquiry. In S. Zein & S. Garton (Eds.), *Early language learning and teacher education: International research and practice* (pp. 41–58). Bristol: Multilingual Matters.

Li, D. (1998). "It's always more difficult than you plan and imagine": Teachers' perceived difficulties in introducing the communicative approach in South Korea. *TESOL Quarterly, 32*(4), 677–703.

Li, M. (2010). EFL teachers and English language education in the PRC: Are they the policy makers? *The Asia-Pacific Education Researcher, 19*(3), 439–451.

Li, M., & Baldauf, R. B., Jr. (2010). Beyond the curriculum: Issues constraining effective English language teaching: A Chinese example. *TESOL Quarterly, 45*(4), 793–803.

Liddicoat, A. J., & Baldauf, R. B., Jr. (Eds.). (2008). *Language planning in local contexts.* Clevedon: Multilingual Matters.

Leung, C. (2013). The "social" in English language teaching: Abstracted norms versus situated enactments. *JELF, 2*(2). 283–313.

Macaro, E. (2018). *English medium instruction*. Oxford: Oxford University Press.

Mann, S. (2005). The language teachers' development. *Language Teaching, 38*, 103–118.

McNamara, T. (2012). English as a lingua franca: The challenge for language testing. *JELF, 1*(1), 199–202.

Nunan, D. (2003). The impact of English as a global language on educational policies and practices in the Asia-Pacific region. *TESOL Quarterly, 37*(4), 589–613.

Pilkinton-Pihko, D. (2013). *English-medium instruction: Seeking assessment criteria for spoken professional English*. Helsinki: University of Helsinki dissertation.

Richards, J. C. (2017). Teaching English through English: Proficiency, pedagogy and performance. *RELC Journal, 48*(1), 7–30.

Ryan, J. G. (2018). Voices from the field: Email interviews with applied linguists in Asia. In R. Barnard & Z. Hasim (Eds.), *English medium instruction programmes: Perspectives from South East Asian universities* (pp. 15–28). London: Routledge.

Schon, D. (1983). *The reflective practitioner*. Boston: Basic Books.

Seidlhofer, B. (2003). *A concept of international English and related issues: From "real English" to "realistic English"?* Strasbourg: Council of Europe.

Shohamy, E. (2013). A critical perspective on the use of English as a medium of instruction at universities. In A. Doiz, D. Lasagabster, & J. M. Sierra (Eds.), *English-medium instruction at universities: Global challenges* (pp. 196–210). Clevedon: Multilingual Matters.

Sifakis, N. (2009). Challenges in teaching ELF in the periphery: The Greek context. *ELT Journal, 63*(3), 230–237.

Trim, J. L. M. (1996). The proposed common European framework for the description of language learning, teaching and assessment. In A. Huhta, V. Kohonen, L. Kurki-Suonio, & S. Luoma (Eds.), *Current developments and alternatives in language assessment* (pp. 415–421). Proceedings of the LTRC. Jyvaskyla: University of Jyvaskyla Press.

Tsui, A. B. M., & Tollefson, J. W. (2007). Language policy and the construction of national cultural identity. In A. B. M. Tsui & J. W. Tollefson (Eds.), *Language policy, culture, and identity in Asian contexts* (pp. 1–21). London: Lawrence Erlbaum.

Verity, D. P. (2000). Side affects: The strategic development of professional satisfaction. In J. P. Lantolf (Ed.), *Sociocultural theory and second language learning* (pp. 179–197). New York: Oxford University Press.

Vygotsky, L. S. (1978). *Mind in society*. Cambridge, MA: Harvard University Press.

Waters, A. (2006). Facilitating follow-up in ELT INSET. *Language Teaching Research, 10*(1), 32–52.

Wedell, M. (2008). Developing a capacity to make "English for everyone" worthwhile: Reconsidering outcomes and how to start achieving them, *International Journal of Educational Development, 28*(6), 628–639.

Woff, D., & De Costa, P. I. (2017). Expanding the language teacher identity landscape: An investigation of the emotions and strategies of a NNEST. *The Modern Language Journal, 101*(Suppl. 2017), 76–90.

Index

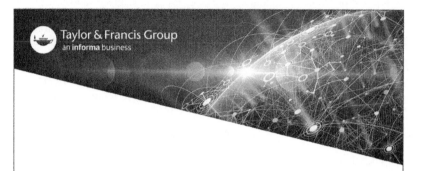

Printed in Great Britain
by Amazon

47623714R10126